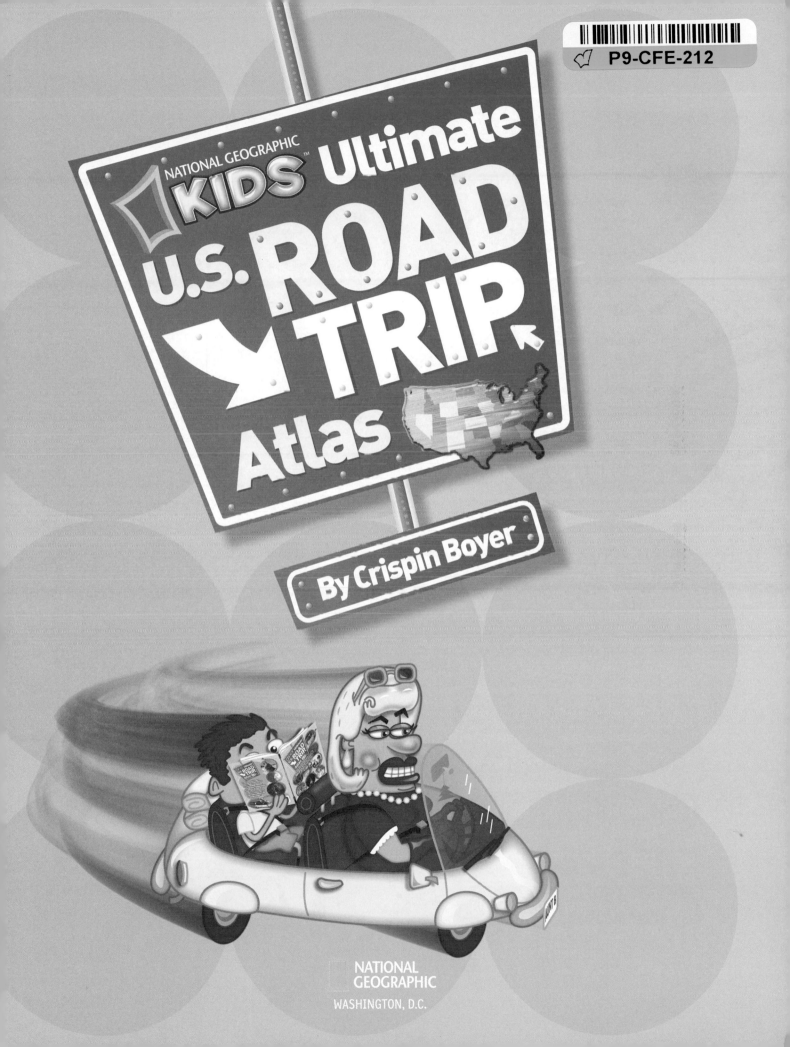

NATIONAL GEOGRAPHIC KIDS

Ultimate U.S. ROAD TRIP Atlas

By Crispin Boyer

NATIONAL GEOGRAPHIC
WASHINGTON, D.C.

TABLE OF CONTENTS

CAR TRIP FUN!

HOW TO USE THIS ATLAS

ROADSIDE ATTRACTIONS

For fun, wacky, and wild side-trip ideas eyeball the list of Roadside Attractions.

STATE FACTS

For the names of state birds, flowers, and animals or trees, look above the state name.

STATE NICKNAME

Do you know your state's nickname? Every state has one! You'll find it below each state name.

WHIMZEYLAND
You'll do a double take when you drive by the wacky bowling-ball sculptures in front of this colorful home in Safety Harbor.

GOOFY GOLF
A popular stop since 1959, this putt-putt course in Panama City features monsters, a volcano, and more!

SUNKEN GARDENS
What started as a St. Petersburg sinkhole 100 years ago is now a lush garden with waterfalls, exotic plants, and flocks of flamingos.

Spanish conquistador Ponce de León never found the Fountain of Youth when he explored Florida 500 years ago, yet the Sunshine State—land of Mickey Mouse, unending beaches, and vibrant cities—still brings out the kid in its many visitors.

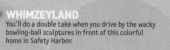

INTRODUCTION

The introductory paragraph offers a fun overview of each state.

TRAFFIC LAWS YOU WON'T BELIEVE

If an elephant is left tied to a parking meter, the parking fee has to be paid just as it would be for a car.

It's illegal to park a pickup truck in your own driveway or in front of your own house on the street.

It's illegal to fish while driving across a bridge.

BOREDOM BUSTER!
Take a picture of every wacky road sign you pass and see who gets the most!

26

TRAFFIC LAWS/ SILLY SIGNS/ FANTASTIC FACTS

Throughout the book, we've included the wackiest laws, the silliest signs, or the most fantastic facts we could find. Look for them on each spread.

BOREDOM BUSTER/GPS BOREDOM BUSTER

For nonstop fun on your road trip, go to the boredom busters. These features ask you to use a camera or phone to take pictures, a smart phone to look up information, or a navigation system to find locations or landmarks.

MAP

To find all the locations mentioned on the page, check out the map! Then look for state capitals, highways, bodies of water, and even national parks.

5 COOL THINGS

These are the five places you must visit while in the state! Follow the pointers from each picture to the map to find out exactly where these cool places are located. Then hit the road!

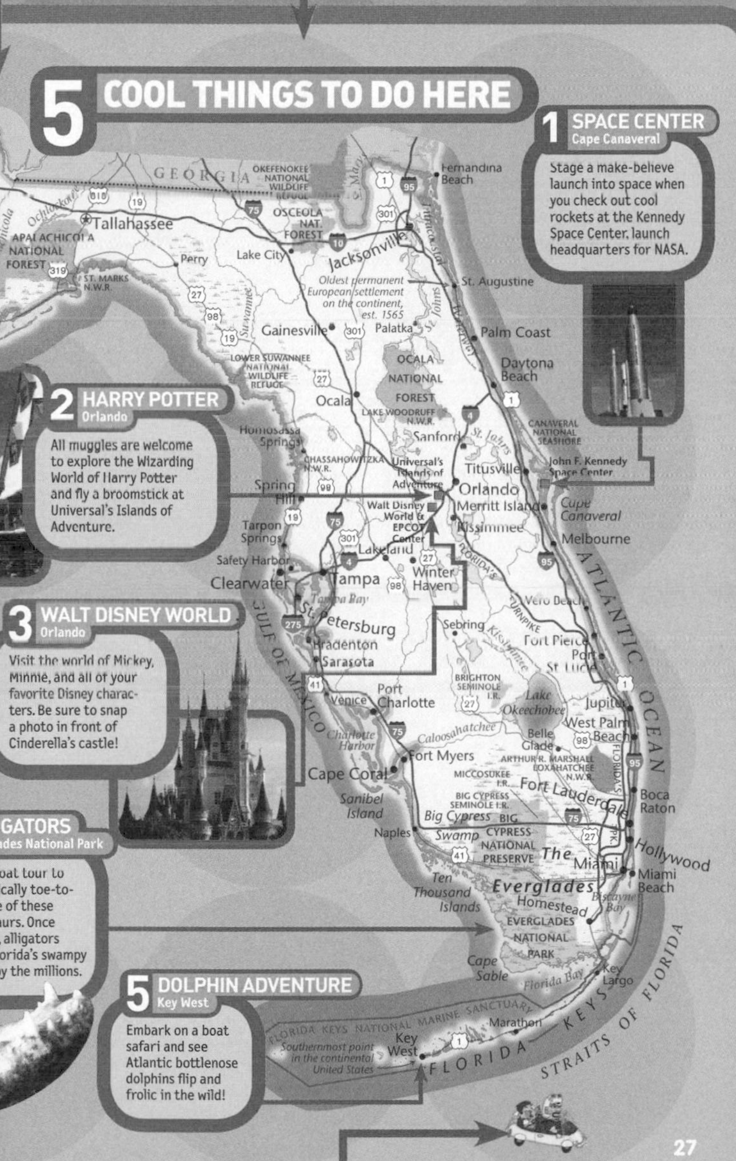

5 COOL THINGS TO DO HERE
1 SPACE CENTER
Cape Canaveral
Stage a make-believe launch into space when you check out cool rockets at the Kennedy Space Center, launch headquarters for NASA.
2 HARRY POTTER
Orlando
All muggles are welcome to explore the Wizarding World of Harry Potter and fly a broomstick at Universal's Islands of Adventure.
3 WALT DISNEY WORLD
Orlando
Visit the world of Mickey, Minnie, and all of your favorite Disney characters. Be sure to snap a photo in front of Cinderella's castle!
GATORS
ades National Park
5 DOLPHIN ADVENTURE
Key West
Embark on a boat safari and see Atlantic bottlenose dolphins flip and frolic in the wild!
GEORGIA
Tallahassee
Jacksonville
Gainesville
Ocala
Orlando
Tampa
St. Petersburg
Sarasota
Fort Myers
Naples
Miami
Key West
GULF OF MEXICO
ATLANTIC OCEAN
STRAITS OF FLORIDA
27

AUNT BERTHA

Meet Aunt Bertha. You'll find her speeding through various pages in this book. Count how many times she appears and then check the answer key on page 122 to see if you're right!

MAP KEY

- Aspen .... town of under 25,000 residents
- Frankfort .... town of 25,000 to 99,999
- San Jose .... city of 100,000 to 999,999
- New York .... city of 1,000,000 and over
- National capital
- State capital
- Fort
- Point of interest
- Mountain peak with elevation above sea level
- Low point with elevation below sea level
- Limited access highway
- Other highway
- Auto ferry
- 80 40 Interstate highway number
- 50 Federal highway number
- 20 State highway number
- 30 Foreign highway number
- Trail
- State or national boundary
- Continental divide
- River
- Intermittent river
- Canal
- Lake and dam
- Intermittent lake
- Dry lake
- Swamp
- Glacier
- Sand
- Lava
- Area below sea level
- Indian Reservation, **IND. RES., I.R.**
- State Park, **S.P.**
  State Historical Park, **S.H.P.**
  State Historic Site, **S.H.S.**
- National Battlefield, **N.B.**
  National Battlefield Park, **N.B.P.**
  National Battlefield Site, **N.B.S.**
  National Historic Landmark
  National Historic Site, **N.H.S.**
  National Historical Area, **N.H.A.**
  National Historical Park, **N.H.P.**
  National Lakeshore
  National Landmark
  National Military Park, **N.M.P.**
  National Memorial, **NAT. MEM.**
  National Monument, **NAT. MON., N.M.**
  National Park, **NAT. PK., N.P.**
  National Parkway
  National Preserve
  National Recreation Area, **N.R.A.**
  National River
  National Riverway
  National Scenic Area
  National Seashore
  National Volcanic Monument
- National Forest, **NAT. FOR., N.F.**
- National Grassland, **N.G.**
- National Wildlife Refuge, **N.W.R.**
  National Conservation Area, **N.C.A.**
- National Marine Sanctuary, **N.M.S.**

UNITED STATES

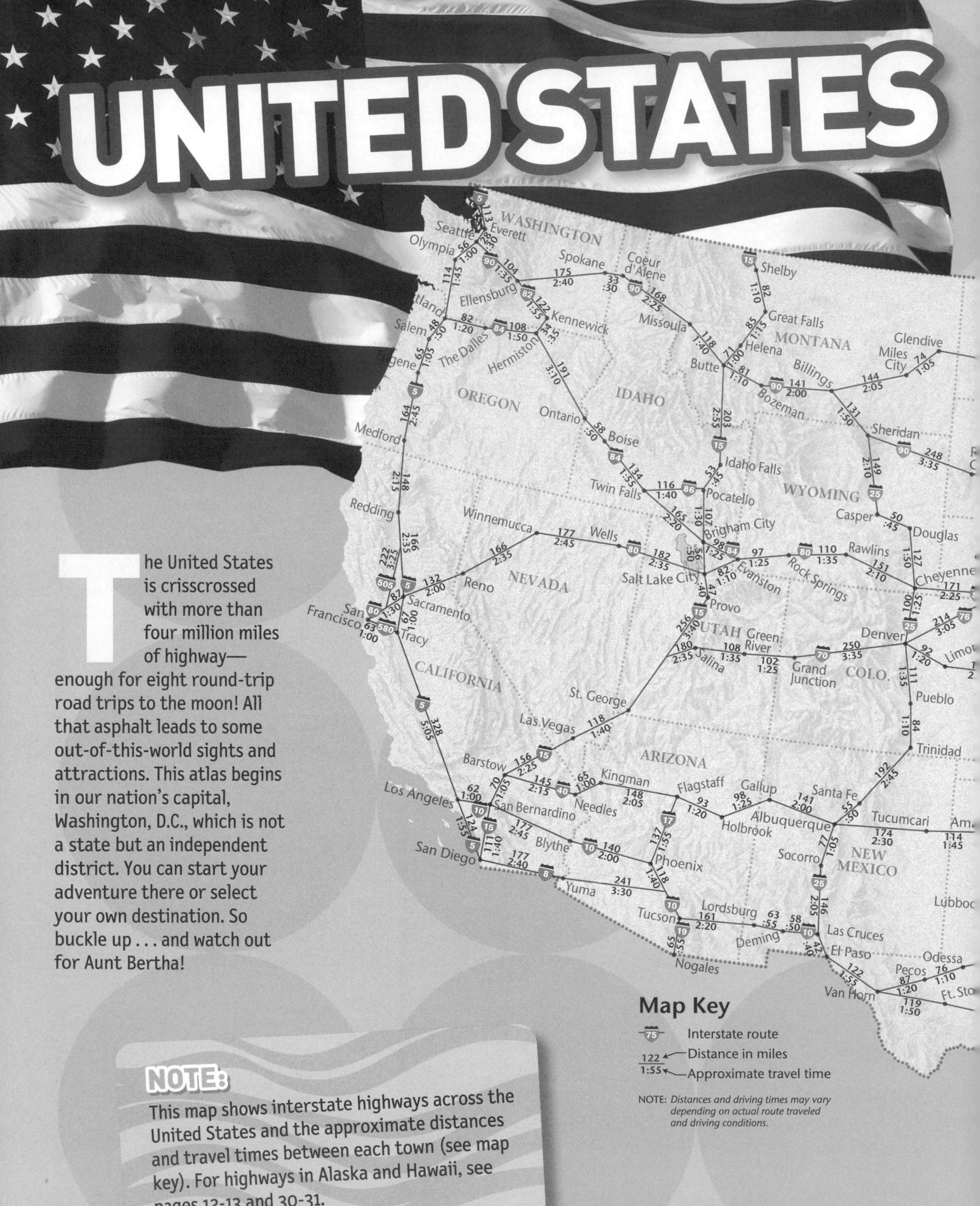

The United States is crisscrossed with more than four million miles of highway—enough for eight round-trip road trips to the moon! All that asphalt leads to some out-of-this-world sights and attractions. This atlas begins in our nation's capital, Washington, D.C., which is not a state but an independent district. You can start your adventure there or select your own destination. So buckle up . . . and watch out for Aunt Bertha!

Map Key

- 75 — Interstate route
- 122 ← Distance in miles
- 1:55 ← Approximate travel time

NOTE: *Distances and driving times may vary depending on actual route traveled and driving conditions.*

NOTE:

This map shows interstate highways across the United States and the approximate distances and travel times between each town (see map key). For highways in Alaska and Hawaii, see pages 12-13 and 30-31.

WASHINGTON, D.C.

Our Nation's CAPITAL

If you think a city full of museums, government offices, and monuments sounds boring, then you haven't been to Washington, D.C. The U.S. capital crams an entire state's worth of historic attractions into the President's backyard.

FANTASTIC WASHINGTON, D.C. FACTS

It might be the capital of the United States, but Washington, D.C., isn't part of any single state. It's an independent federal district.

Think your local library has a lot of books? The Library of Congress has more than 800 miles of bookshelves!

The President's home wasn't officially called the White House until 1901. Before that it held several names, including the President's Palace.

BOREDOM BUSTER!

The Washington Monument is one of D.C.'s most visited sights. At more than 555 feet tall, it's also one of the city's tallest structures. Lie on your back and point your camera up for a fun shot!

Roadside Attractions

MADAME TUSSAUDS

The D.C. branch of the famous wax museum lets you meet every U.S. President, or at least their eerily life-like wax incarnations.

MUSEUM OF CRIME & PUNISHMENT

Pirates, bankrobbers, and other seedy sorts get locked away for eternity in exhibits that show how crime doesn't pay.

NATIONAL GEOGRAPHIC MUSEUM

Expeditions and adventure stories come to life at the National Geographic Society's base of operations.

2 GIANT PANDAS
National Zoo

Fewer than 1,600 of these magnificent black-and-white bears are left in the world. Meet two of them at this famous zoo.

3 AIR & SPACE MUSEU
National Mall

Take a voyage through the evolution of flight—from the Wright brothers' rickety first airplane to the Apollo 11 moon module—at this out-of-this-world Smithsonian museum.

5 COOL THINGS TO DO HERE

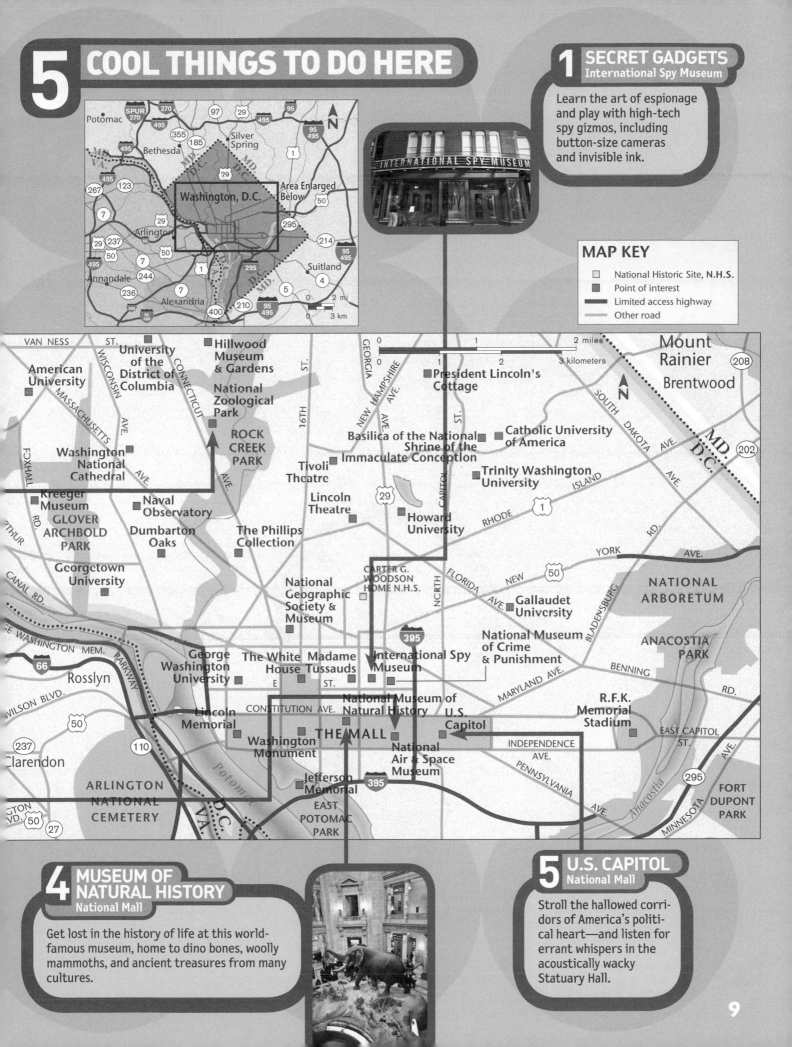

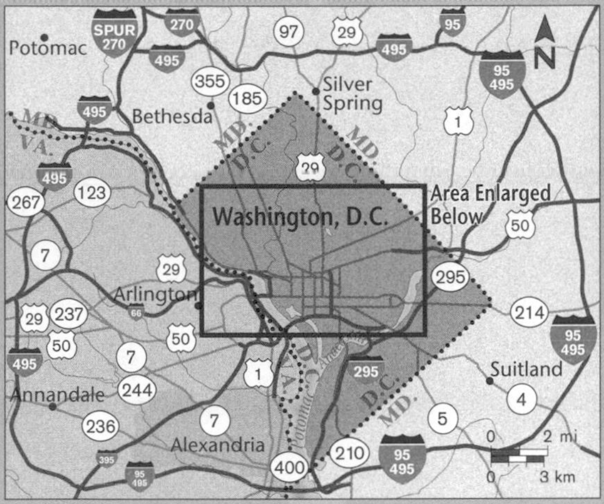

1 SECRET GADGETS
International Spy Museum

Learn the art of espionage and play with high-tech spy gizmos, including button-size cameras and invisible ink.

MAP KEY

- National Historic Site, **N.H.S.**
- Point of interest
- Limited access highway
- Other road

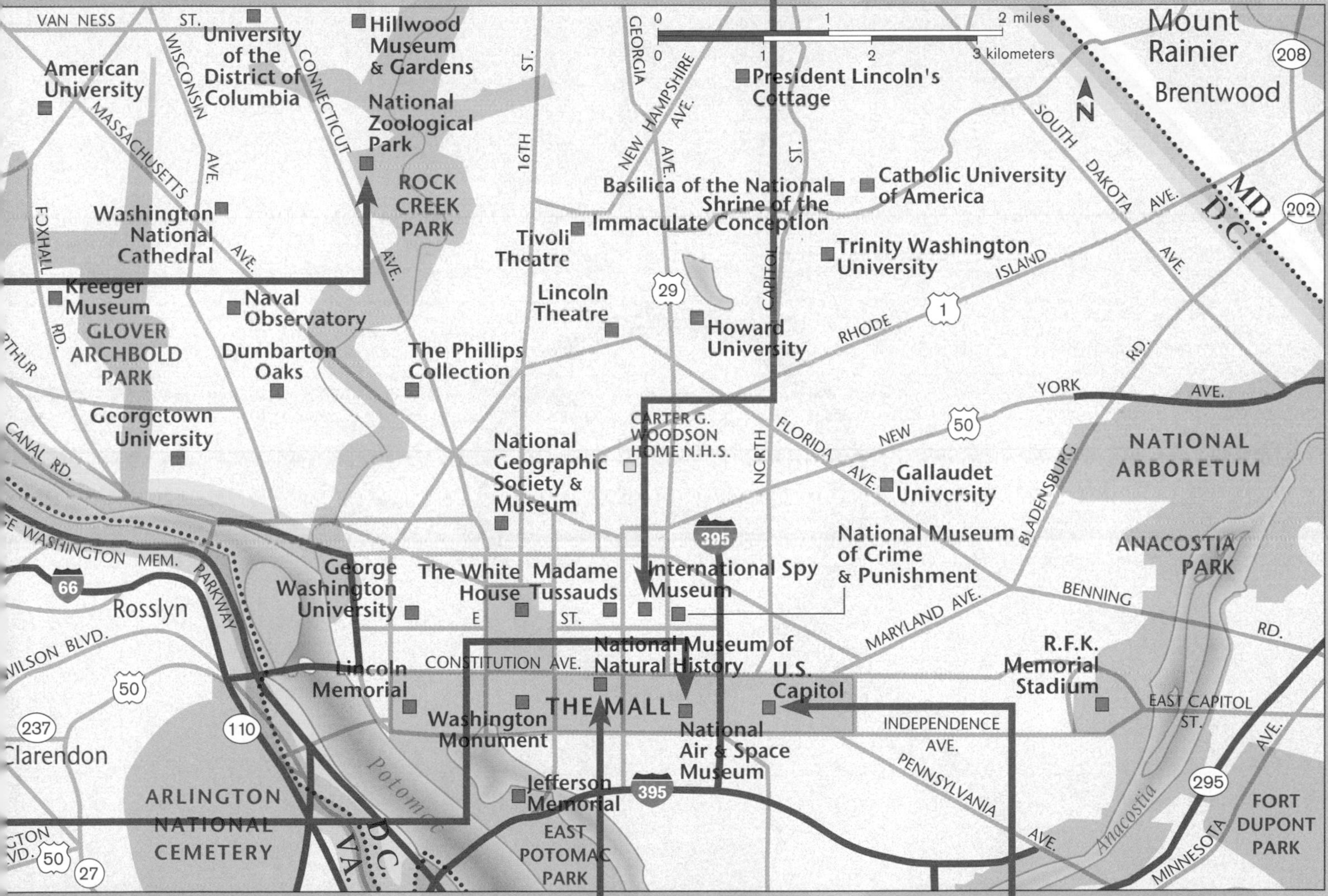

4 MUSEUM OF NATURAL HISTORY
National Mall

Get lost in the history of life at this world-famous museum, home to dino bones, woolly mammoths, and ancient treasures from many cultures.

5 U.S. CAPITOL
National Mall

Stroll the hallowed corridors of America's political heart—and listen for errant whispers in the acoustically wacky Statuary Hall.

STATE BIRD: yellowhammer

STATE FLOWER: camellia

STATE TREE: southern longleaf pine

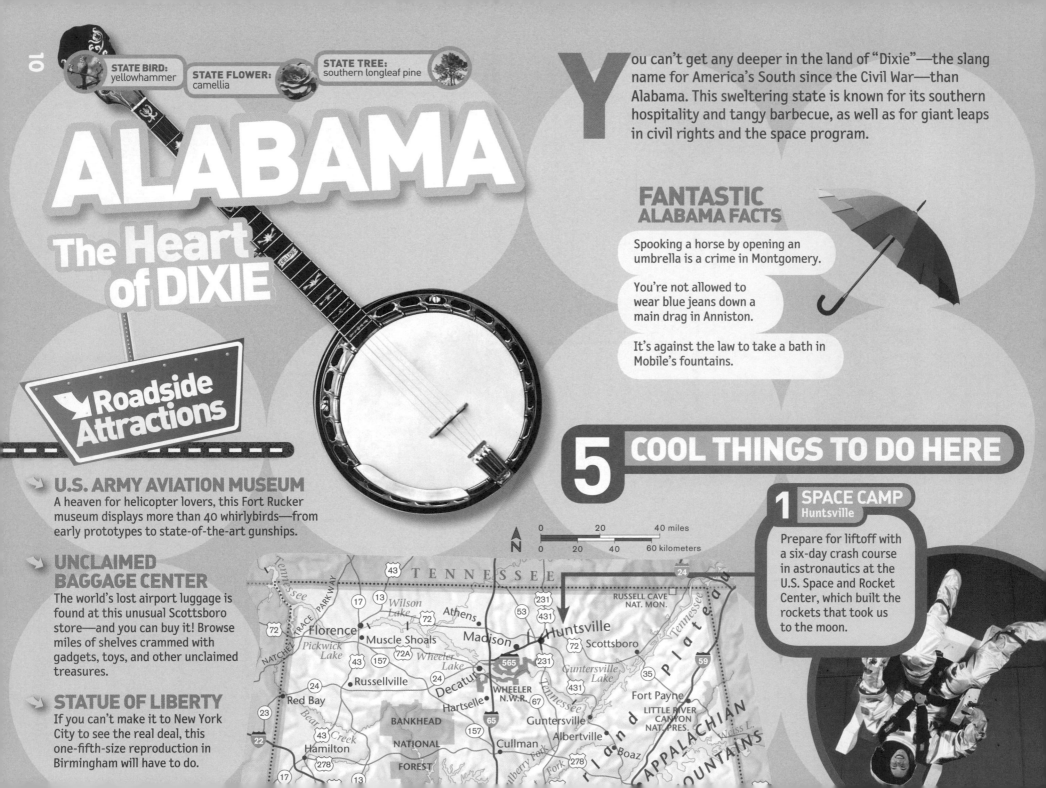

ALABAMA
The Heart of DIXIE

You can't get any deeper in the land of "Dixie"—the slang name for America's South since the Civil War—than Alabama. This sweltering state is known for its southern hospitality and tangy barbecue, as well as for giant leaps in civil rights and the space program.

FANTASTIC ALABAMA FACTS

Spooking a horse by opening an umbrella is a crime in Montgomery.

You're not allowed to wear blue jeans down a main drag in Anniston.

It's against the law to take a bath in Mobile's fountains.

Roadside Attractions

U.S. ARMY AVIATION MUSEUM
A heaven for helicopter lovers, this Fort Rucker museum displays more than 40 whirlybirds—from early prototypes to state-of-the-art gunships.

UNCLAIMED BAGGAGE CENTER
The world's lost airport luggage is found at this unusual Scottsboro store—and you can buy it! Browse miles of shelves crammed with gadgets, toys, and other unclaimed treasures.

STATUE OF LIBERTY
If you can't make it to New York City to see the real deal, this one-fifth-size reproduction in Birmingham will have to do.

5 COOL THINGS TO DO HERE

1 SPACE CAMP
Huntsville

Prepare for liftoff with a six-day crash course in astronautics at the U.S. Space and Rocket Center, which built the rockets that took us to the moon.

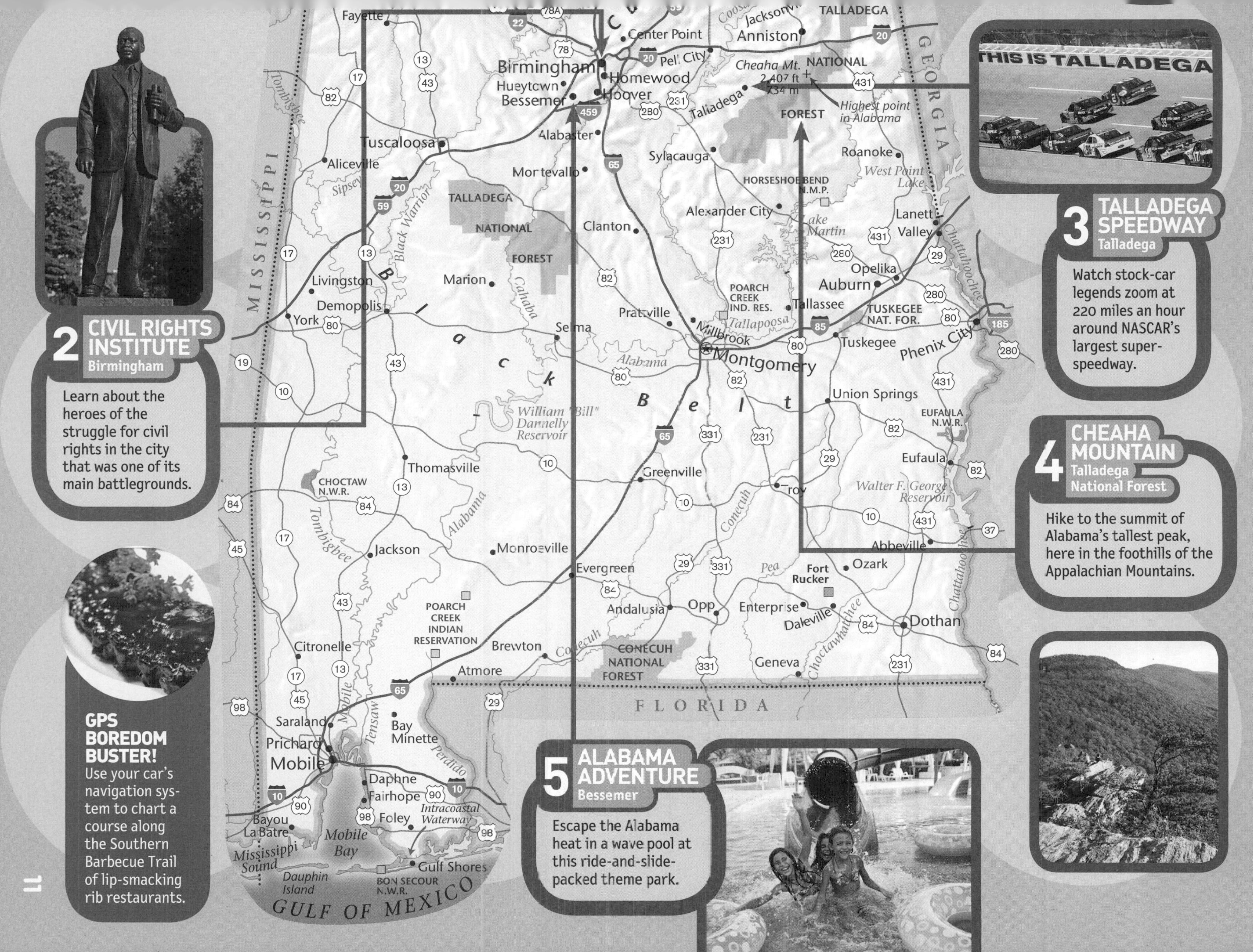

2 CIVIL RIGHTS INSTITUTE
Birmingham

Learn about the heroes of the struggle for civil rights in the city that was one of its main battlegrounds.

GPS BOREDOM BUSTER!
Use your car's navigation system to chart a course along the Southern Barbecue Trail of lip-smacking rib restaurants.

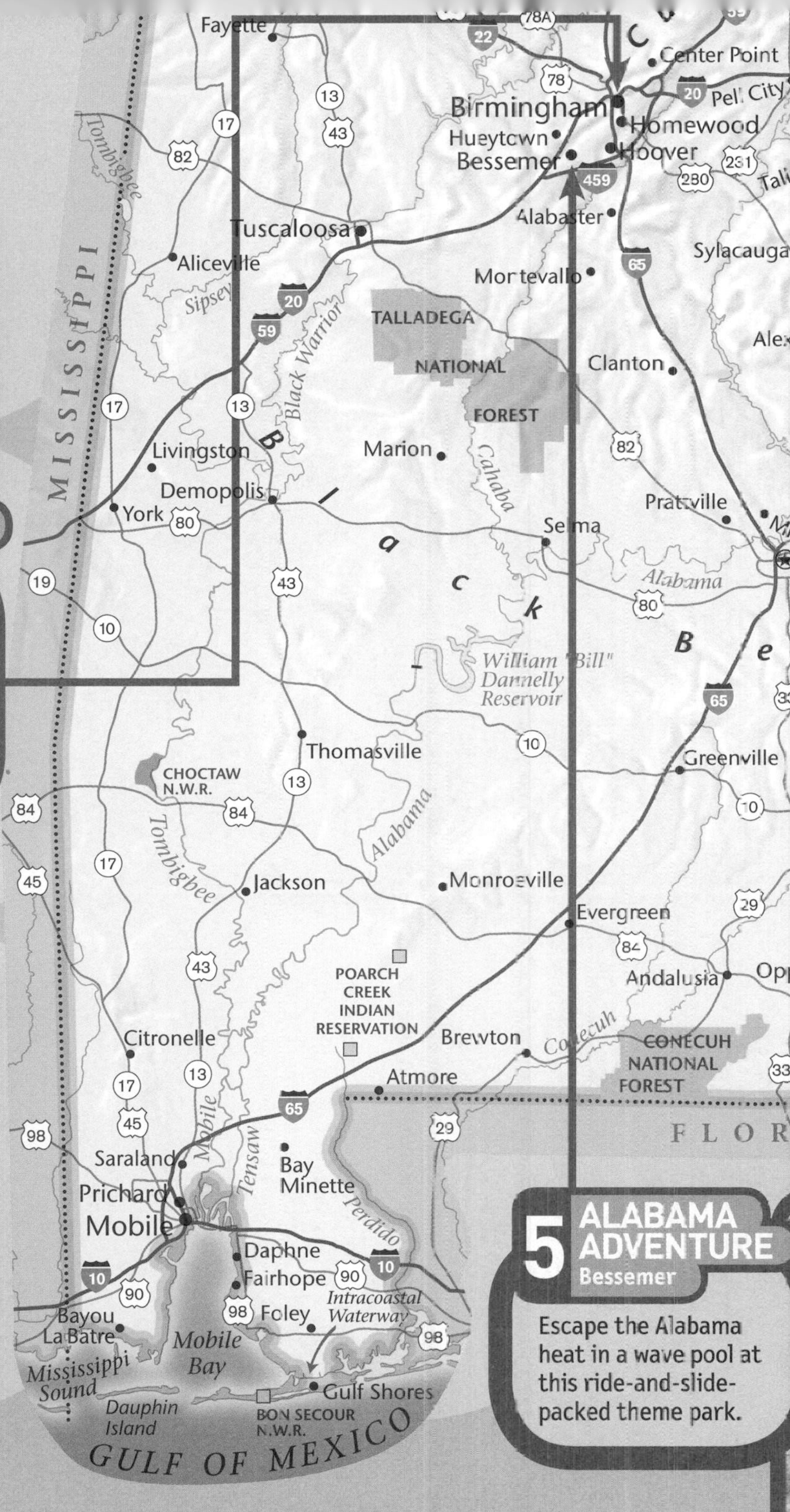

3 TALLADEGA SPEEDWAY
Talladega

Watch stock-car legends zoom at 220 miles an hour around NASCAR's largest superspeedway.

4 CHEAHA MOUNTAIN
Talladega National Forest

Hike to the summit of Alabama's tallest peak, here in the foothills of the Appalachian Mountains.

5 ALABAMA ADVENTURE
Bessemer

Escape the Alabama heat in a wave pool at this ride-and-slide-packed theme park.

STATE BIRD: willow ptarmigan

STATE FLOWER: forget-me-not

STATE ANIMAL: moose

ALASKA

The Last Frontier STATE

Calling Alaska big is like saying water is wet. The 49th state is more than twice the size of the second largest, Texas. From its towering terrain to its ten-foot Kodiak bears, everything in Alaska is epic.

FANTASTIC ALASKA FACTS

America's northernmost, westernmost, and easternmost points by longitude are all in Alaska.

Alaskan fishermen have the most dangerous job in America.

Barrow, Alaska, goes through three months of daylight in the summer and two months of darkness in the winter.

Roadside Attractions

ALASKA RAPTOR CENTER

Injured bald eagles, owls, and falcons get a second chance at this rehab facility for rescued birds of prey in Sitka.

EL DORADO GOLD MINE

This working mine near Fairbanks is a mother lode of Alaskan gold-mining history. Visiting prospectors can even pan for gold!

TOTEM HERITAGE CENTER

This museum in Ketchikan preserves ornate 19th-century totem poles from native Alaskan villages.

1 ALASKA RAILROAD TOUR
Denali National Park

Watch grizzly bears, caribou, and moose whiz by as you ride the rails through this vast wilderness dominated by Mount McKinley, North America's tallest peak.

CHUKCHI SEA

RUSSIA

Bering Strait

only 2.5 miles from Russia

Little Diomede I.

BERING LAND BR NAT. PRES

Taylor

Teller

Sew Penir

Nome

Co

St. Lawrence Island

ALASKA MARITIME N.W.R.

KRUSEN NAT MONU

Po Ho

Nort Sou

Yukon Delta

Emmonak

Mountain Village

Hooper Bay

YUKON DELTA

St. Matthew I.

ALASKA MARITIME N.W.R.

Nelson I.

NATIONA

WILDLIFE

BERING SEA

Nunivak I.

REF

St. Paul

Pribilof Islands

ALASKA MARITIME N.W.R.

Br

Attu I.

NEAR IS.

Agattu I.

RAT ISLANDS

Kiska I.

Amchitka I.

Semisopochnoi Island

Garelot I.

Tanaga I.

Adak I.

Amlia I.

Atka I.

Seguam I.

Yunaska I.

Islands of Four Mountains

ANDREANOF ISLANDS

ALASKA

MARITIME

NATIONAL WILDLIFE REFUGE

IZEMBEK N.W.R.

Unimak I.

Unalaska I.

Umnak I.

Dutch Harbor

Unalaska

Sanak I.

Alas Alaska

N

0 100 200 miles

0 100 200 300 kilometer

GPS BOREDOM BUSTER!
Much of Alaska is reachable only by boat or plane. Use your car's navigation system to see where you can go by road and where you can't.

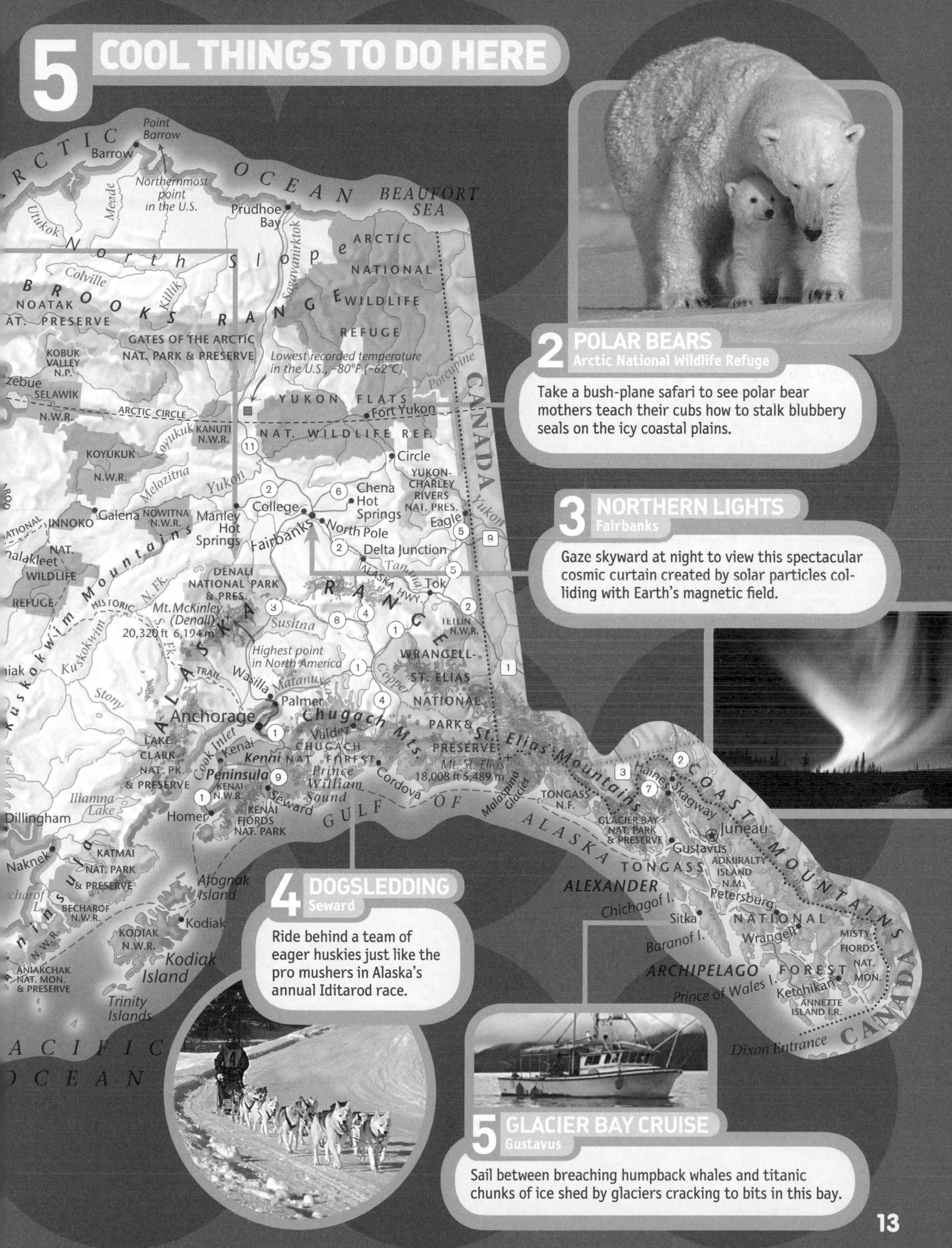

5 COOL THINGS TO DO HERE

2 POLAR BEARS
Arctic National Wildlife Refuge

Take a bush-plane safari to see polar bear mothers teach their cubs how to stalk blubbery seals on the icy coastal plains.

3 NORTHERN LIGHTS
Fairbanks

Gaze skyward at night to view this spectacular cosmic curtain created by solar particles colliding with Earth's magnetic field.

4 DOGSLEDDING
Seward

Ride behind a team of eager huskies just like the pro mushers in Alaska's annual Iditarod race.

5 GLACIER BAY CRUISE
Gustavus

Sail between breaching humpback whales and titanic chunks of ice shed by glaciers cracking to bits in this bay.

STATE BIRD: cactus wren

STATE FLOWER: saguaro cactus blossom

STATE ANIMAL: ringtail cat

ARIZONA

The Grand Canyon STATE

Your eyeballs and brain will have a disconnect when you visit Arizona, a land of mind-boggling heights and unreal lowlands. The first time you peer over the rim of the Grand Canyon, the state's greatest natural treasure, you won't believe your eyes.

Roadside Attractions

ROOSTER COGBURN OSTRICH RANCH

You've never been to a petting zoo like this one in Picacho! Visitors can feed the ranch's big birds by hand. (Don't worry—ostriches don't have teeth.)

METEOR CRATER

An asteroid smacked into the desert near Winslow 50,000 years ago; today it's a mile-wide tourist attraction full of trails and interactive exhibits.

BIOSPHERE 2

Scientists in the 1990s sealed themselves into this enclosed ecosystem near Tucson to study humanity's effect on the environment. Today you can tour its artificial rain forest, coral reef, and desert habitats.

5 COOL THINGS TO DO HERE

1 GRAND CANYON SKYWALK
Grand Canyon West

Walk where eagles soar along this glass-bottomed sidewalk perched 4,000 feet above the floor of the Grand Canyon, one of the natural wonders of the world.

2 TRAIL RIDE
Monument Valley

Mount up for a wild ride among flat-top buttes and mesas made famous by countless Westerns.

FANTASTIC ARIZONA FACTS

Arizona has more land set aside for Native Americans than any other state.

Unlike most of the U.S., Arizona doesn't observe daylight savings time. You'll be an hour ahead if you visit during the summer!

Camels were once imported from the Middle East to carry goods across Arizona for the U.S. Army.

3 ANTELOPE CANYON
Page

Stroll through a geological watercolor painting at this frequently photographed canyon.

4 CANYON DE CHELLY
Near Tsaile

Imagine living in the walls of these spectacular thousand-foot cliffs, home to the Navajo people and other Native American cultures throughout history.

5 O.K. CORRAL
Tombstone

Dodge a hail of (phony) bullets during daily reenactments of the Wild West's most famous gunfight in this once lawless mining town.

BOREDOM BUSTER!
Watch for a speedy brown bird bolting through Arizona's red-rocked deserts—it's a roadrunner! Reach quickly for your camera and try to snap a photo of one.

5 COOL THINGS TO DO HERE

1 OZARK MEDIEVAL FORTRESS
Lead Hill

The Ozark Mountains may be 5,000 miles and 800 years from medieval Europe, but that hasn't stopped a team of crafty historians from constructing a castle here using methods from the Middle Ages.

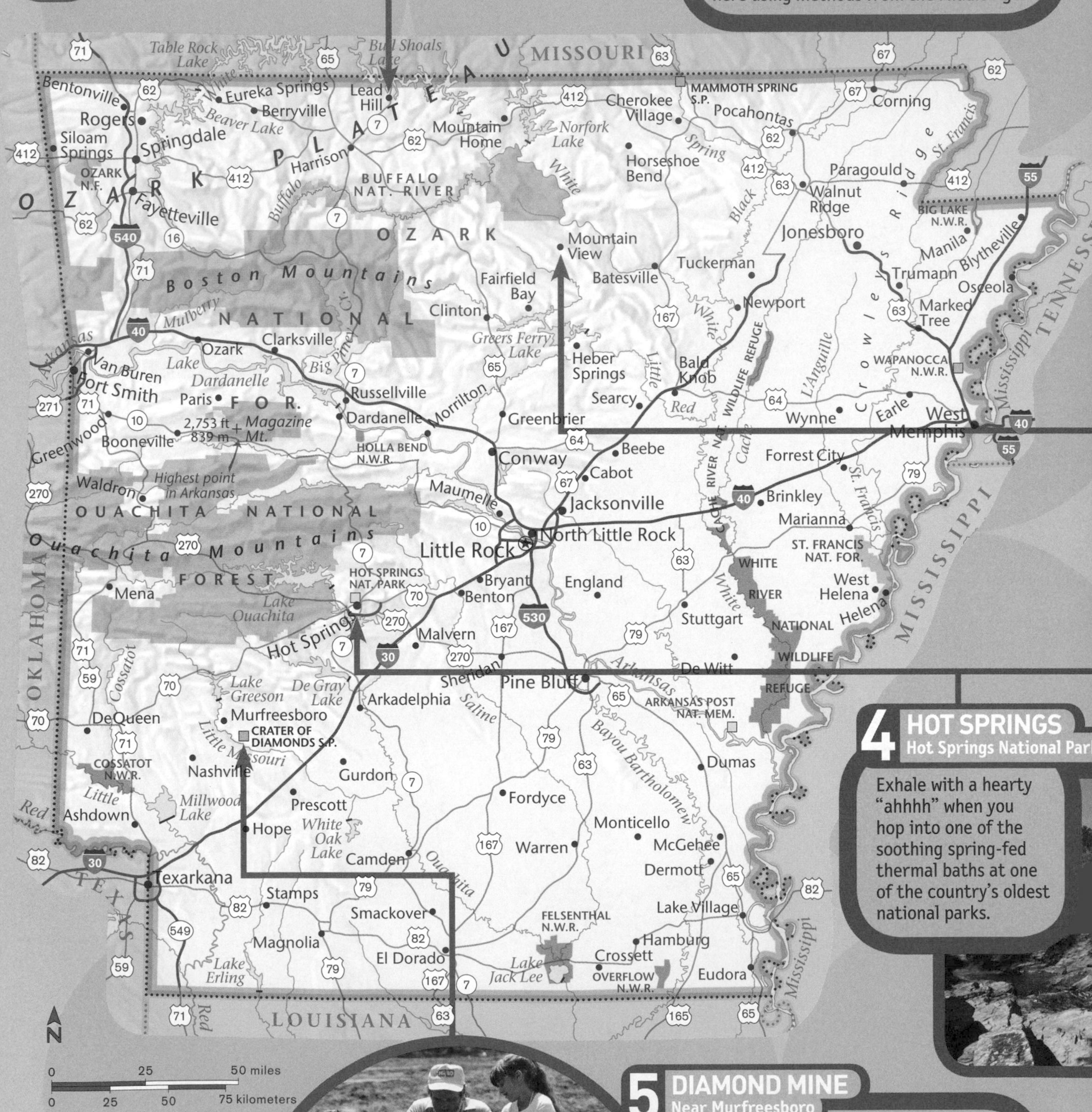

4 HOT SPRINGS
Hot Springs National Par

Exhale with a hearty "ahhhh" when you hop into one of the soothing spring-fed thermal baths at one of the country's oldest national parks.

5 DIAMOND MINE
Near Murfreesboro

Finders are keepers at Crater of Diamonds State Park, the world's only diamond mine where the public can prospect for precious stones.

STATE BIRD: mockingbird

STATE FLOWER: apple blossom

STATE ANIMAL: white-tailed deer

ARKANSAS

The Natural STATE

2 TREETOP ADVENTURE
Mountain View

Dangle dozens of feet in the air as you hop from platform to platform and tiptoe on tightropes at this high-wire adventure park.

3 MAGIC SPRINGS & CRYSTAL FALLS
Hot Springs

Break a sweat on this theme park's twisting coasters before cooling off in its water park.

For outdoor enthusiasts, Arkansas is a full-service destination. Its rugged Ozark Plateau is a mountainous playground for hikers, campers, and mountain bikers, who can cap off their strenuous excursions with a soothing soak in the state's many natural hot springs.

TRAFFIC LAWS YOU WON'T BELIEVE

It's illegal to walk your cow down Main Street in Little Rock after 1 p.m. on Sundays.

Flirting on the street could land you in jail for 30 days.

You can't honk your horn in front of Little Rock sandwich shops after 9 p.m.

Roadside Attractions

BIG CAT REFUGE
Abandoned lions, tigers, and even a bear roam their new homes at Turpentine Creek Wildlife Refuge in Eureka Springs.

BLANCHARD SPRINGS CAVERN
Spelunk a newly opened section of this cave system in Mountain View to reach a cluster of towering subterranean columns appropriately named the Titans.

WWII SUBMARINE
Ponder life at sea in an oversize sardine can when you tour the still working U.S.S. *Razorback* at North Little Rock's Inland Maritime Museum.

BOREDOM BUSTER!
Former President Bill Clinton was born in Arkansas. Use your camera to snap pictures of any Clinton-themed roadside stops and see who can get the most!

CALIFORNIA

The Golden STATE

STATE BIRD: California quail

STATE FLOWER: golden poppy

STATE ANIMAL: California grizzly bear

From its scorching deserts to its snow-capped mountains, California is a state of extremes. The southern half is home to Hollywood and surf culture. Coastal redwoods in the north tower to dizzying heights. Maybe it's not just looking up at those tall trees that's making you wobble; this is earthquake country!

TRAFFIC LAWS YOU WON'T BELIEVE

Love ice cream? Well, in Carmel, it is illegal to eat the delicious treat while standing on a sidewalk.

In Arcadia, peacocks have the right of way to cross any street, even driveways.

In Baldwin Park, it is illegal to ride your bicycle in a swimming pool.

5 COOL THINGS TO DO HERE

1 REDWOODS
Crescent City

Pitch a tent among towering redwoods that started as saplings a thousand years ago.

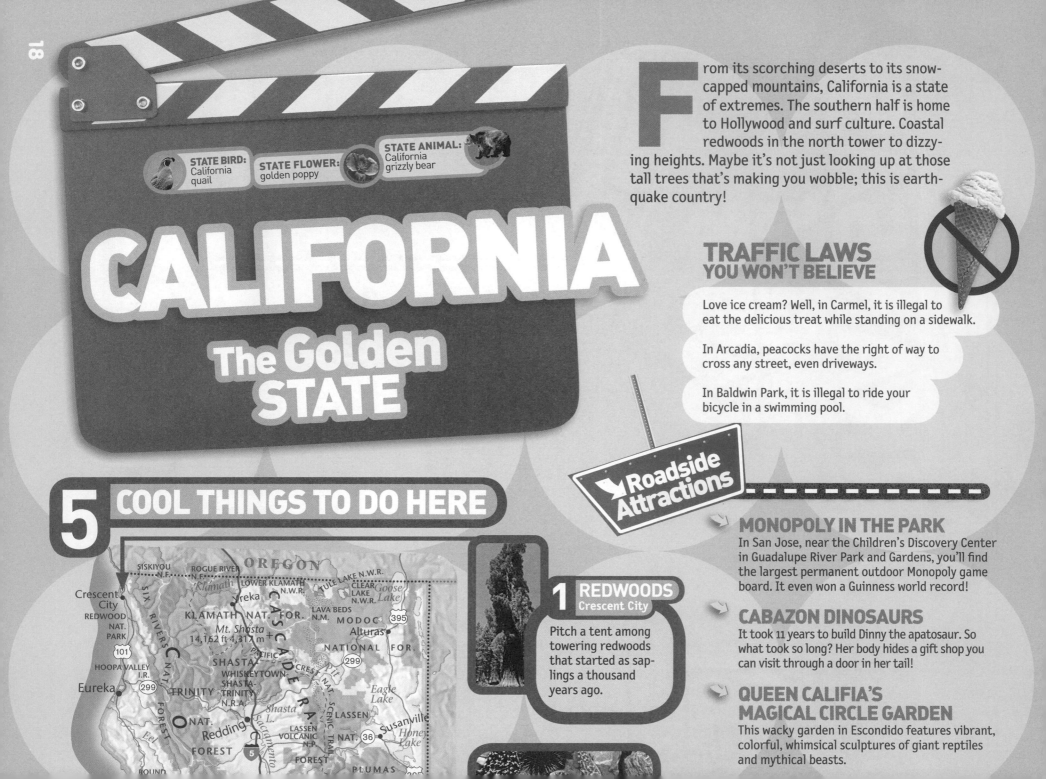

Roadside Attractions

MONOPOLY IN THE PARK

In San Jose, near the Children's Discovery Center in Guadalupe River Park and Gardens, you'll find the largest permanent outdoor Monopoly game board. It even won a Guinness world record!

CABAZON DINOSAURS

It took 11 years to build Dinny the apatosaur. So what took so long? Her body hides a gift shop you can visit through a door in her tail!

QUEEN CALIFIA'S MAGICAL CIRCLE GARDEN

This wacky garden in Escondido features vibrant, colorful, whimsical sculptures of giant reptiles and mythical beasts.

2 POINT LOBOS
Carmel

Splish and splash in tide pools or at the beach at Point Lobos State Reserve in Carmel Highlands.

BOREDOM BUSTER! Take pictures of all the cool things you see as you ride along in the car and then make your own map of your California road trip.

3 SAND DUNES
Death Valley

Hike among the sunny dunes of North America's hottest desert.

4 UNIVERSAL STUDIOS
Los Angeles

Ride roaring roller coasters based on Hollywood blockbusters.

5 SAN DIEGO ZOO
San Diego

Say hello to thousands of animals—from peacocks to pandas—at one of the world's largest zoos.

STATE BIRD: lark bunting

STATE FLOWER: Rocky Mountain columbine

STATE ANIMAL: Rocky Mountain bighorn sheep

COLORADO

The Centennial STATE

If Colorado's breathtaking Rocky Mountain scenery doesn't make your head spin, the thin air will! With 54 peaks towering above 14,000 feet, Colorado is the tallest state in the country. Its old mining towns have become havens for hearty adventurers seeking high-altitude hikes and world-class skiing.

TRAFFIC LAWS YOU WON'T BELIEVE

Better become an expert skier before visiting Vail. It's illegal to crash into any signs, lift towers, or other obstacles on the slopes!

Firing a catapult on Aspen's streets is against the law.

You're not allowed to roll boulders on the streets of Boulder!

Roadside Attractions

U.S. MINT

This U.S. government moneymaking factory in Denver mints a whole mountain range of spare change—more than 50 million coins a day!

UFO WATCHTOWER

The owner of this two-story platform in the San Luis Valley—a UFO hot spot—invites passersby to stop and watch the skies for alien visitors.

GARDEN OF THE GODS

Towering formations of red sandstone frame the distant snow-capped peaks of the Rocky Mountains at this geological wonderland near Colorado Springs.

1 DINOSAUR FOSSILS
Dinosaur National Monument

Count the dinosaur bones embedded in a cliff face inside the Dinosaur Quarry Visitor Center on the Utah border.

3 VAIL
Vail

Never run out of powdery trails at the largest ski resort in the country.

Only spot in the U.S. where the borders of 4 states come together

BOREDOM BUSTER!
Keep an eye out for signs marking the Continental Divide, the line along the Rockies that separates rivers between the Atlantic and Pacific Oceans.

5 COOL THINGS TO DO HERE

2 PIKES PEAK
Near Colorado Springs

Drive to the 14,115-foot summit of the country's most visited mountain and take in the view that inspired "America the Beautiful."

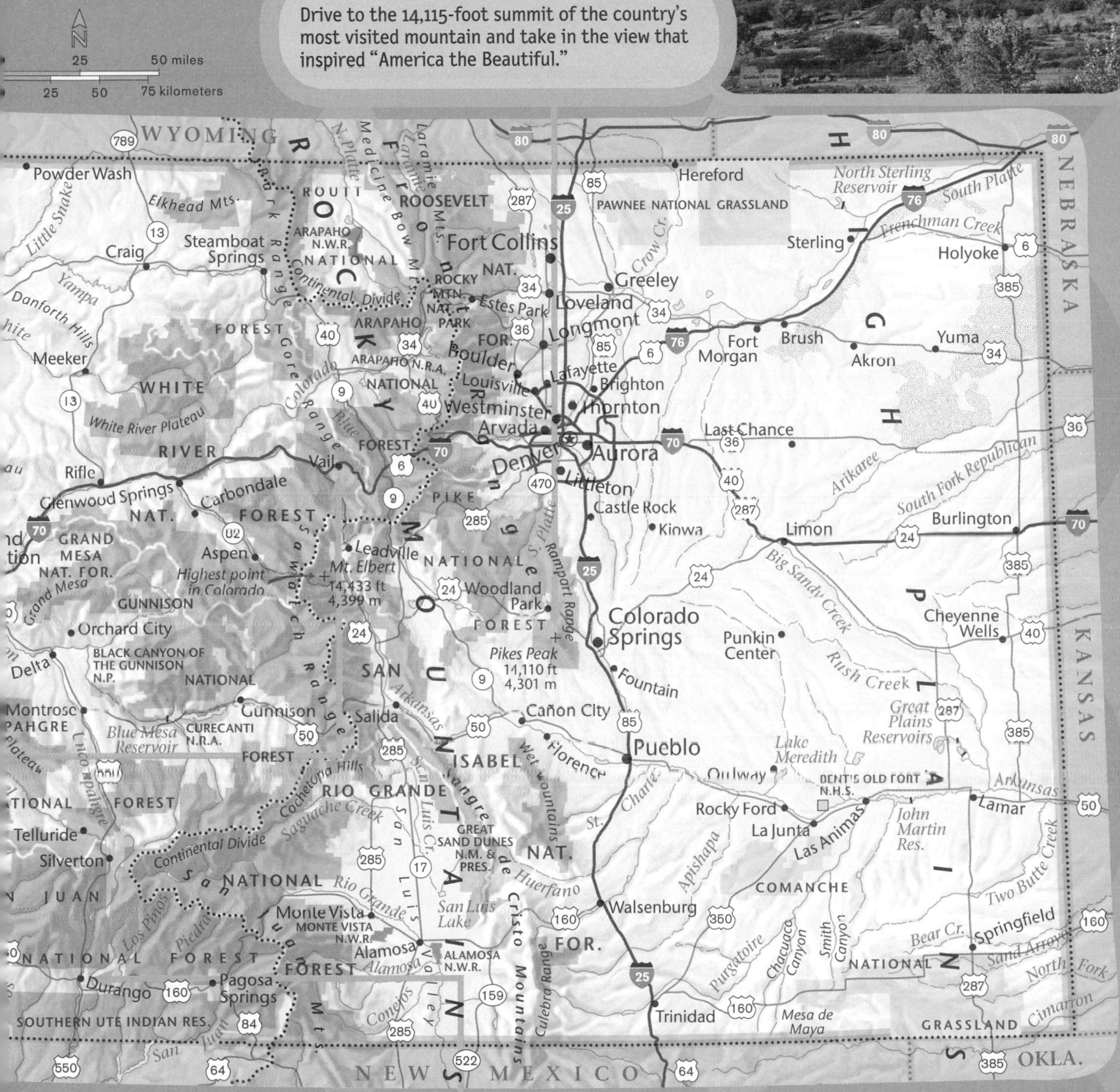

N

25 50 miles

25 50 75 kilometers

4 CLIFF PALACE
Mesa Verde National Park

Explore the largest (150 rooms!) cliff dwelling in America—and wonder why its ancestral Puebloan builders abandoned it 700 years ago.

5 RAILROAD TOUR
Durango

Climb aboard an 1882 locomotive and ride the rails through the San Juan Mountains to the mining town of Silverton.

5 COOL THINGS TO DO HERE

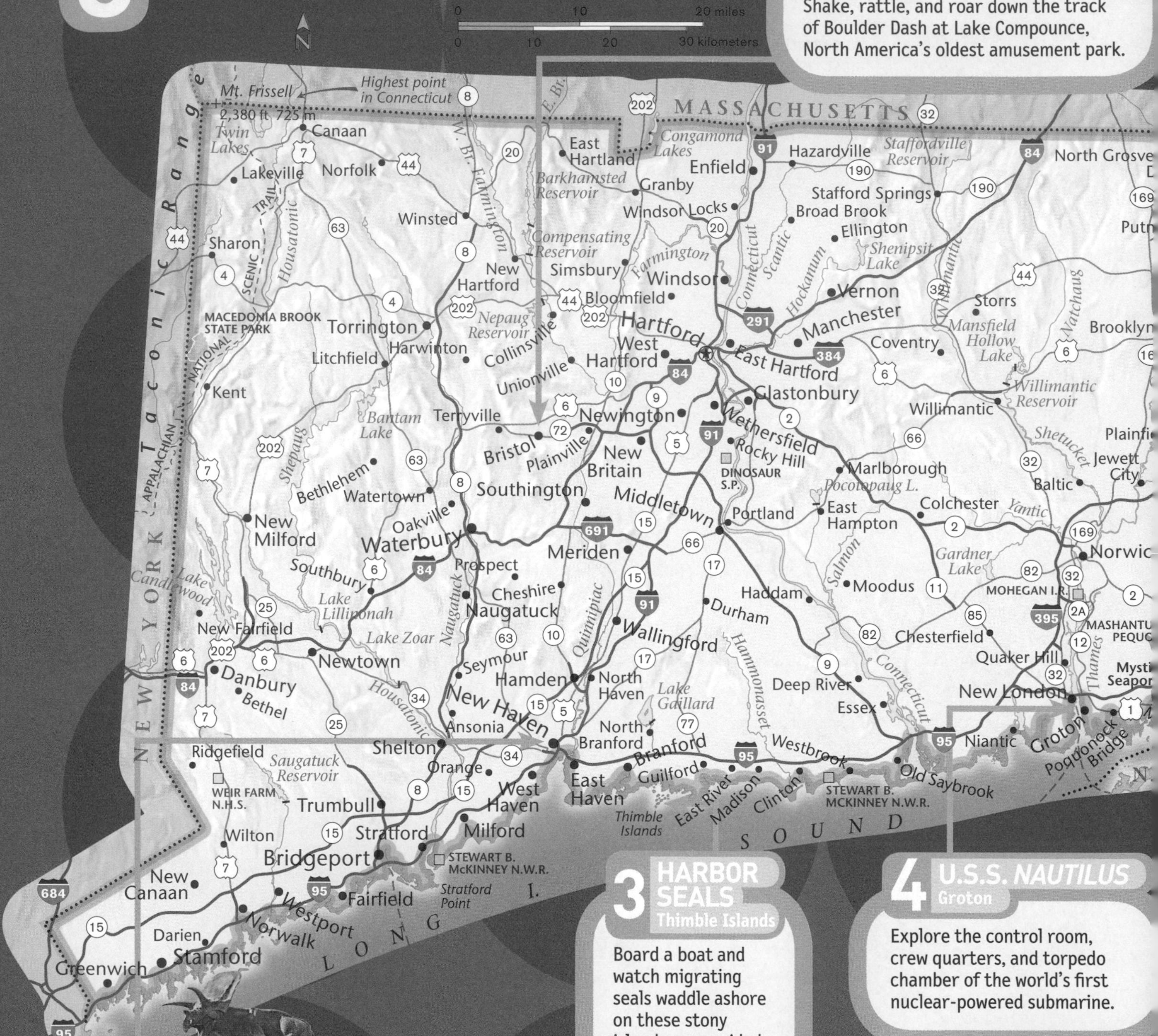

1 WOODEN ROLLER COASTER
Bristol

Shake, rattle, and roar down the track of Boulder Dash at Lake Compounce, North America's oldest amusement park.

2 *TOROSAURUS*
New Haven

Dinosaurs died out 65 million years ago, but their sculptures and fossilized skeletons still rule at Yale University's Peabody Museum of Natural History.

3 HARBOR SEALS
Thimble Islands

Board a boat and watch migrating seals waddle ashore on these stony islands once raided by the piratical Captain Kidd.

4 U.S.S. *NAUTILUS*
Groton

Explore the control room, crew quarters, and torpedo chamber of the world's first nuclear-powered submarine.

CONNECTICUT

The Constitution STATE

5 MYSTIC SEAPORT
Mystic

Finding this restored 18th-century whaling village is easy—just look for the towering masts of its old schooners and square-rigged ships.

Tour this southwestern corner of New England, and you'll soon see why so many people from New York City come here for a break from the bustle. Connecticut is a land of scenic seascapes, lush landscapes, and laid-back adventures.

BICYCLES 65 SPEED LIMIT

TRAFFIC LAWS YOU WON'T BELIEVE

Police can pull you over if you ride your bicycle faster than 65 miles an hour.

In Hartford, it's illegal to cross a street while walking on your hands.

Fire trucks can't exceed 25 miles an hour in New Britain—even if they're racing to a fire!

GPS BOREDOM BUSTER!
For such a small state, Connecticut sure has a lot of lakes—more than a thousand! How many can you find with your car's navigation system?

Roadside Attractions

FROG BRIDGE
Gigantic bronze frogs crouch atop oversize thread spools on this unusual bridge in Willimantic.

GARBAGE MUSEUM
To show how much garbage the average person tosses each year, this Stratford museum created Trash-o-saurus, a dinosaur made from a ton of actual trash!

MARK TWAIN HOUSE
Some claim this Hartford home of the famous author was built to resemble a Mississippi steamboat. Learn the truth when you take the tour.

STATE BIRD: blue hen chicken

STATE FLOWER: peach blossom

STATE ANIMAL: gray fox

DELAWARE

The First STATE

#1

#1

#1

Delaware is a small state best known for big business, but that doesn't mean it's a boring place to visit! Miles of Atlantic Ocean beaches beckon surfers and fishermen. Inland, you'll find massive mansions, fun museums, and the historic landmarks of this first colony to become a U.S. state.

TRAFFIC LAWS YOU WON'T BELIEVE

You can't cook inside your car on Fenwick Island.

If Halloween falls on a Sunday, kids in Rehoboth Beach have to trick or treat the night before.

Take Fido for a walk in South Bethany without a doggy-doo bag and you risk paying a $100 fine!

Roadside Attractions

MILES THE MONSTER

Beware of the 50-foot concrete creature clutching a race car at the Dover International Speedway.

GIANT STETHOSCOPE

This oversize medical tool hangs from a steel sculpture of a doctor's bag in front of a Newark hospital. At least Miles the Monster knows where to go for a checkup!

MYSTERIOUS MERMAN

The Zwaanendael Museum in Lewes is home to a half-monkey/half-fish monstrosity cobbled together in the 19th century as a sideshow oddity.

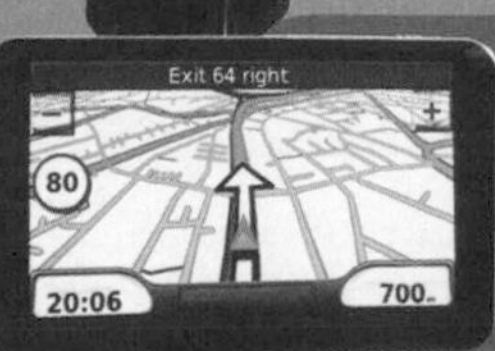

GPS BOREDOM BUSTER!

A portion of the Delaware's border is called the "Twelve-Mile Circle." Use your car's navigation system to find this unusual feature and guess how it got its name.

Map scale:
0 5 10 miles
0 5 10 15 kilometers
N

PENNSYLVANIA

Highest point in Delaware
448 ft
137 m

52
Winterthur Museum & Gardens
95
202
13
Claymont
7
41
141
Elsmere
Marshallton
2
Newport
202
Wilmington
295
Newark
95
13
9
295
Brookside
13
New Castle
NEW JERSEY
896
Bear
40
DELAWARE MEMORIAL BRIDGE
Christina
40
Glasgow
301
Delaware City
Chesapeake and Delaware Canal
Pea Patch Island
St. Georges
Port Penn
13
Reedy I.
Middletown
301
Noxontown Pond
9
Odessa
Townsend
Liston Pt.
1
Smyrna
Bombay Hook Island
13
BOMBAY HOOK
Clayton
NATIONAL
Leipsic
WILDLIFE
300
Goose Point
Cheswold
REFUGE
Deepwater Point
St. Jones
Dover International Speedway
8
Dover
9
Camden
10
1
Marydel
Kitts Hummock
10
13
Bowers Beach
Felton
Frederica
1
14
Slaughter Beach
Harrington
Houston
Milford
Lincoln
PRIME HOOK
NATIONAL
13
WILDLIFE
113
REFUGE
Greenwood
Ellendale
Broadkill Beach
1
Milton
Cape Henlopen
9
Lewes
404
Lewes & Rehoboth Canal
Harbeson
Rehoboth Beach
Midway
1
9
Dewey Beach
404
Georgetown
Rehoboth Bay
Seaford
9
Oak Orchard
Indian River Bay
Indian River Inlet
Blades
Millsboro
1
Laurel
Ocean View
Bethany Beach
Dagsboro
Assawoman Canal
South Bethany
13
Frankford
113
Fenwick Island
Delmar
Selbyville
528
50

Delaware Bay

Delaware River

Brandywine Creek

Choptank

Marshyhope Creek

Nanticoke

Smyrna

Cypress Swamp

ATLANTIC OCEAN

MARYLAND

DELMARVA PENINSULA

5 COOL THINGS TO DO HERE

3 TALL SHIP
Wilmington

Hoist the sails of this working reproduction of the colonial ship *Kalmar Nyckel*, which embarks from ports throughout the state.

4 HAGLEY MUSEUM & LIBRARY
Wilmington

Learn how American industry began with a bang at the gunpowder factories of this outdoor museum.

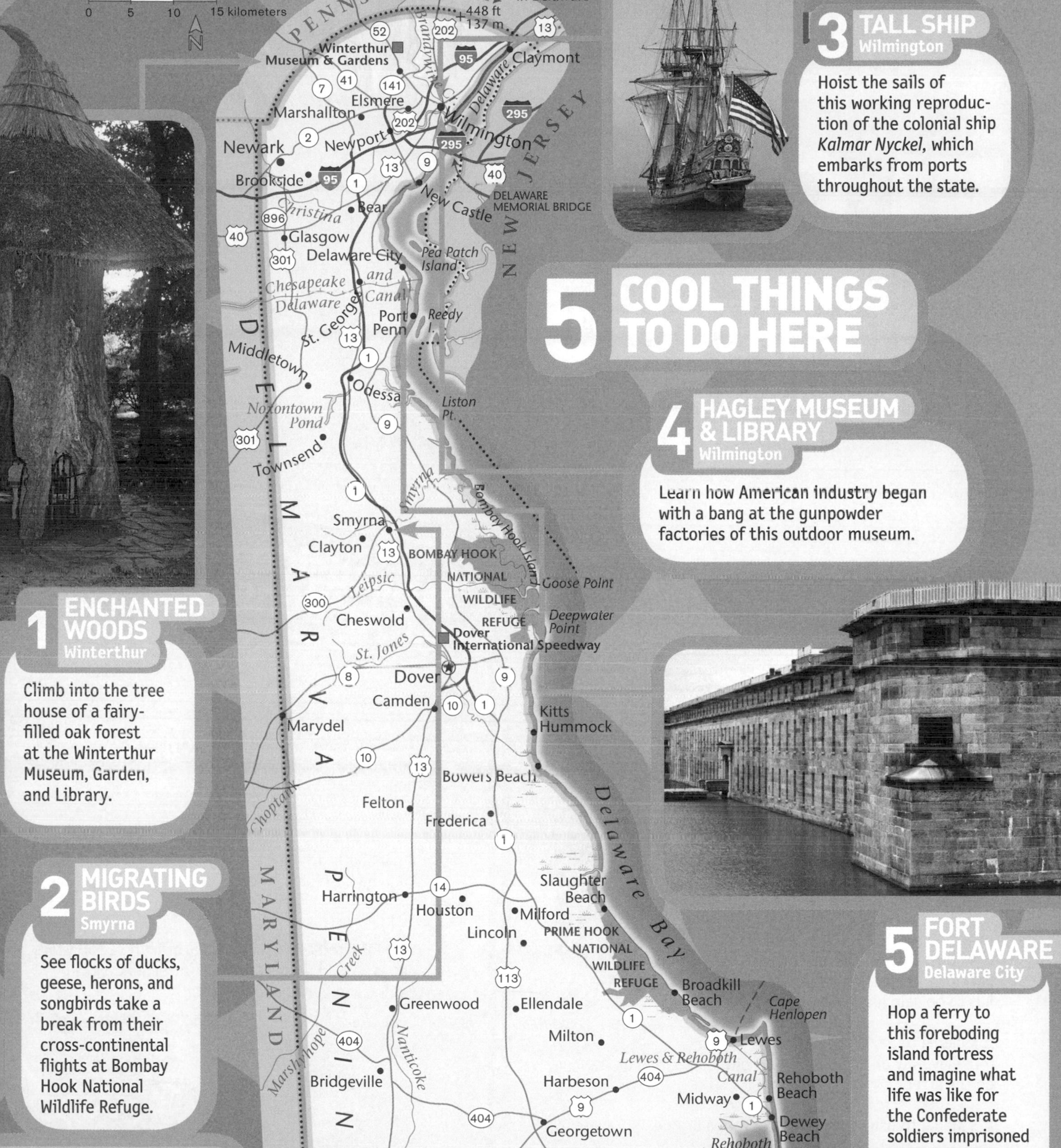

1 ENCHANTED WOODS
Winterthur

Climb into the tree house of a fairy-filled oak forest at the Winterthur Museum, Garden, and Library.

2 MIGRATING BIRDS
Smyrna

See flocks of ducks, geese, herons, and songbirds take a break from their cross-continental flights at Bombay Hook National Wildlife Refuge.

5 FORT DELAWARE
Delaware City

Hop a ferry to this foreboding island fortress and imagine what life was like for the Confederate soldiers imprisoned here during the Civil War.

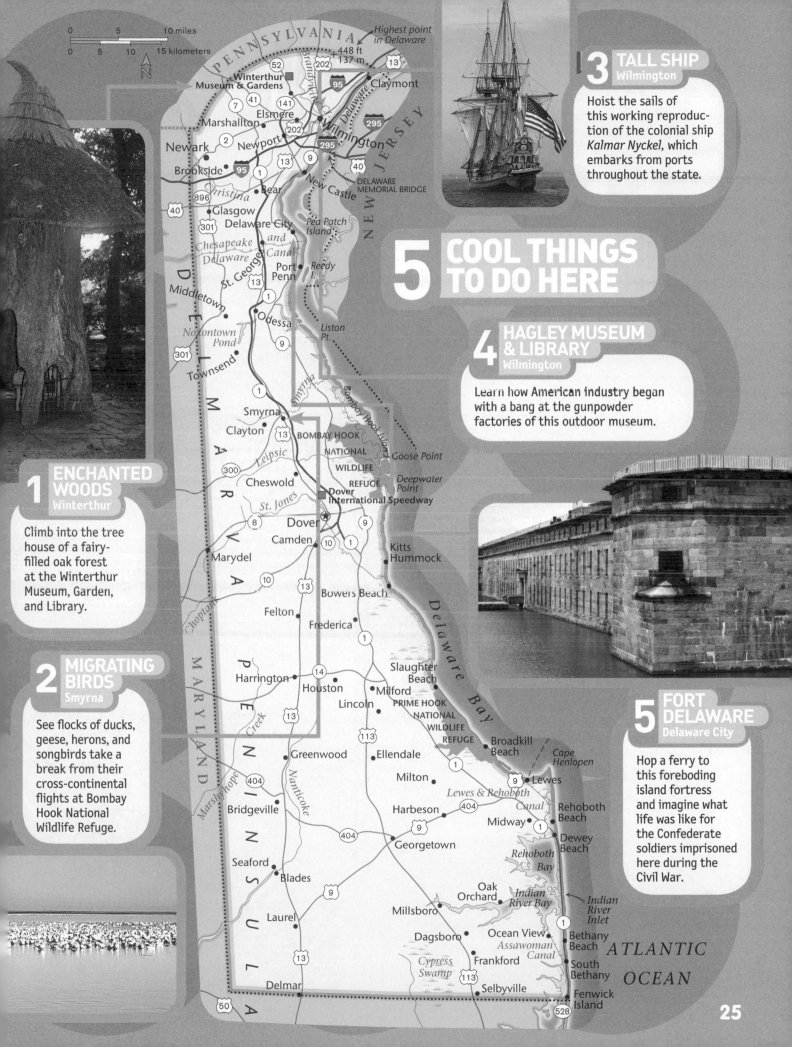

STATE BIRD: mockingbird

STATE FLOWER: orange blossom

STATE ANIMAL: panther

FLORIDA

The Sunshine STATE

Highest point in Florida
Britton H
345 ft
29
105
Perdido
Crestview
For
Wa
Bea
98
Pensacola
GULF ISLANDS NAT. SEASHORE
0 25 50 75 m
0 25 50 75 100 kilomete
N

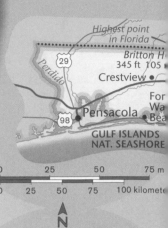

Spanish conquistador Ponce de León never found the Fountain of Youth when he explored Florida 500 years ago, yet the Sunshine State—land of Mickey Mouse, unending beaches, and vibrant cities—still brings out the kid in its many visitors.

WHIMZEYLAND

You'll do a double take when you drive by the wacky bowling-ball sculptures in front of this colorful home in Safety Harbor.

GOOFY GOLF

A popular stop since 1959, this putt-putt course in Panama City features monsters, a volcano, and more!

SUNKEN GARDENS

What started as a St. Petersburg sinkhole 100 years ago is now a lush garden with waterfalls, exotic plants, and flocks of flamingos.

TRAFFIC LAWS YOU WON'T BELIEVE

If an elephant is left tied to a parking meter, the parking fee has to be paid just as it would be for a car.

It's illegal to park a pickup truck in your own driveway or in front of your own house on the street.

It's illegal to fish while driving across a bridge.

BOREDOM BUSTER!
Take a picture of every wacky road sign you pass and see who gets the most!

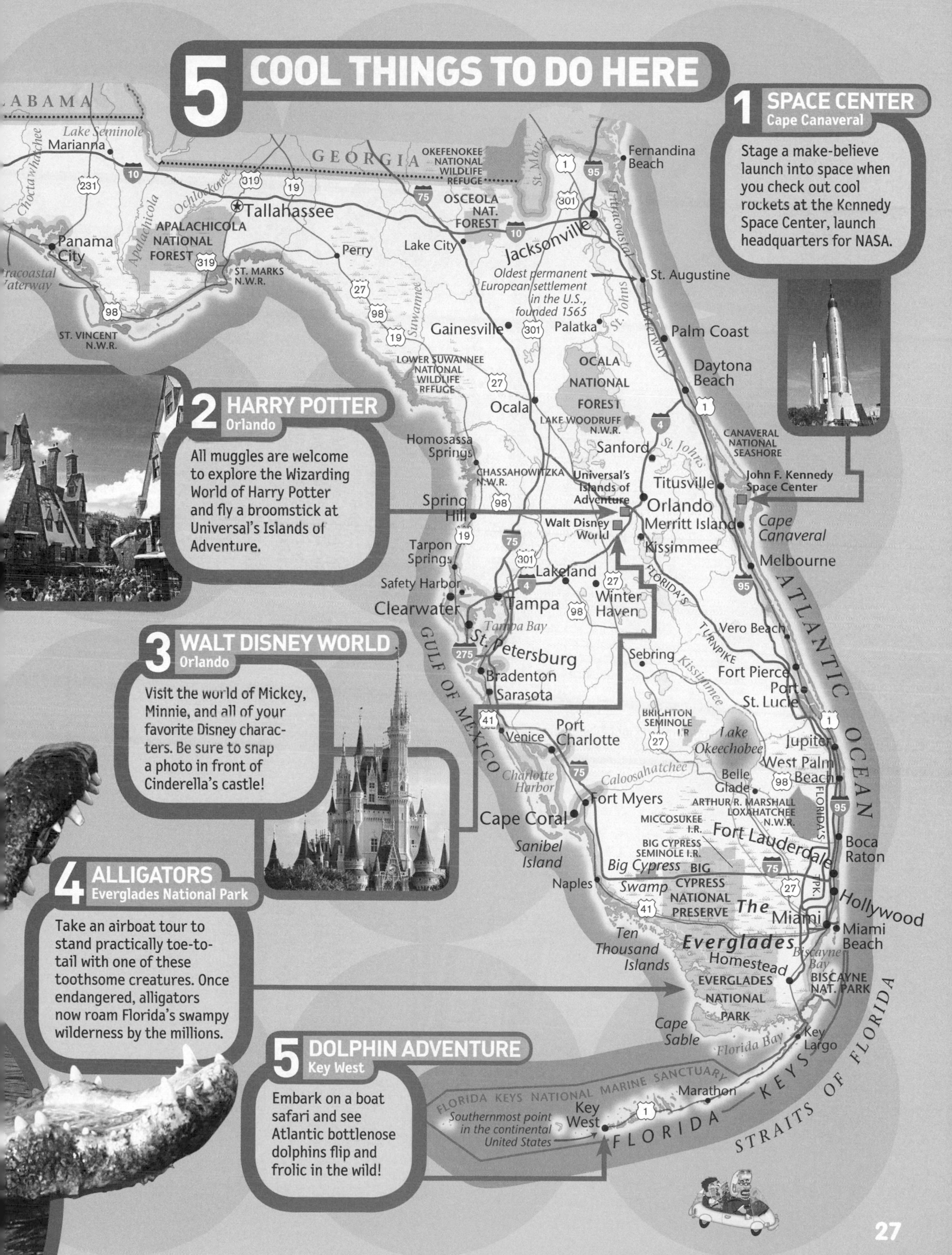

5 COOL THINGS TO DO HERE

1 SPACE CENTER
Cape Canaveral

Stage a make-believe launch into space when you check out cool rockets at the Kennedy Space Center, launch headquarters for NASA.

2 HARRY POTTER
Orlando

All muggles are welcome to explore the Wizarding World of Harry Potter and fly a broomstick at Universal's Islands of Adventure.

3 WALT DISNEY WORLD
Orlando

Visit the world of Mickey, Minnie, and all of your favorite Disney characters. Be sure to snap a photo in front of Cinderella's castle!

4 ALLIGATORS
Everglades National Park

Take an airboat tour to stand practically toe-to-tail with one of these toothsome creatures. Once endangered, alligators now roam Florida's swampy wilderness by the millions.

5 DOLPHIN ADVENTURE
Key West

Embark on a boat safari and see Atlantic bottlenose dolphins flip and frolic in the wild!

ALABAMA

Lake Seminole
Marianna
Choctawhatchee
231
10
Ochlockonee
310
19
GEORGIA
OKEFENOKEE NATIONAL WILDLIFE REFUGE
St. Marys
1
95
OSCEOLA NAT. FOREST
75
Fernandina Beach
★ Tallahassee
Apalachicola
Panama City
APALACHICOLA NATIONAL FOREST
319
Perry
Lake City
10
301
Jacksonville
Intracoastal Waterway
98
ST. MARKS N.W.R.
27
Oldest permanent European settlement in the U.S., founded 1565
St. Augustine
Intracoastal Waterway
ST. VINCENT N.W.R.
Suwannee
98
19
Gainesville
301
Palatka
St. Johns
Palm Coast
LOWER SUWANNEE NATIONAL WILDLIFE REFUGE
27
Ocala
OCALA NATIONAL FOREST
LAKE WOODRUFF N.W.R.
4
Daytona Beach
1
Homosassa Springs
CHASSAHOWITZKA N.W.R.
Sanford
St. Johns
CANAVERAL NATIONAL SEASHORE
Spring Hill
98
Universal's Islands of Adventure
Titusville
John F. Kennedy Space Center
Tarpon Springs
19
Walt Disney World
Orlando
Merritt Island
Cape Canaveral
Safety Harbor
301
Lakeland
Kissimmee
75
4
Winter Haven
FLORIDA'S
Melbourne
Clearwater
Tampa
27
98
95
Tampa Bay
St. Petersburg
Vero Beach
275
Sebring
Kissimmee
Fort Pierce
Bradenton
Sarasota
BRIGHTON SEMINOLE I.R.
Lake Okeechobee
Port St. Lucie
GULF OF MEXICO
41
Port Charlotte
27
Jupiter
Venice
FLORIDA'S TURNPIKE
Charlotte Harbor
75
Caloosahatchee
West Palm Beach
1
Belle Glade
98
Fort Myers
ARTHUR R. MARSHALL LOXAHATCHEE N.W.R.
Cape Coral
MICCOSUKEE I.R.
Fort Lauderdale
95
Sanibel Island
BIG CYPRESS SEMINOLE I.R.
Boca Raton
Big Cypress
BIG CYPRESS NATIONAL PRESERVE
75
Naples
Swamp
27
Hollywood
41
The Everglades
Miami
Ten Thousand Islands
Biscayne Bay
Miami Beach
Homestead
EVERGLADES NATIONAL PARK
BISCAYNE NAT. PARK
Cape Sable
Florida Bay
Key Largo
ATLANTIC OCEAN
FLORIDA KEYS NATIONAL MARINE SANCTUARY
Southernmost point in the continental United States
Marathon
Key West
1
FLORIDA KEYS
STRAITS OF FLORIDA

STATE BIRD: brown thrasher

STATE FLOWER: Cherokee rose

STATE TREE: live oak

GEORGIA

The Peach STATE

Its countryside ravaged and its capital in flames, Georgia was the last place you'd want to visit 150 years ago at the end of the Civil War. Today, this comeback state is full of must-see destinations, from energetic Atlanta to laid-back barrier islands.

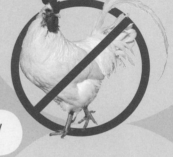

Roadside Attractions

LUNCH BOX MUSEUM
Forget the plastic pail you use to haul your PB&J today. This museum in Columbus is devoted entirely to old-school metal lunch boxes adorned with the images of TV characters and superheroes.

BRUCE WEINER MICROCAR MUSEUM
Today's compact cars look like gas-guzzling monster trucks compared to the vintage European "bubble cars" at this Eatonton museum, home of the world's largest collection of itty-bitty autos.

PEANUT MONUMENT
In a nutshell, this Ashburn roadside monument honors the "Peanut Capital of the World."

TRAFFIC LAWS YOU WON'T BELIEVE

Chickens can't cross public roads in Athens-Clarke County.

Slingshots are outlawed on the streets of Columbus.

State senators can drive as fast as they want when the legislature is in session.

5 COOL THINGS TO DO HERE

1 AMICALOLA FALLS
Amicalola Falls State Park

Climb steep stairways alongside this tumbling torrent in the Blue Ridge Mountains, not far from the start of the famous Appalachian Trail, which meanders all the way to Maine.

2 GEORGIA AQUARIUM
Atlanta

Say hello to beluga whales and hop in the water with whale sharks at the world's largest aquarium.

3 STONE MOUNTAIN
Stone Mountain Park

This granite dome, emblazoned with sculptures of Confederate leaders of the Civil War, towers 1,700 feet above the countryside. On a clear day, you can see all the way to the Appalachian Mountains from its summit.

4 GOLDEN ISLES
St. Simons Island

Play on the golden beaches of this resort island, one of several barrier islands famous for historic sites, nature trails, and watersports.

5 WILD ADVENTURES
Valdosta

Whoop and holler on looping roller coasters, then embark on an African safari at this theme park that doubles as a zoo.

BOREDOM BUSTER!
Take pictures of all the antebellum—meaning pre–Civil War—buildings you pass and see who gets the most. (Hint: If the house is fronted by white columns, like the house above, take a picture!)

STATE BIRD: Hawaiian goose

STATE FLOWER: hibiscus

STATE ANIMAL: monk seal

HAWAII

The Aloha STATE

Thrust into the middle of the Pacific Ocean by volcanic eruption long ago, the Hawaiian Islands are a tropical paradise of lush jungles, awesome waterfalls, and turquoise waters. Six million tourists flock to the newest U.S. state each year to frolic on golden beaches and experience ancient Polynesian culture.

FANTASTIC HAWAII FACTS

The Hawaiian Islands are actually the tips of an immense submarine mountain range.

"Aloha" is an all-purpose Hawaiian word. Use it to say hello, goodbye, and to express affection.

Hawaiian sand comes in a rainbow of colors: black, red—even green!

Roadside Attractions

ALOHA ELVIS STATUE

This bronze statue in Honolulu catches the king of rock and roll in mid-croon, just as he appeared in a concert here in 1973.

HALONA BLOWHOLE

Fed by an ancient lava tube, this seaside rock formation in Oahu blasts seawater 30 feet high.

HONOLULU SURFING MUSEUM

Surfboards of every era—including the heavy planks of the ancient Hawaiians—line the walls of this fascinating repository of surf history and folklore.

BOREDOM BUSTER!

Use your camera to take action shots of surfers riding waves. Award yourself bonus points if you catch any surfers hanging ten (riding with every toe over the board's nose).

5 COOL THINGS TO DO HERE

1 HUMPBACK WHALES
Lahaina

Watch 40-ton leviathans create incredible splashes off the west coast of Maui.

2 SNORKEL ADVENTURE
Molokini Island

Dive headfirst into an undersea world teeming with tropical fish, sea turtles—and, yes, the occasional shark!

3 HELICOPTER TOUR
Waimea Canyon

oar above the waterfalls nd rugged cliffs of Kauai's Grand Canyon of the Pacific."

4 SURFING
Honolulu

Learn what Hawaiians call the "sport of kings" in the land where it was invented. The easy rollers on Oahu's Waikiki Beach are best for watermen-in-training.

5 KILAUEA VOLCANO
Hawaii Volcanoes National Park

Watch the Big Island of Hawaii grow inch by inch as molten lava spews into the sea to form new land.

STATE BIRD: mountain bluebird

STATE FLOWER: syringa

STATE TREE: western white pine

IDAHO

The Gem STATE

Maybe it's the state's creepily named geographical features (Hells Canyon! Craters of the Moon!) or the misconception that it's one gigantic potato field, but Idaho doesn't rank high as a tourist hot spot. Your gain! Investigate the state's uncrowded scenic wonders and pretend you discovered them yourself!

Roadside Attractions

IDAHO POTATO MUSEUM

No spud detail is spared at this building in Blackfoot devoted to the history and deep-fried uses of Idaho's most famous crop.

CITY OF ROCKS

Stone formations in this Alamo reserve almost look manmade. See rocks in the shapes of cities, castles, and animals—all the products of natural erosion.

SHOSHONE ICE CAVES

Residents from nearby Shoshone once chipped ice chunks from this chilly lava tube to keep their drinks cold. Now the caves make a refreshing roadside escape from Idaho's sweltering summer heat.

WHAT A SILLY SIGN!

CHICKEN DINNER RD

HWY 55

What really happened to the chicken that crossed the road? This oddly named street in Caldwell might finally solve the mystery.

5 COOL THINGS TO DO HERE

CANADA
3
21
1
95
KOOTENAI N.W.R.
KOOTENAI
Priest Lake
Pend Oreille
Kootenai
Selkirk Mtns.
Bonners Ferry
IDAHO
2
Cabinet Mtns.
200
Sandpoint
Pend Oreille Lake
Priest
NAT.
R
O
C
B
Post
PANHANDLE
Clark Fo

1 HELLS CANYON
Hells Canyon National Recreation Area

Take a wild boat cruise through canyon walls that tower a mile high in North America's deepest river gorge.

2 MOUNTAIN LAKES
Sawtooth National Recreation Area

Camp alongside pristine lakes that reflect the jutting peaks of the Sawtooths, one of the Rockies' many ranges.

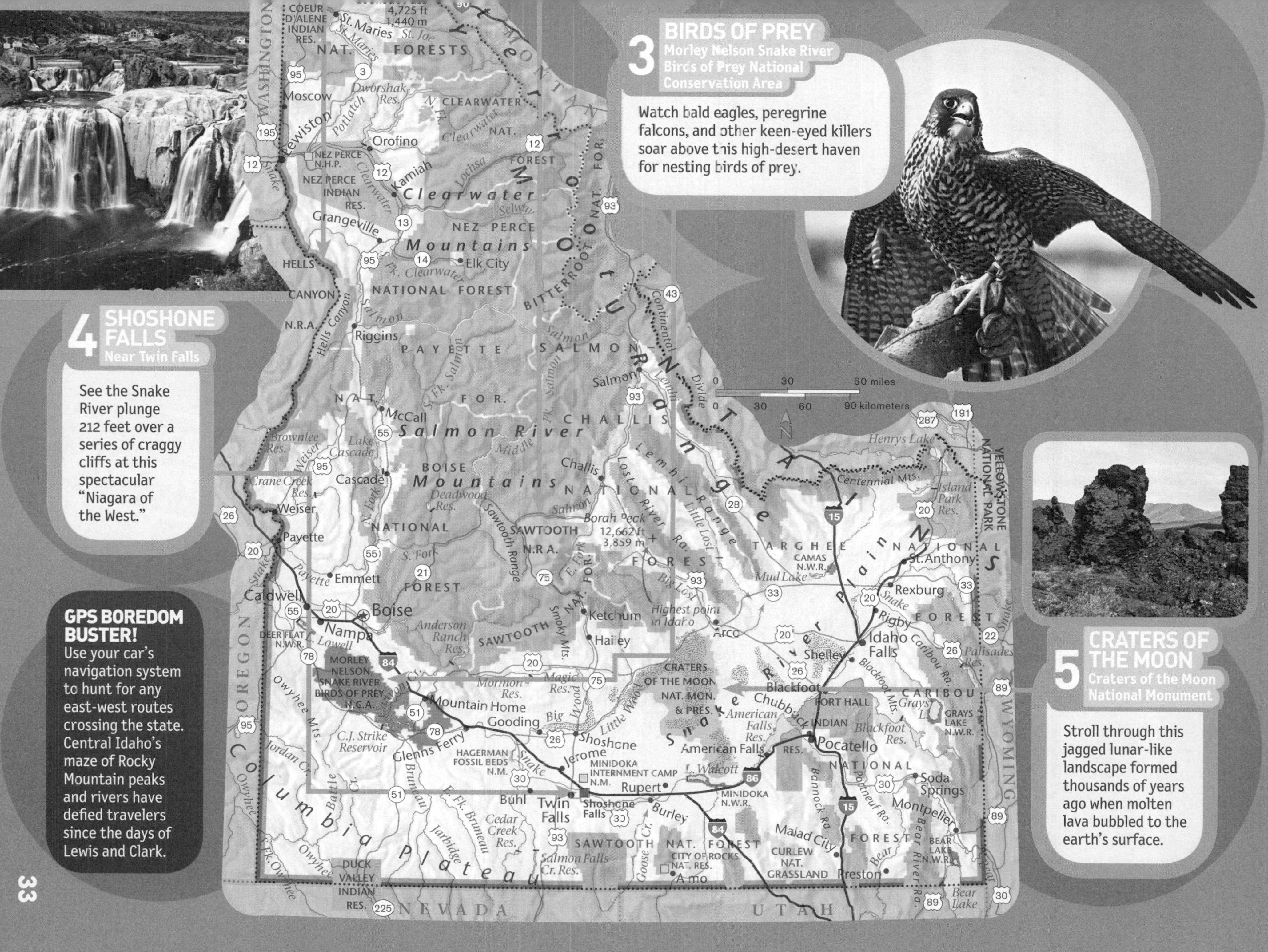

3 BIRDS OF PREY
Morley Nelson Snake River Birds of Prey National Conservation Area

Watch bald eagles, peregrine falcons, and other keen-eyed killers soar above this high-desert haven for nesting birds of prey.

4 SHOSHONE FALLS
Near Twin Falls

See the Snake River plunge 212 feet over a series of craggy cliffs at this spectacular "Niagara of the West."

5 CRATERS OF THE MOON
Craters of the Moon National Monument

Stroll through this jagged lunar-like landscape formed thousands of years ago when molten lava bubbled to the earth's surface.

GPS BOREDOM BUSTER!
Use your car's navigation system to hunt for any east-west routes crossing the state. Central Idaho's maze of Rocky Mountain peaks and rivers have defied travelers since the days of Lewis and Clark.

STATE BIRD: cardinal

STATE FLOWER: violet

STATE ANIMAL: white-tailed deer

ILLINOIS

The Land of LINCOLN

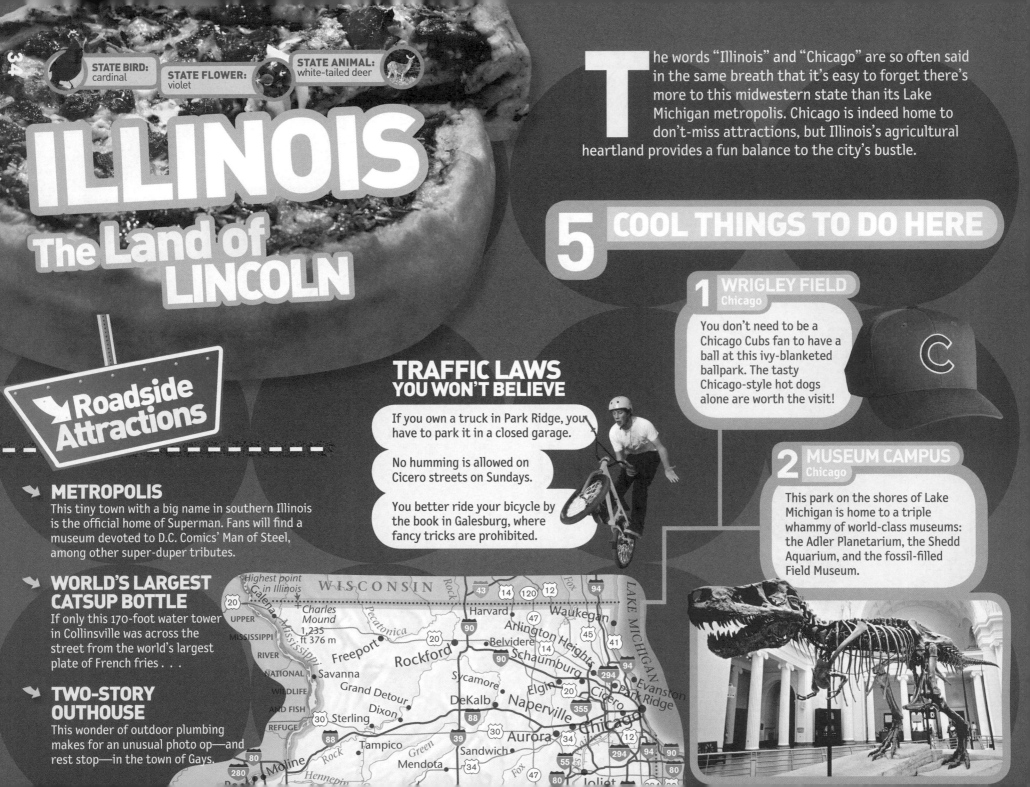

The words "Illinois" and "Chicago" are so often said in the same breath that it's easy to forget there's more to this midwestern state than its Lake Michigan metropolis. Chicago is indeed home to don't-miss attractions, but Illinois's agricultural heartland provides a fun balance to the city's bustle.

Roadside Attractions

METROPOLIS

This tiny town with a big name in southern Illinois is the official home of Superman. Fans will find a museum devoted to D.C. Comics' Man of Steel, among other super-duper tributes.

WORLD'S LARGEST CATSUP BOTTLE

If only this 170-foot water tower in Collinsville was across the street from the world's largest plate of French fries . . .

TWO-STORY OUTHOUSE

This wonder of outdoor plumbing makes for an unusual photo op—and rest stop—in the town of Gays.

TRAFFIC LAWS YOU WON'T BELIEVE

If you own a truck in Park Ridge, you have to park it in a closed garage.

No humming is allowed on Cicero streets on Sundays.

You better ride your bicycle by the book in Galesburg, where fancy tricks are prohibited.

5 COOL THINGS TO DO HERE

1 WRIGLEY FIELD
Chicago

You don't need to be a Chicago Cubs fan to have a ball at this ivy-blanketed ballpark. The tasty Chicago-style hot dogs alone are worth the visit!

2 MUSEUM CAMPUS
Chicago

This park on the shores of Lake Michigan is home to a triple whammy of world-class museums: the Adler Planetarium, the Shedd Aquarium, and the fossil-filled Field Museum.

3 COOL CANYONS
Starved Rock State Park

It's hard to believe this geological wonderland of waterfalls and sandstone cliffs is within 100 miles of Chicago's skyscrapers.

4 MILLER PARK ZOO
Bloomington

Visit red pandas, sea lions, and bald eagles at this zoo filled with wildlife of the land, sea, and air.

5 ANCIENT CITY
Cahokia Mounds State Historic Site

Investigate the mysterious prehistoric culture of Cahokia, a mound city that rivaled medieval London in size centuries before Columbus reached America.

GPS BOREDOM BUSTER!
Use your car's navigation system to search for all the historic sites tied to Abraham Lincoln, who practiced law in central Illinois before becoming President.

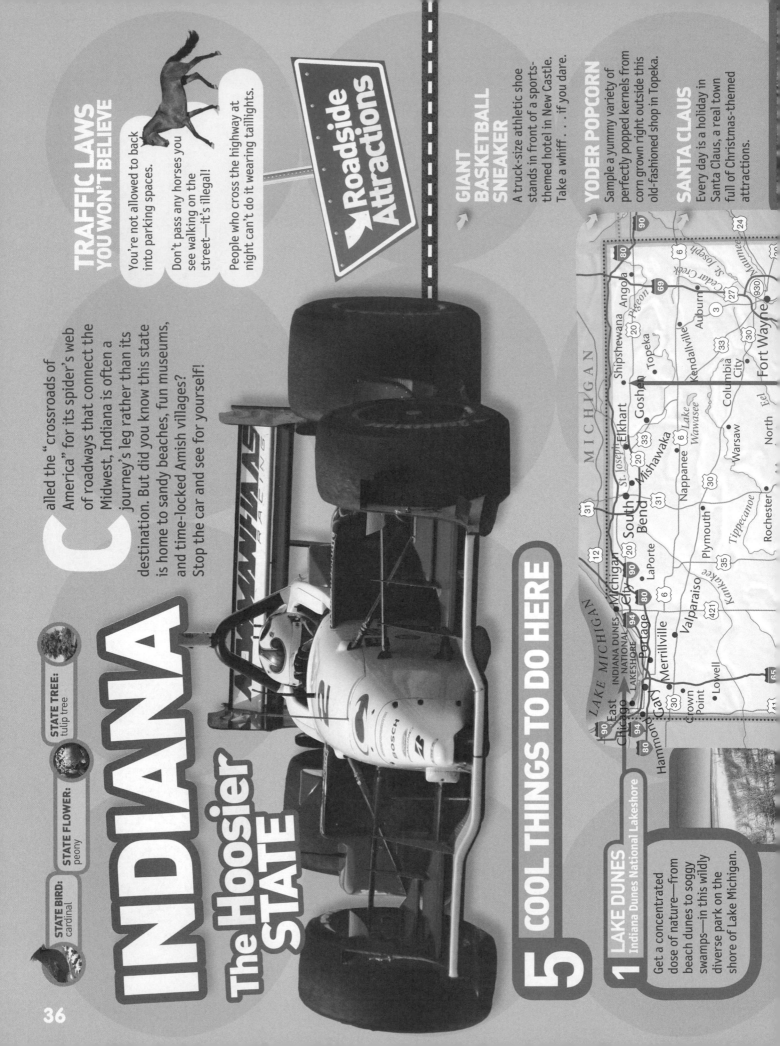

STATE BIRD: cardinal **STATE FLOWER:** peony **STATE TREE:** tulip tree

INDIANA
The Hoosier STATE

Called the "crossroads of America" for its spider's web of roadways that connect the Midwest, Indiana is often a journey's leg rather than its destination. But did you know this state is home to sandy beaches, fun museums, and time-locked Amish villages? Stop the car and see for yourself!

TRAFFIC LAWS YOU WON'T BELIEVE

You're not allowed to back into parking spaces.

Don't pass any horses you see walking on the street—it's illegal!

People who cross the highway at night can't do it wearing taillights.

GIANT BASKETBALL SNEAKER
A truck-size athletic shoe stands in front of a sports-themed hotel in New Castle. Take a whiff . . . if you dare.

YODER POPCORN
Sample a yummy variety of perfectly popped kernels from corn grown right outside this old-fashioned shop in Topeka.

SANTA CLAUS
Every day is a holiday in Santa Claus, a real town full of Christmas-themed attractions.

5 COOL THINGS TO DO HERE

1 LAKE DUNES
Indiana Dunes National Lakeshore

Get a concentrated dose of nature—from beach dunes to soggy swamps—in this wildly diverse park on the shore of Lake Michigan.

2 AMISH COUNTRY
Shipshewana

Tour the villages and sample the homemade treats of Indiana's Amish, a community that embraces 19th-century living for religious reasons.

3 CHILDREN'S MUSEUM
Indianapolis

Touching the exhibits is encouraged at this popular hands-on science museum.

4 RACE CARS
Indianapolis

Climb into the cockpit of a sleek race car at the Indianapolis Motor Speedway Hall of Fame Museum.

5 HEDGE LABYRINTH
New Harmony

Make your way through the confounding hedge maze of this serene historic town.

BOREDOM BUSTER!
No one knows for sure why Indiana is called the Hoosier State. Use a smart phone to research the many theories and choose the most likely among them.

STATE BIRD: eastern goldfinch

STATE FLOWER: wild rose

STATE TREE: oak

IOWA

The Hawkeye STATE

Rolling hills, big red barns, and endless stalks of corn rush past your window as you ride through Iowa. To see the state's most valuable resource, however, you'll need to pull over and get your hands dirty. Iowa's black soil is the most fertile in the country.

TRAFFIC LAWS YOU WON'T BELIEVE

You'll never hear the catchy tune of an ice cream truck in Indianola, which banned the vehicles.

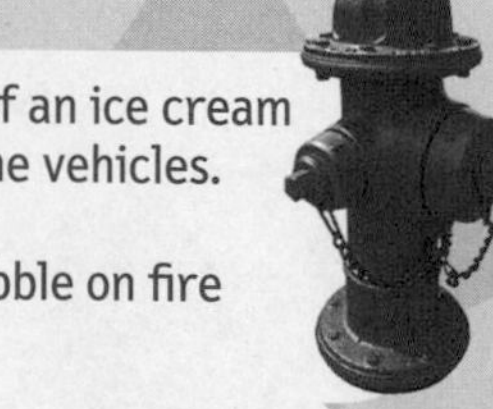

Hungry horses aren't allowed to nibble on fire hydrants in Marshalltown.

You'll need permission from Mount Vernon's city council if you plan to toss bricks onto a highway.

BOREDOM BUSTER!
Use a smart phone to look up all the famous people born in Iowa and see who can find the most!

Roadside Attractions

VERMEER WINDMILL

Take a peek at the gears and grain-grinding power of the country's tallest working windmill, towering above the Dutch-settled town of Pella.

BUFFALO BILL MUSEUM

Learn about one of the Wild West's most colorful cowboys in LeClaire, birthplace of William F. "Buffalo Bill" Cody.

AMERICAN GOTHIC HOUSE

Re-create the famous painting "American Gothic" by posing in front of the historic house in Eldon that inspired it.

5 COO

THINGS TO DO HERE

1 ADVENTURELAND
Altoona

Strap into any of the many roller coasters at this homegrown amusement park.

2 MYSTERIOUS MOUNDS
Near Marquette

Native Americans built sacred mounds in the shape of birds and bears long ago. Explore the Effigy Mounds National Monument to find out why.

3 HOT-AIR BALLOONS
Indianola

Bone up on the history of hot-air flight at the National Balloon Museum, then hop aboard a basket at Z-Balloon Adventures for some silent soaring.

4 LIVING HISTORY FARMS
Urbandale

Take a fascinating look at where your food comes from by exploring three historic farms—including one run by Native Americans.

5 FOSSILS
Coralville

A 1993 flood scoured away trees and soil at the Devonian Fossil Gorge, revealing the petrified skeletons of sea creatures that died 150 million years before the age of dinosaurs.

STATE BIRD: western meadowlark

STATE FLOWER: sunflower

STATE ANIMAL: buffalo

KANSAS

The Sunflower STATE

That hint of earthy flavor in your bread? That's Kansas you're tasting! Most of America's wheat grows here in the nation's geographic heart, but there's more to the state than amber waves of grain, dust storms, and the occasional tornado.

TRAFFIC LAWS YOU WON'T BELIEVE

It's illegal to ride a zebra down the road in Derby.

Better pull over if you see a marching band coming your way in Topeka, where driving through parades is not allowed.

Singing on Topeka's streets at night is a big no-no.

Roadside Attractions

ROCK CITY

The sandstone boulders scattered around this park near Minneapolis aren't petrified dinosaur eggs. They're actually geological leftovers from when Kansas was covered by a vast inland sea.

DOROTHY'S HOUSE

How do you find the house that fell on the wicked witch in *The Wizard of Oz?* Follow the yellow brick road in Liberal, of course.

MUSEUM OF WORLD TREASURES

T. rex fossils, ancient Egyptian mummies, and other artifacts fill three floors of time-tripping exhibits in Wichita.

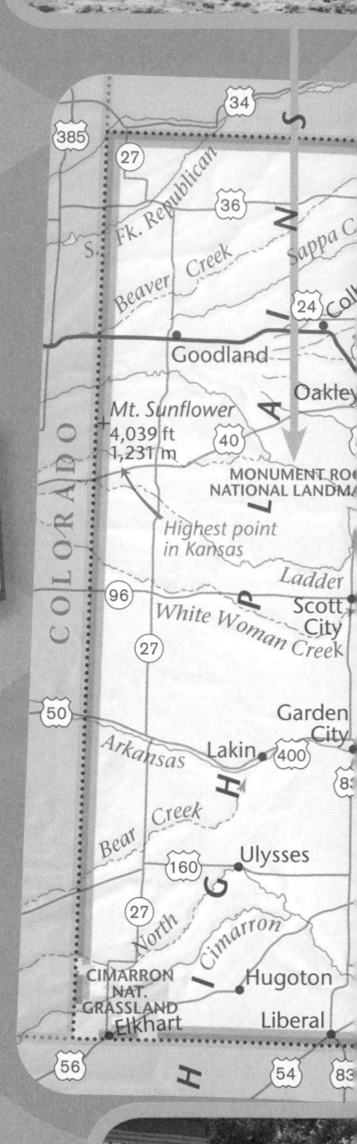

BOREDOM BUSTER!
Take a picture of every tornado-shelter sign you pass and see who can get the most!

5 COOL THINGS TO DO HERE

1 MONUMENT ROCKS
Near Oakley

Explore an alien landscape of towering chalk formations in the vast prairie-land of northwestern Kansas.

2 TALLGRASS PRAIRIE
Flint Hills

Watch fireflies flit above this green and golden oasis, all that remains of a vast sea of grass that once covered 140 million acres of North America.

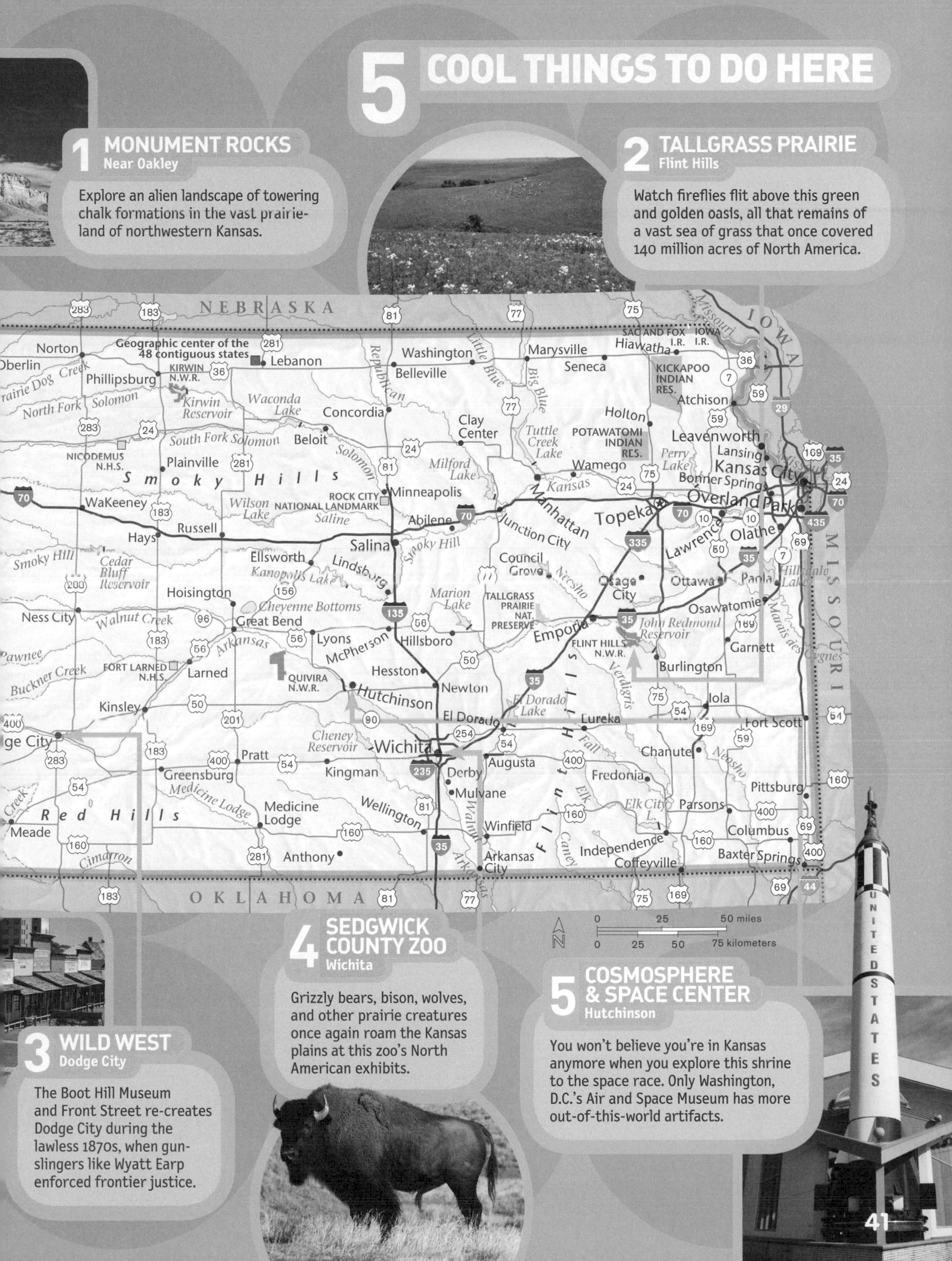

3 WILD WEST
Dodge City

The Boot Hill Museum and Front Street re-creates Dodge City during the lawless 1870s, when gunslingers like Wyatt Earp enforced frontier justice.

4 SEDGWICK COUNTY ZOO
Wichita

Grizzly bears, bison, wolves, and other prairie creatures once again roam the Kansas plains at this zoo's North American exhibits.

5 COSMOSPHERE & SPACE CENTER
Hutchinson

You won't believe you're in Kansas anymore when you explore this shrine to the space race. Only Washington, D.C.'s Air and Space Museum has more out-of-this-world artifacts.

STATE BIRD: cardinal

STATE FLOWER: goldenrod

STATE ANIMAL: gray squirrel

KENTUCKY

The Bluegrass STATE

Kentucky is famous for two distinct sounds: the thunderous gallop of thoroughbred horses and the toe-tapping twang of bluegrass music. You're bound to hear one or the other as you ramble from the state's Appalachian highlands to its rolling farmland.

FANTASTIC KENTUCKY FACTS

Over 147 million ounces of gold are locked away in Fort Knox, the world's most secure vault.

Abraham Lincoln and Jefferson Davis—the respective presidents of the Union and the Confederacy during the Civil War—were both born in Kentucky.

Eastern Kentucky is home to so many country-music stars that a stretch of highway was renamed the "Country Music Highway."

GPS BOREDOM BUSTER!
Use your car's navigation system to find a horse ranch near you—then snap a photo of a thoroughbred galloping through a roadside pasture!

Roadside Attractions

INTERNATIONAL BLUEGRASS MUSEUM

Listen and learn at this Owensboro museum dedicated to the music of Kentucky's bluegrass plains.

KENTUCKY FRIED CHICKEN MUSEUM

Harland Sanders—aka Colonel Sanders to fast-food aficionados—opened his first restaurant in Corbin. Visit it to find a barrel of his secret recipe.

KENTUCKY CASTLE

Perched in the rolling pasturelands of Versailles, this themed hotel looks just like a medieval fortress. Well, if you ignore the swimming pool and tennis courts.

5 COOL THINGS TO DO HERE

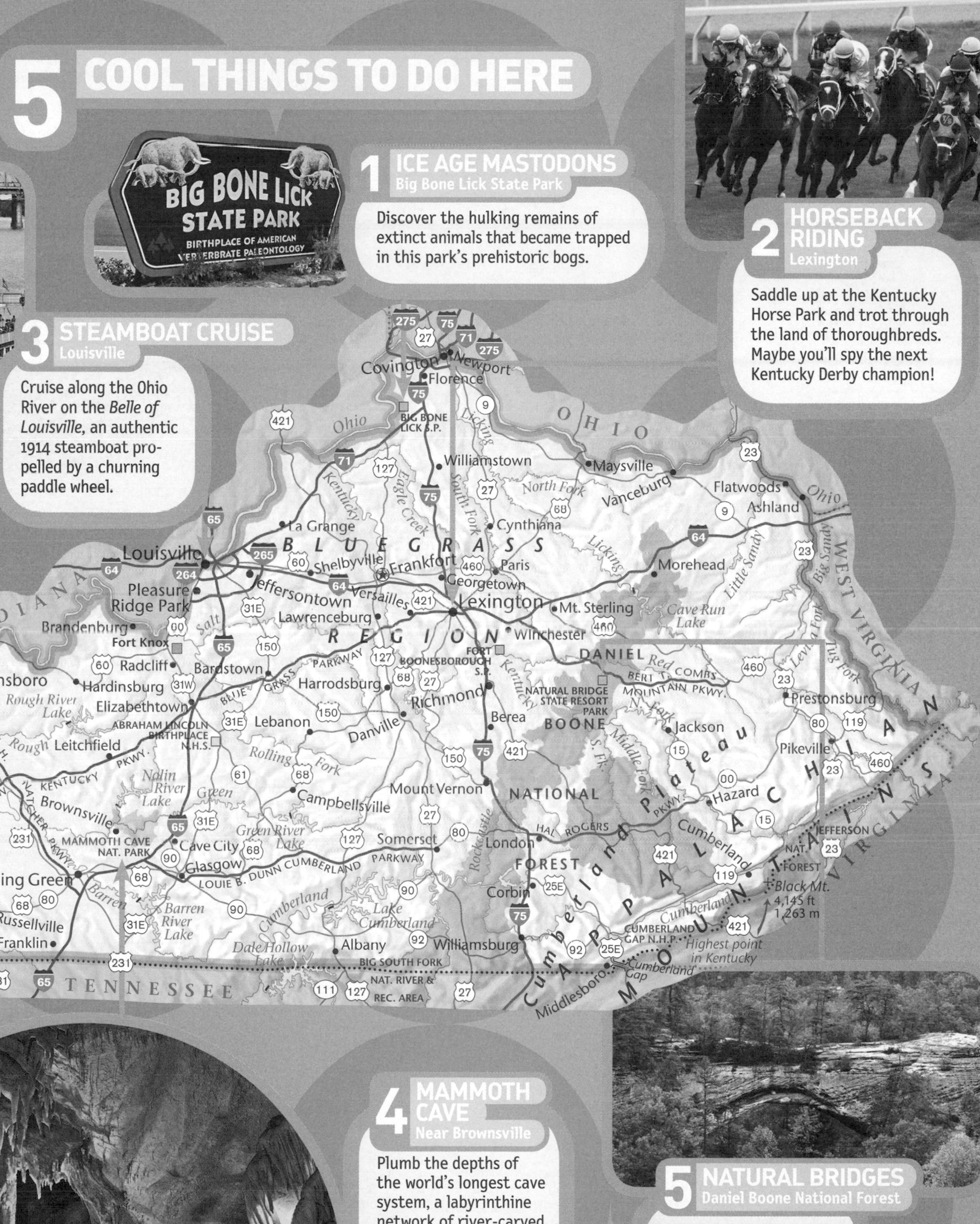

1 ICE AGE MASTODONS
Big Bone Lick State Park

Discover the hulking remains of extinct animals that became trapped in this park's prehistoric bogs.

2 HORSEBACK RIDING
Lexington

Saddle up at the Kentucky Horse Park and trot through the land of thoroughbreds. Maybe you'll spy the next Kentucky Derby champion!

3 STEAMBOAT CRUISE
Louisville

Cruise along the Ohio River on the *Belle of Louisville*, an authentic 1914 steamboat propelled by a churning paddle wheel.

4 MAMMOTH CAVE
Near Brownsville

Plumb the depths of the world's longest cave system, a labyrinthine network of river-carved limestone that stretches for nearly 400 miles!

5 NATURAL BRIDGES
Daniel Boone National Forest

Hike among the hundreds of spectacular sandstone formations of Natural Bridge State Resort Park.

5 COOL THINGS TO DO HERE

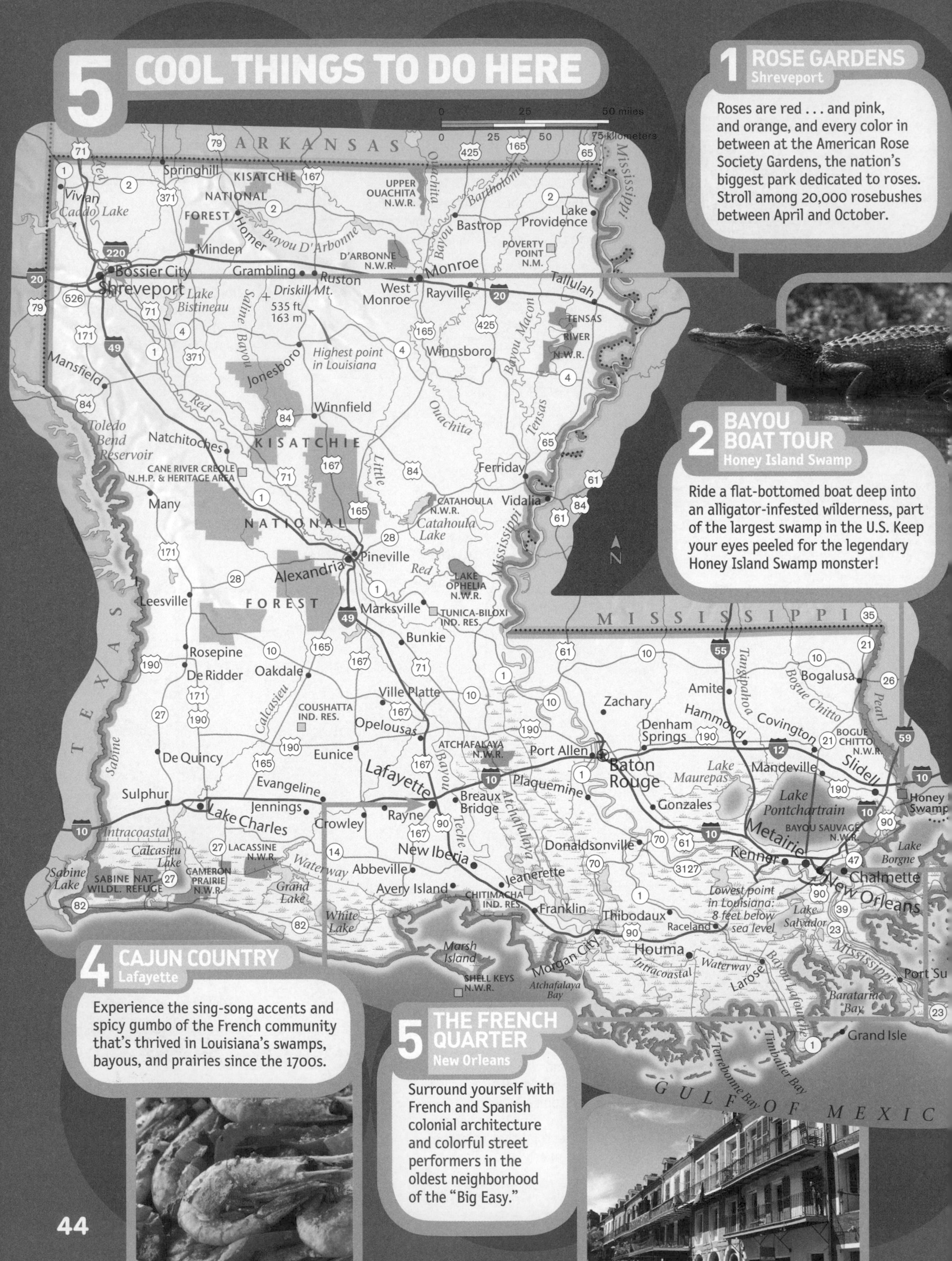

1 ROSE GARDENS
Shreveport

Roses are red . . . and pink, and orange, and every color in between at the American Rose Society Gardens, the nation's biggest park dedicated to roses. Stroll among 20,000 rosebushes between April and October.

2 BAYOU BOAT TOUR
Honey Island Swamp

Ride a flat-bottomed boat deep into an alligator-infested wilderness, part of the largest swamp in the U.S. Keep your eyes peeled for the legendary Honey Island Swamp monster!

4 CAJUN COUNTRY
Lafayette

Experience the sing-song accents and spicy gumbo of the French community that's thrived in Louisiana's swamps, bayous, and prairies since the 1700s.

5 THE FRENCH QUARTER
New Orleans

Surround yourself with French and Spanish colonial architecture and colorful street performers in the oldest neighborhood of the "Big Easy."

STATE BIRD: brown pelican

STATE FLOWER: magnolia

STATE TREE: bald cypress

LOUISIANA

The Pelican STATE

Infused with pirate lore and voodoo magic, rooted in French and Spanish traditions, Louisiana is like a foreign country on American soil. Its Deep South volcanic Cajun cuisine, sultry swamps, and surreal celebrations will take your senses on a roller-coaster ride.

3 AQUARIUM OF THE AMERICAS
New Orleans

This famous aquarium's clear tunnels and titanic tanks let you get as close as possible to aquatic life without getting wet.

TRAFFIC LAWS YOU WON'T BELIEVE

You're not allowed to cure voodoo curses on the streets of New Orleans.

Alligators must stay at least 200 yards away from the Mardi Gras Parade route.

Planting a tree near New Orleans streets or highways is a crime.

GPS BOREDOM BUSTER!

Use your car's navigation system to find all the locations named after Jean Lafitte, a 19th-century pirate who became a New Orleans folk hero.

Roadside Attractions

THE BIEDENHARN MUSEUM & GARDENS

Take a stroll through the historic home and magical gardens of Joseph A. Biedenharn, the first bottler of Coca-Cola.

MARDI GRAS WORLD

Can't make the annual Mardi Gras party? Visit Blaine Kern's Mardi Gras World in New Orleans to see how the parade's magical floats get made.

INSECTARIUM

This New Orleans museum is infested with insects, but don't call the exterminator! The butterflies, spiders, and swarms of bugs here are all part of the exhibits.

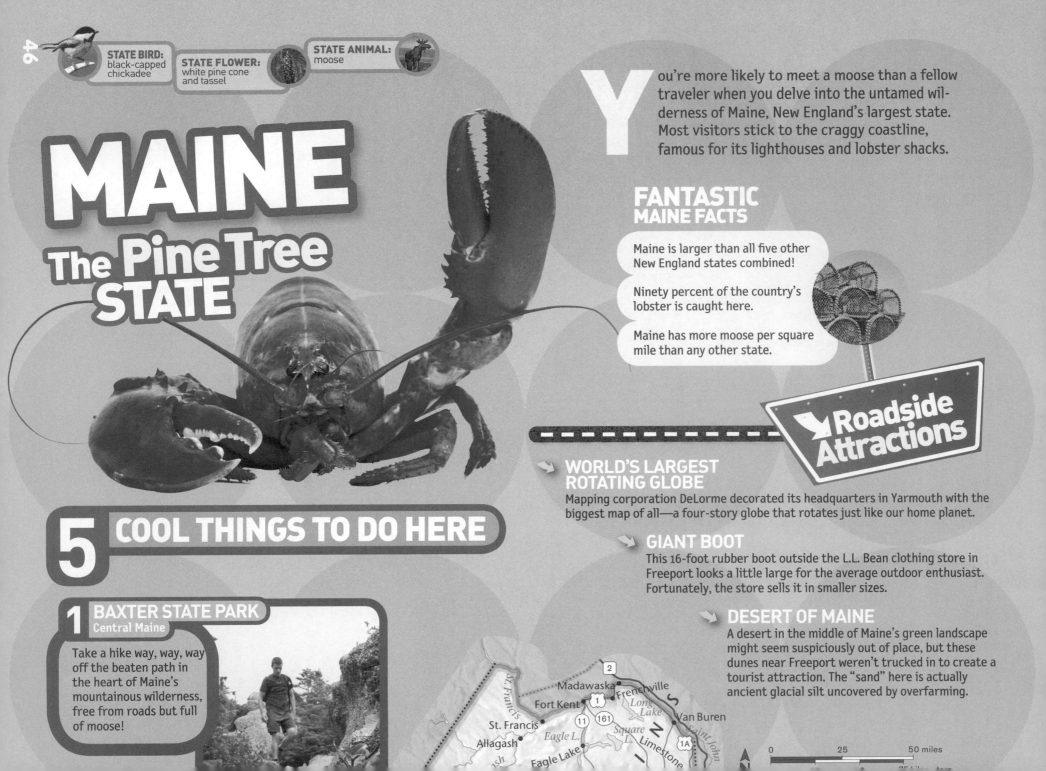

STATE BIRD: black-capped chickadee

STATE FLOWER: white pine cone and tassel

STATE ANIMAL: moose

MAINE

The Pine Tree STATE

You're more likely to meet a moose than a fellow traveler when you delve into the untamed wilderness of Maine, New England's largest state. Most visitors stick to the craggy coastline, famous for its lighthouses and lobster shacks.

FANTASTIC MAINE FACTS

Maine is larger than all five other New England states combined!

Ninety percent of the country's lobster is caught here.

Maine has more moose per square mile than any other state.

Roadside Attractions

WORLD'S LARGEST ROTATING GLOBE

Mapping corporation DeLorme decorated its headquarters in Yarmouth with the biggest map of all—a four-story globe that rotates just like our home planet.

GIANT BOOT

This 16-foot rubber boot outside the L.L. Bean clothing store in Freeport looks a little large for the average outdoor enthusiast. Fortunately, the store sells it in smaller sizes.

DESERT OF MAINE

A desert in the middle of Maine's green landscape might seem suspiciously out of place, but these dunes near Freeport weren't trucked in to create a tourist attraction. The "sand" here is actually ancient glacial silt uncovered by overfarming.

St. Francis
Madawaska
Frenchville
Fort Kent
Long Lake
Van Buren
Saint John
St. Francis
Eagle L.
Square L.
Limestone
Allagash
Eagle Lake
2
1
11
161
1A
0 25 50 miles

5 COOL THINGS TO DO HERE

1 BAXTER STATE PARK
Central Maine

Take a hike way, way, way off the beaten path in the heart of Maine's mountainous wilderness, free from roads but full of moose!

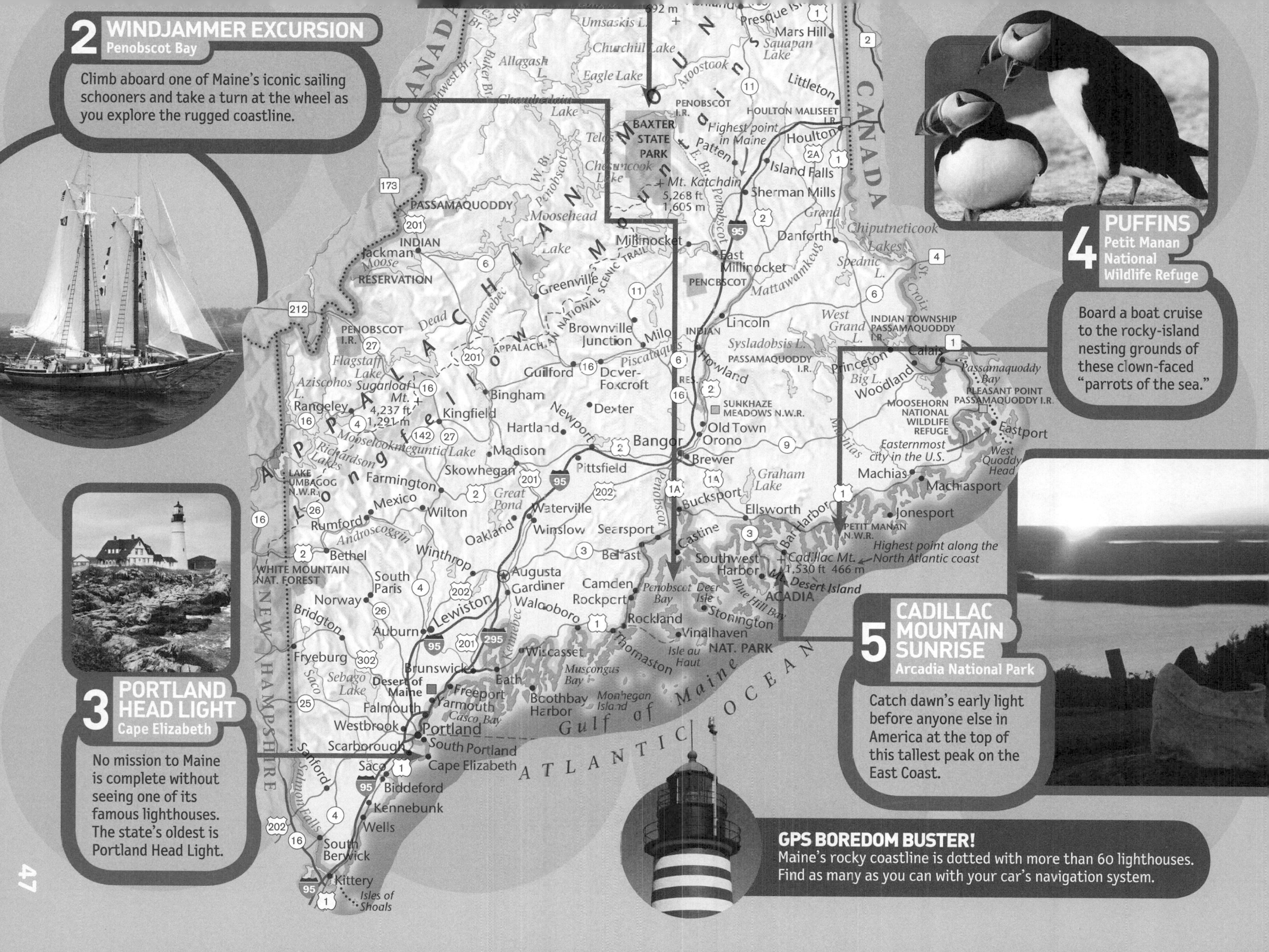

2 WINDJAMMER EXCURSION
Penobscot Bay

Climb aboard one of Maine's iconic sailing schooners and take a turn at the wheel as you explore the rugged coastline.

3 PORTLAND HEAD LIGHT
Cape Elizabeth

No mission to Maine is complete without seeing one of its famous lighthouses. The state's oldest is Portland Head Light.

4 PUFFINS
Petit Manan National Wildlife Refuge

Board a boat cruise to the rocky-island nesting grounds of these clown-faced "parrots of the sea."

5 CADILLAC MOUNTAIN SUNRISE
Arcadia National Park

Catch dawn's early light before anyone else in America at the top of this tallest peak on the East Coast.

GPS BOREDOM BUSTER!

Maine's rocky coastline is dotted with more than 60 lighthouses. Find as many as you can with your car's navigation system.

STATE BIRD: Baltimore oriole

STATE FLOWER: black-eyed Susan

STATE TREE: white oak

MARYLAND

The Old Line STATE

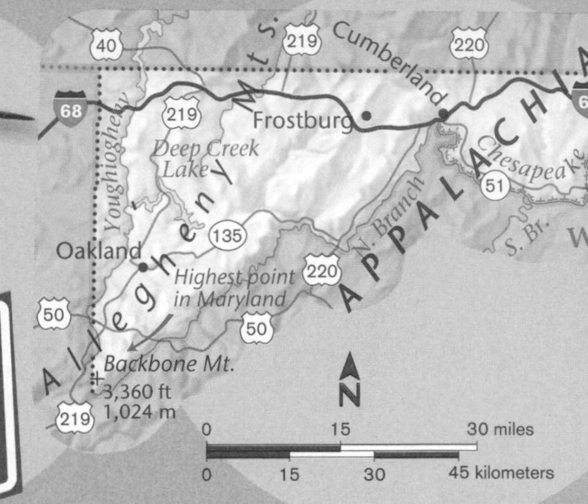

Roadside Attractions

Here's a tip to making the most of your trip to Maryland: Come in a crabby mood! This seaside state is famous for its blue crab, caught fresh and feisty from Chesapeake Bay. Seafood not your style? Plenty of other nice—often nautical—attractions await.

FANTASTIC MARYLAND FACTS

Poet Francis Scott Key wrote the national anthem in 1814 after he watched the British Royal Navy bombard Fort McHenry.

Maryland gave up some of its land to help form the U.S. capital—Washington, D.C.

The average depth of Chesapeake Bay and its tributaries is only 21 feet.

NATIONAL MUSEUM OF DENTISTRY

Dental hygiene gets its due at this Baltimore exhibit featuring feats of jaw strength, whopping whale teeth, and George Washington's false choppers (find out if they were really made of wood).

B&O RAILROAD MUSEUM

Railroad history's mightiest locomotives fill this big Baltimore building—and spill into the parking lot.

GEPPI'S ENTERTAINMENT MUSEUM

Comic books, vintage toys, and classic TV shows are on loving display at this Baltimore shrine to pop culture.

GPS BOREDOM BUSTER!

Maryland is less than two miles wide near the town of Hancock. Find this narrow patch with your car's navigation system—then go walk across the state!

5 COOL THINGS TO DO HERE

1 NATIONAL AQUARIUM
Baltimore

See dolphins, jellyfish, and some truly wild Australian reptiles at this aquarium on Baltimore's Inner Harbor.

2 MARYLAND SCIENCE CENTER
Baltimore

Pretend you're a paleontologist or an astronomer for a day at this museum that takes a hands-on approach to science.

3 TRIMPER'S RIDES
Ocean City

Ride old-fashioned merry-go-rounds and modern coasters at this century-old boardwalk amusement park.

4 CHESAPEAKE BAY CRUISE
Annapolis

No visit to "America's sailing capital" is complete without a day cruise along this inland coastline, or join a kayak tour and see historic Annapolis from a different perspective.

5 WILD HORSES
Assateague State Park

Some believe the wild horses that roam this small coastal island are descended from a herd of shipwreck survivors.

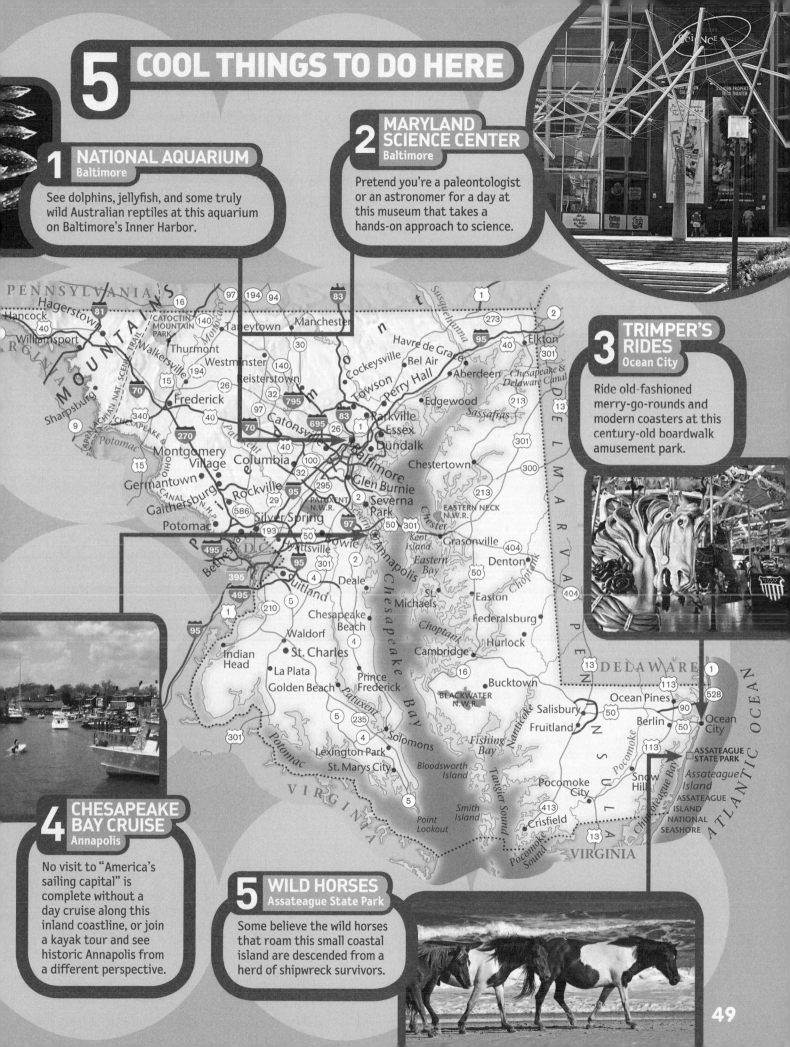

STATE BIRD: black-capped chickadee

STATE FLOWER: mayflower

STATE TREE: American elm

MASSACHUSETTS

The Bay STATE

The Pilgrims who established the Plymouth Colony started a sensible local tradition with their first Thanksgiving—visitors to Massachusetts have lots to be thankful for! The state is rich in restful seaside villages and historic sites from every American era.

Roadside Attractions

MAPPARIUM

Visitors to the Mary Baker Eddy Library in Boston get a new perspective on the world when they walk through the center of this three-story globe.

WHALING MUSEUM

The pursuit of whale oil and blubber was once big business in Massachusetts. This museum in New Bedford highlights the whaling trade's ships, tools, and dangers.

THE BUTTERFLY PLACE

Hundreds of butterflies flutter around this indoor garden in Westford.

WHAT A SILLY SIGN!

The town of Webster has a sign that seems to go on forever. It reads "Lake Chargoggagoggmanchauggagoggchaubunagungamaugg," which is the Native American name of a nearby lake. Not surprisingly, locals prefer to call it Lake Webster.

3 OLD STURBRIDGE VILLAGE

Sturbridge

Experience ye olde New England at this 200-acre village staffed by historical interpreters who convince you it's 1840.

BOREDOM BUSTER!
Both basketball and chocolate-chip cookies have their origins in Massachusetts. Use a smart phone to look up other famous inventions of this New England state.

5 COOL THINGS TO DO HERE

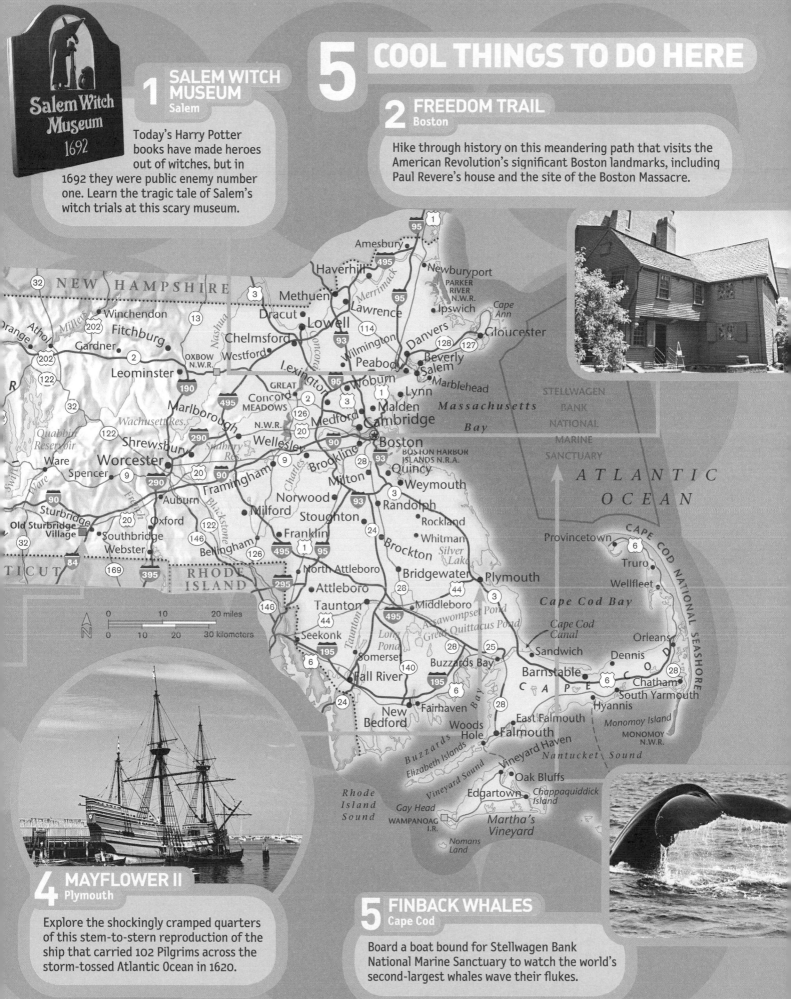

1 SALEM WITCH MUSEUM
Salem

Today's Harry Potter books have made heroes out of witches, but in 1692 they were public enemy number one. Learn the tragic tale of Salem's witch trials at this scary museum.

2 FREEDOM TRAIL
Boston

Hike through history on this meandering path that visits the American Revolution's significant Boston landmarks, including Paul Revere's house and the site of the Boston Massacre.

4 MAYFLOWER II
Plymouth

Explore the shockingly cramped quarters of this stem-to-stern reproduction of the ship that carried 102 Pilgrims across the storm-tossed Atlantic Ocean in 1620.

5 FINBACK WHALES
Cape Cod

Board a boat bound for Stellwagen Bank National Marine Sanctuary to watch the world's second-largest whales wave their flukes.

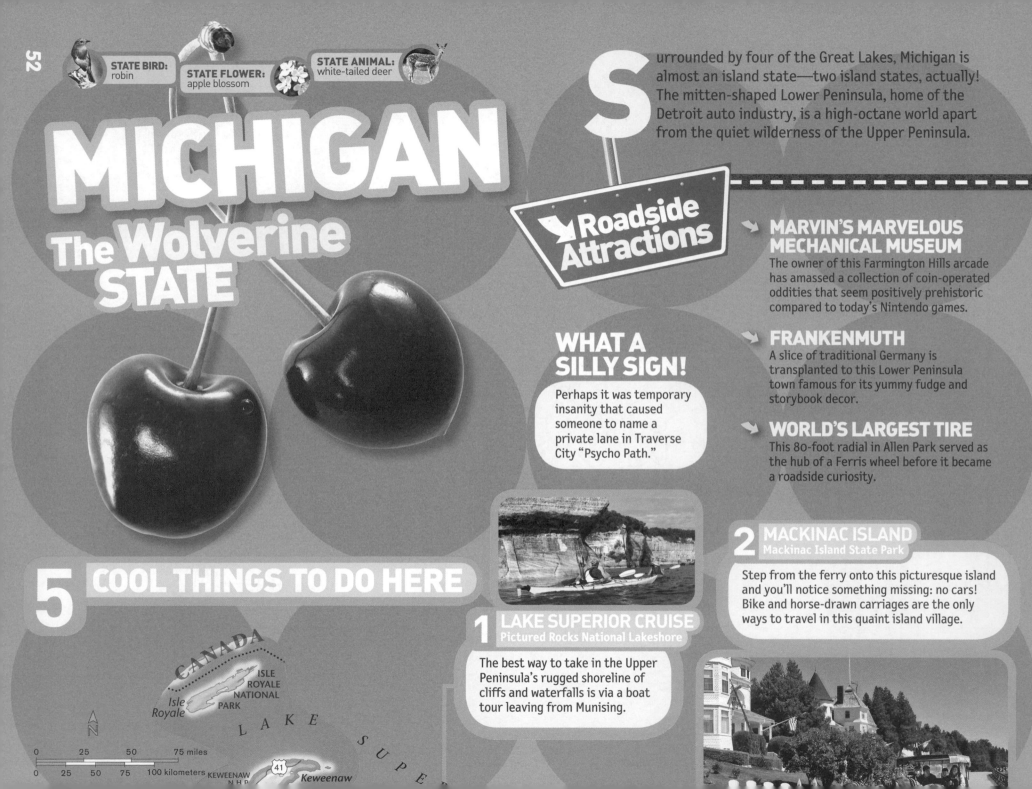

STATE BIRD: robin

STATE FLOWER: apple blossom

STATE ANIMAL: white-tailed deer

MICHIGAN

The Wolverine STATE

Surrounded by four of the Great Lakes, Michigan is almost an island state—two island states, actually! The mitten-shaped Lower Peninsula, home of the Detroit auto industry, is a high-octane world apart from the quiet wilderness of the Upper Peninsula.

MARVIN'S MARVELOUS MECHANICAL MUSEUM

The owner of this Farmington Hills arcade has amassed a collection of coin-operated oddities that seem positively prehistoric compared to today's Nintendo games.

FRANKENMUTH

A slice of traditional Germany is transplanted to this Lower Peninsula town famous for its yummy fudge and storybook decor.

WORLD'S LARGEST TIRE

This 80-foot radial in Allen Park served as the hub of a Ferris wheel before it became a roadside curiosity.

WHAT A SILLY SIGN!

Perhaps it was temporary insanity that caused someone to name a private lane in Traverse City "Psycho Path."

5 COOL THINGS TO DO HERE

CANADA
ISLE ROYALE NATIONAL PARK
Isle Royale
LAKE SUPE
N
0 25 50 75 miles
0 25 50 75 100 kilometers
KEWEENAW NHP
41
Keweenaw

1 LAKE SUPERIOR CRUISE
Pictured Rocks National Lakeshore

The best way to take in the Upper Peninsula's rugged shoreline of cliffs and waterfalls is via a boat tour leaving from Munising.

2 MACKINAC ISLAND
Mackinac Island State Park

Step from the ferry onto this picturesque island and you'll notice something missing: no cars! Bike and horse-drawn carriages are the only ways to travel in this quaint island village.

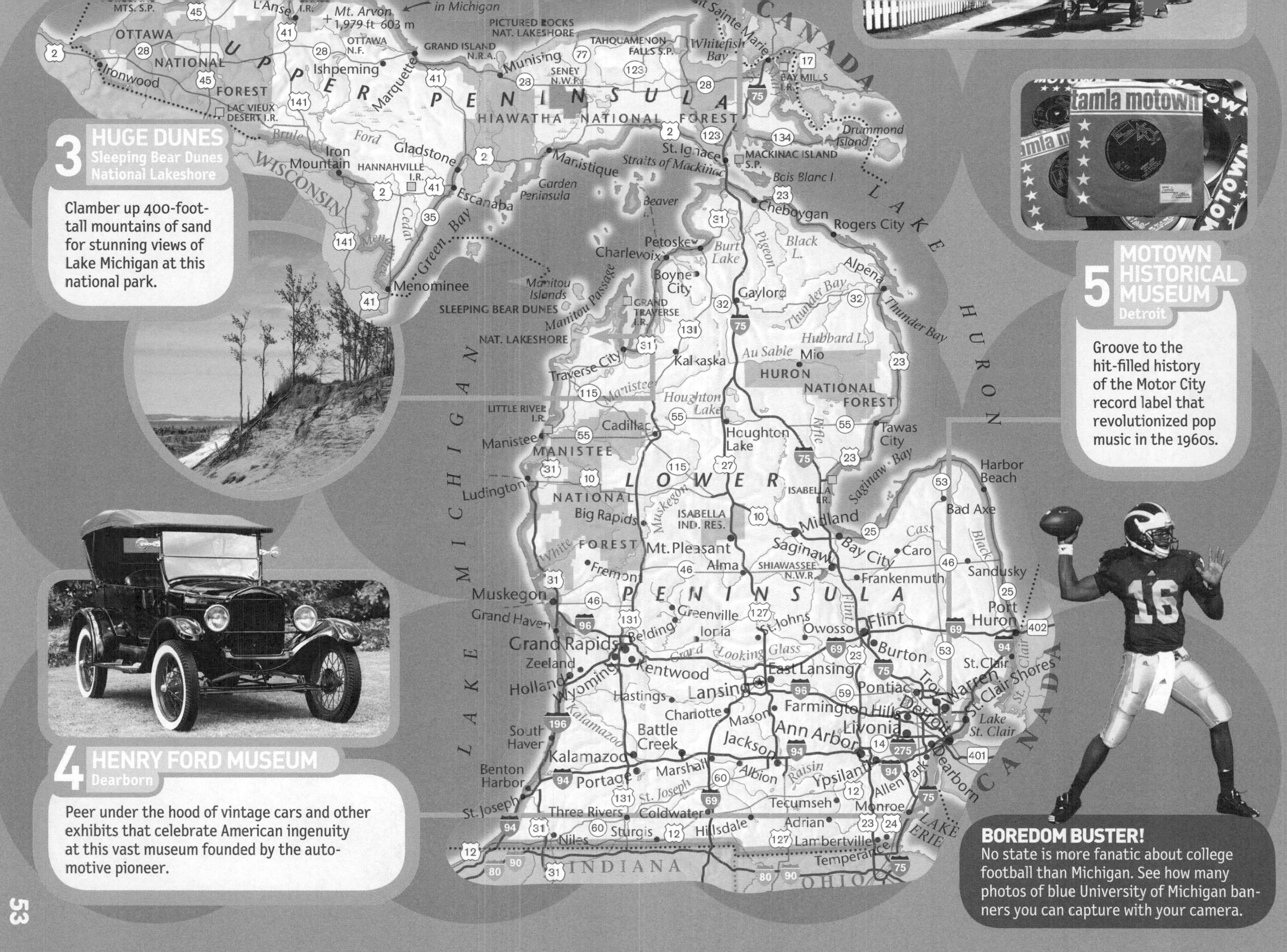

3 HUGE DUNES
Sleeping Bear Dunes National Lakeshore

Clamber up 400-foot-tall mountains of sand for stunning views of Lake Michigan at this national park.

4 HENRY FORD MUSEUM
Dearborn

Peer under the hood of vintage cars and other exhibits that celebrate American ingenuity at this vast museum founded by the automotive pioneer.

5 MOTOWN HISTORICAL MUSEUM
Detroit

Groove to the hit-filled history of the Motor City record label that revolutionized pop music in the 1960s.

BOREDOM BUSTER!
No state is more fanatic about college football than Michigan. See how many photos of blue University of Michigan banners you can capture with your camera.

STATE BIRD: common loon
STATE FLOWER: pink and white lady's slipper
STATE TREE: Norway pine

MINNESOTA
The Land of 10,000 LAKES

You're bound to find whatever floats your boat in Minnesota, home to more lakes than any state except Alaska. Trade in your car for a canoe and you'll never grow tired of exploring the wet wilds—at least until the brutally cold winters drive you indoors.

Roadside Attractions

WORLD'S LARGEST BALL OF TWINE
This 13-foot boulder of solid twine in Darwin has become an icon of oddball roadside attractions.

SOUDAN UNDERGROUND MINE
Don a hard hat and ride an elevator half a mile underground to an old iron mine.

PAUL BUNYAN AND BABE THE OX
Tall tales don't get any taller than those of Paul Bunyan, the mythical lumberjack who created Minnesota's lakes with his boot prints. See towering statues of this larger-than-life folk hero and his blue-hued sidekick in Bemidji.

FANTASTIC MINNESOTA FACTS

The "Land of 10,000 Lakes" nickname shortchanges the state by a few thousand lakes.

Even in the dead of winter, people in Minneapolis can get around town wearing short sleeves. The city has a network of heated tunnels!

Waterskiing was invented in Minnesota in 1922.

5 COOL THINGS TO DO HERE

1 WOLVES
Voyageurs National Park

Listen for the howl of the timber wolf when you visit this watery wilderness. It's a sanctuary for the secretive animals.

RED LAKE IND. RES.
Lake of the Woods
75
59
12
CANADA
89
The "Northwest Angle"

2 CANOEING
Boundary Waters Canoe Area Wilderness

Motorboats are forbidden in this vast expanse of forest-fringed streams and lakes, a paradise for paddlers.

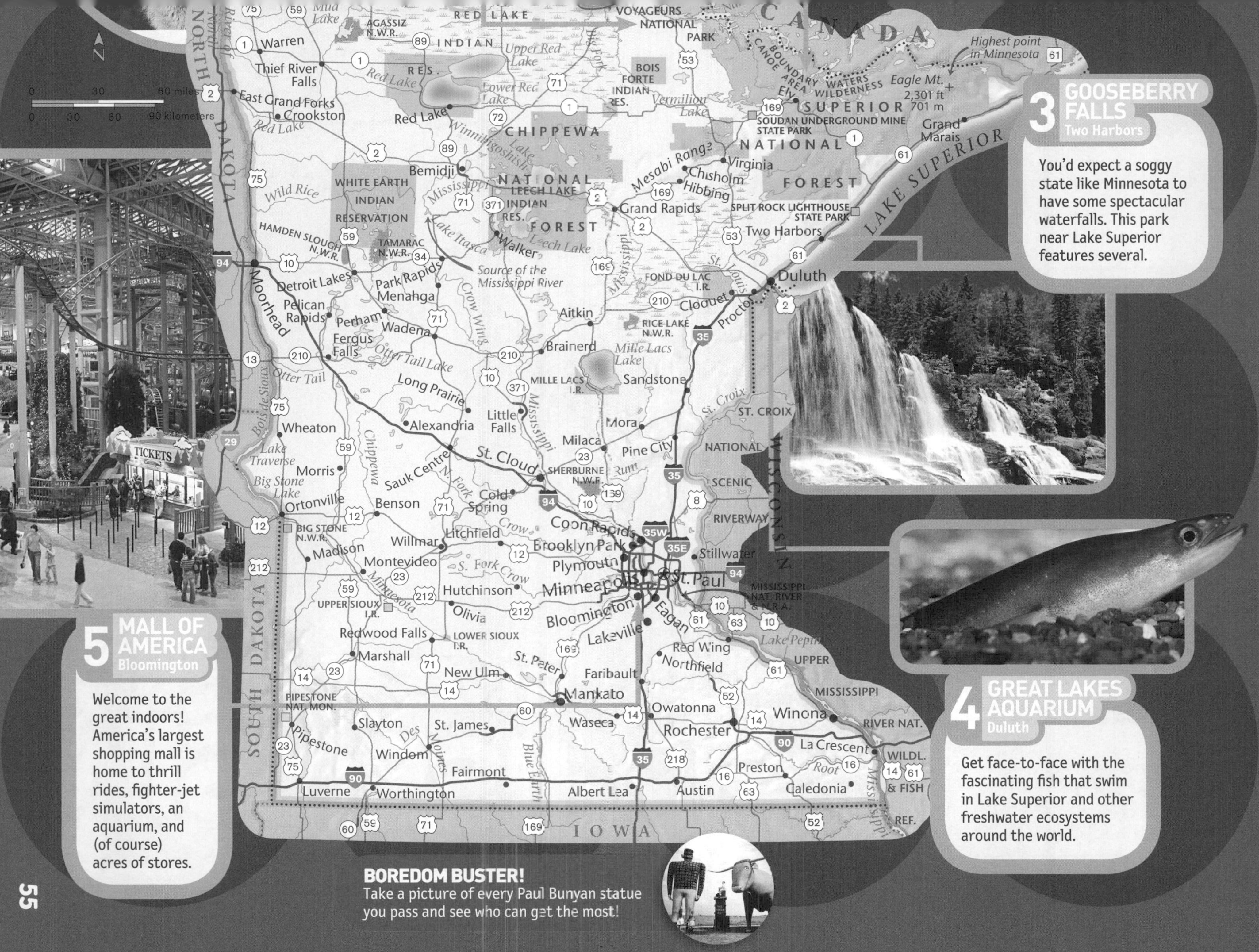

3 GOOSEBERRY FALLS
Two Harbors

You'd expect a soggy state like Minnesota to have some spectacular waterfalls. This park near Lake Superior features several.

4 GREAT LAKES AQUARIUM
Duluth

Get face-to-face with the fascinating fish that swim in Lake Superior and other freshwater ecosystems around the world.

5 MALL OF AMERICA
Bloomington

Welcome to the great indoors! America's largest shopping mall is home to thrill rides, fighter-jet simulators, an aquarium, and (of course) acres of stores.

BOREDOM BUSTER!
Take a picture of every Paul Bunyan statue you pass and see who can get the most!

STATE BIRD: mockingbird **STATE FLOWER:** magnolia **STATE ANIMAL:** white-tailed deer

MISSISSIPPI
The Magnolia STATE

You won't get the whole Mississippi experience if you just tour its casino steamboats, scenic byways, and pre–Civil War plantations. This state must be heard as well as seen! Blues music, born on the banks of the Mississippi, is a vital part of any Deep South excursion.

Roadside Attractions

BIRTHPLACE OF KERMIT THE FROG
Kermit creator Jim Henson was born in Leland, where you'll find an exhibit honoring the man and his muppets at the Chamber of Commerce.

GRACELAND TOO
This house in Holly Springs isn't so much a replica of Elvis Presley's Memphis estate as a shrine. The place is packed floor-to-ceiling with all manner of Elvis merchandise.

COCA-COLA MUSEUM
This restored candy store in Vicksburg sits where Coca-Cola was first bottled in 1894. See the original bottling equipment while gobbling down ice-cream floats.

5 COOL THINGS TO DO HERE

1 DELTA BLUES
Clarksdale

Soak in the soulful sounds of Mississippi blues music at the Delta Blues Museum.

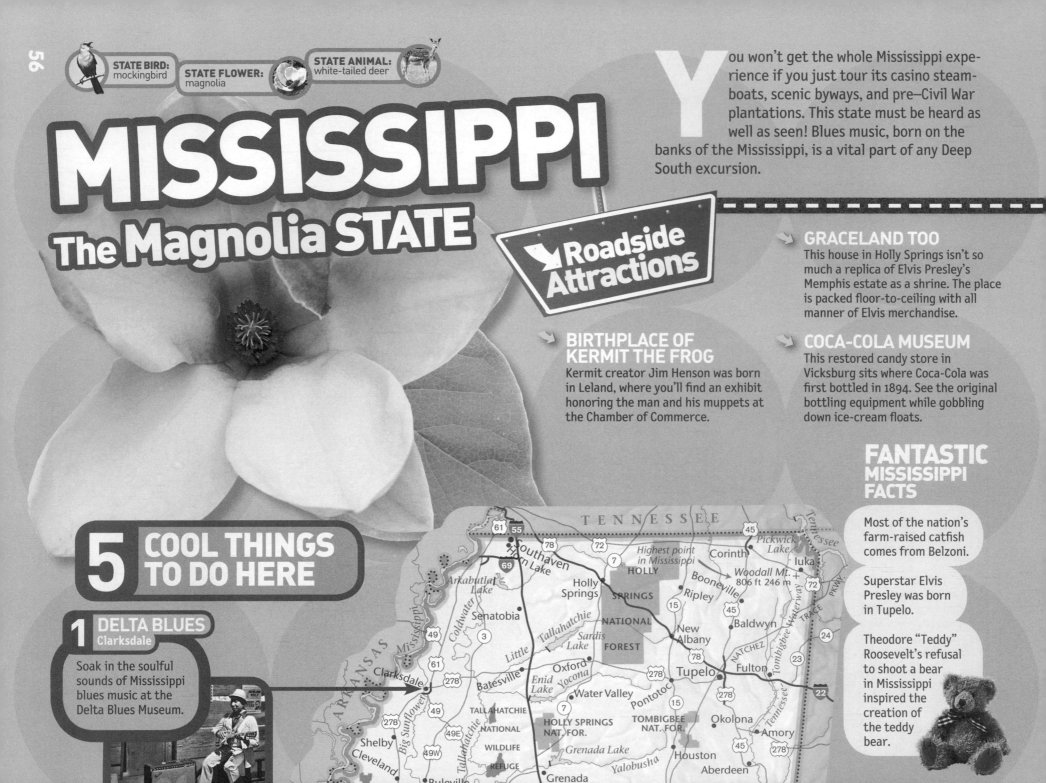

FANTASTIC MISSISSIPPI FACTS

- Most of the nation's farm-raised catfish comes from Belzoni.
- Superstar Elvis Presley was born in Tupelo.
- Theodore "Teddy" Roosevelt's refusal to shoot a bear in Mississippi inspired the creation of the teddy bear.

4 STENNIS SPHERE
Stennis Space Center

Practice landing a space shuttle simulator at this NASA facility that puts rocket engines through their paces.

5 GULF ISLANDS
Gulf Islands National Seashore

Swim, sunbathe, or explore Civil War forts on these barrier islands off the Mississippi coast.

GPS BOREDOM BUSTER!
Use your car's navigation system to find steamboats you can visit along the Mississippi River.

2 PETRIFIED FOREST
Flora

Before they were felled by a flood and turned to stone over millions of years, the ancient trees in this fascinating forest stood over a hundred feet tall.

MISSISSIPPI
PETRIFIED FOREST

3 NATCHEZ TRACE PARKWAY
Natchez

Take a leisurely drive through Mississippi's unspoiled forests on this former buffalo trail that traverses the state.

Map labels

ALABAMA

LOUISIANA

GULF OF MEXICO

Mississippi

Tombigbee
Noxubee
Big Black
Yazoo
Pearl
Leaf
Chickasawhay
Pascagoula
Black Creek
Bogue Chitto
Homochitto

NOXUBEE N.W.R.
TOMBIGBEE NATIONAL FOREST
MORGAN BRAKE N.W.R.
HILLSIDE N.W.R.
PANTHER SWAMP N.W.R.
DELTA NAT. FOREST
YAZOO N.W.R.
BIENVILLE NATIONAL FOREST
FOREST
MISSISSIPPI CHOCTAW I.R.
HOMOCHITTO NATIONAL FOREST
ST. CATHERINE CREEK N.W.R.
DE SOTO NATIONAL FOREST
MISSISSIPPI SANDHILL CRANE N.W.R.
GULF ISLANDS NATIONAL SEASHORE
BOGUE CHITTO N.W.R.

Mississippi Petrified Forest
Vicksburg N.M.P.
Stennis Space Center

Cleland
Greenville
Hollandale
Belzoni
Yazoo City
Vaughan
Canton
Carthage
Ridgeland
Flora
Jackson
Clinton
Brandon
Vicksburg
Magee
Crystal Springs
Hazlehurst
Brookhaven
Centreville
McComb
Natchez
Kosciusko
Louisville
Philadelphia
Meridian
Newton
Forest
Laurel
Collins
Columbia
Ellisville
Hattiesburg
Petal
Wiggins
Poplarville
Picayune
Long Beach
Gulfport
Biloxi
Ocean Springs
Pascagoula
Moss Point
Bay St. Louis
Waynesboro
Quitman
Lucedale

Mississippi Sound

N

0 25 50 miles
0 25 50 75 kilometers

57

5 COOL THINGS TO DO HERE

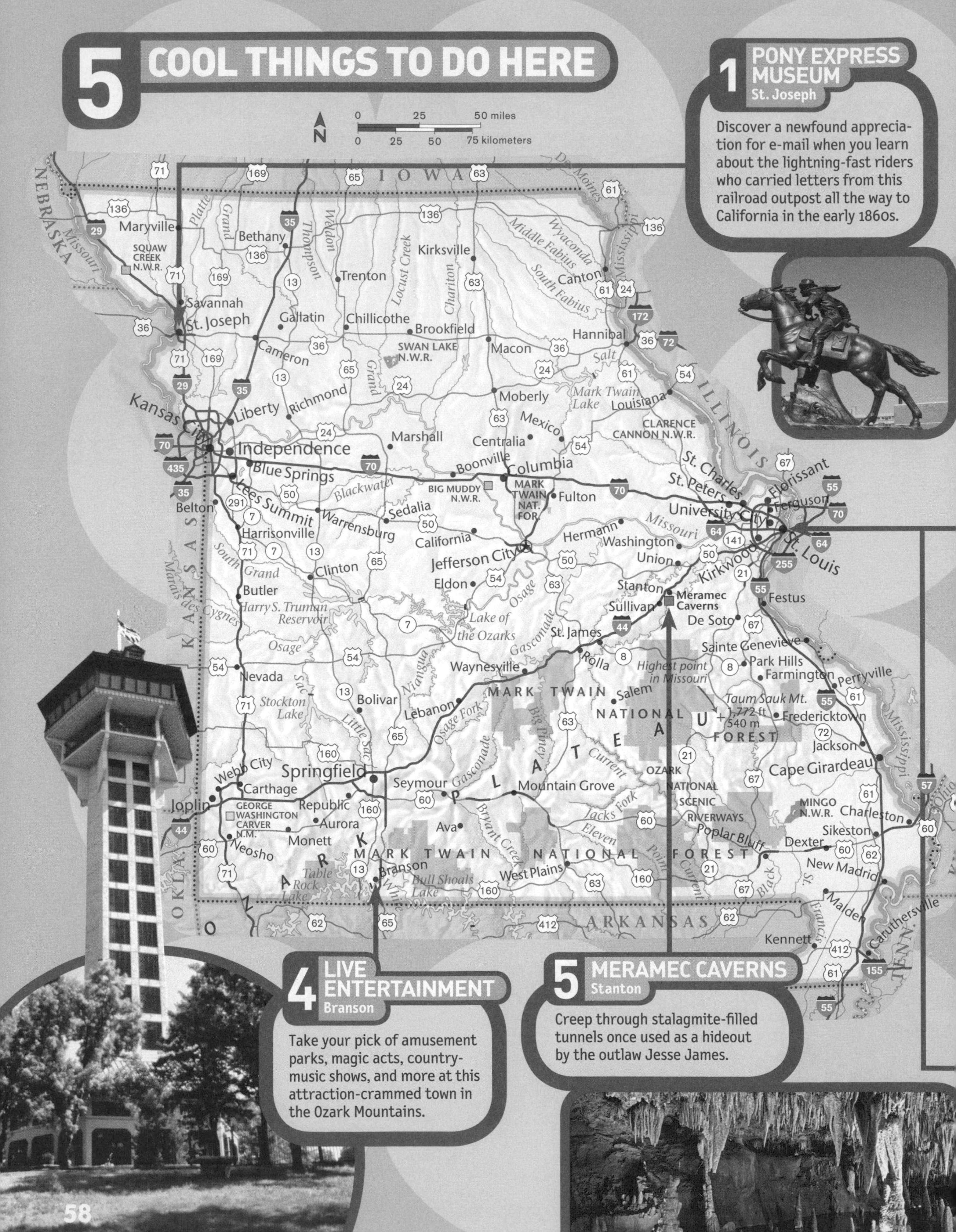

1 PONY EXPRESS MUSEUM
St. Joseph

Discover a newfound appreciation for e-mail when you learn about the lightning-fast riders who carried letters from this railroad outpost all the way to California in the early 1860s.

4 LIVE ENTERTAINMENT
Branson

Take your pick of amusement parks, magic acts, country-music shows, and more at this attraction-crammed town in the Ozark Mountains.

5 MERAMEC CAVERNS
Stanton

Creep through stalagmite-filled tunnels once used as a hideout by the outlaw Jesse James.

Map scale: 0 25 50 miles / 0 25 50 75 kilometers

Map labels (selection):

NEBRASKA, IOWA, ILLINOIS, KANSAS, OKLAHOMA, ARKANSAS, TENNESSEE

Maryville, Bethany, Kirksville, Canton, Trenton, Savannah, St. Joseph, Gallatin, Chillicothe, Brookfield, Hannibal, Macon, Cameron, Swan Lake N.W.R., Moberly, Louisiana, Liberty, Richmond, Kansas City, Independence, Blue Springs, Marshall, Centralia, Mexico, Columbia, Boonville, Clarence Cannon N.W.R., St. Charles, St. Peters, Florissant, University City, Ferguson, Belton, Lees Summit, Harrisonville, Warrensburg, Sedalia, California, Hermann, Washington, Union, Stanton, Meramec Caverns, Sullivan, Festus, De Soto, Kirkwood, St. Louis, Butler, Jefferson City, Eldon, Clinton, Lake of the Ozarks, St. James, Rolla, Sainte Genevieve, Park Hills, Farmington, Perryville, Nevada, Waynesville, Salem, Taum Sauk Mt. 1,772 ft 540 m, Fredericktown, Jackson, Bolivar, Lebanon, Mountain Grove, Cape Girardeau, Webb City, Carthage, Springfield, Seymour, Joplin, George Washington Carver N.M., Republic, Aurora, Ava, Poplar Bluff, Charleston, Sikeston, Dexter, Neosho, Monett, Branson, West Plains, New Madrid, Table Rock Lake, Bull Shoals Lake, Kennett, Malden, Caruthersville

Squaw Creek N.W.R., Big Muddy N.W.R., Mark Twain Nat. For., Harry S. Truman Reservoir, Stockton Lake, Mingo N.W.R., Mark Twain National Forest, Ozark National Scenic Riverways, Ozark Plateau, Highest point in Missouri

Rivers: Missouri, Mississippi, Des Moines, Platte, Grand, Thompson, Weldon, Chariton, Locust Creek, Middle Fabius, South Fabius, Wyaconda, Salt, Mark Twain Lake, Blackwater, Osage, Gasconade, Niangua, South Grand, Marais des Cygnes, Sac, Little Sac, Osage Fork, Big Piney, Current, Jacks Fork, Eleven Point, Bryant Creek, Black, St. Francis, White, Ohio

STATE BIRD: bluebird

STATE FLOWER: white hawthorn

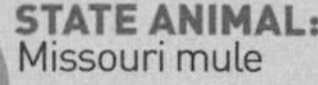

STATE ANIMAL: Missouri mule

MISSOURI

The Show Me STATE

2 GATEWAY ARCH
St. Louis

Squeeze into a tiny tram and ride to the top of this 630-foot steel monument to America's pioneering spirit.

When explorers Meriwether Lewis and William Clark set out to chart the American West in 1804, they used Missouri as their launching point. A sense of adventure has thrived in this "gateway to the West" ever since.

TRAFFIC LAWS YOU WON'T BELIEVE

In University City, you're not allowed to honk someone else's horn.

Milkmen in St. Louis aren't allowed to run while on the job.

It's against the law in University City to ask anyone to watch your parked car for you.

MARK TWAIN CAVE
The famous author chased bats in this creepy cavern while growing up in Hannibal. He later used it as a setting in *The Adventures of Tom Sawyer.*

GRANT'S FARM
Zebra, antelope, and other exotic animals roam this St. Louis safari park.

TITANIC MUSEUM
It's hard to miss Branson's ship-shaped museum for the doomed passenger liner.

BOREDOM BUSTER!
Missouri once raised more mules (for its westbound wagon trains) than any other state. See how many mules you can capture with your camera today!

3 CITY MUSEUM
St. Louis

Scramble around a dream jungle gym made of fighter jets, fire engines, and over-size Slinky toys suspended 25 feet high!

STATE BIRD: western meadowlark

STATE FLOWER: bitterroot

STATE ANIMAL: grizzly bear

MONTANA

The BIG SKY COUNTRY

Seeing why Montana is nicknamed "Big Sky Country" is easy: Just look up! A canopy of blue stretches from horizon to horizon over the wide-open prairies in the east and the snowcapped Rocky Mountains in the west. Don't look up too long, though—Big Sky Country is also grizzly bear country!

WHAT A SILLY SIGN!

Bad Route Road off Interstate 94 in Montana's eastern prairieland doesn't sound like the most inviting road-trip detour, but at least it has a rest area!

EXIT 192
Bad Route Road
1 MILE
REST AREA

Roadside Attractions

SMOKEJUMPERS BASE

You think fighting fires in a burning building takes guts? The men and women of the Aerial Fire Depot in Missoula jump out of planes to battle remote forest blazes. Meet these daredevils and see their gear.

WORLD'S LARGEST STEER

A two-ton bovine named Steer Montana became the state's hottest hoofed celebrity in the 1920s. See his stuffed body at the O'Fallon Historical Museum in Baker.

45TH PARALLEL MARKER

This plain wooden sign near the north entrance of Yellowstone National Park is positioned exactly halfway between the Equator and the North Pole.

3 VIRGINIA CITY

Virginia City

Pan for gold in this pioneer ghost town, unchanged for 150 years.

BOREDOM BUSTER!

Snap camera pics of the Rocky Mountains and Montana's wide-open prairies. Print them out as Big Sky Country postcards when you get home!

5 COOL THINGS TO DO HERE

1 GRIZZLY BEARS
Glacier National Park

Big solitary beasts dwell in the forests, meadows, and glacier-carved valleys of Montana's most beautiful park. Keep your distance, though—grizzlies are no teddy bears!

2 BEARTOOTH HIGHWAY
Red Lodge

Brave perilous switchbacks and summer snowstorms as you drive up, up, and up this breathtaking stretch of high-altitude highway in the Rocky Mountains.

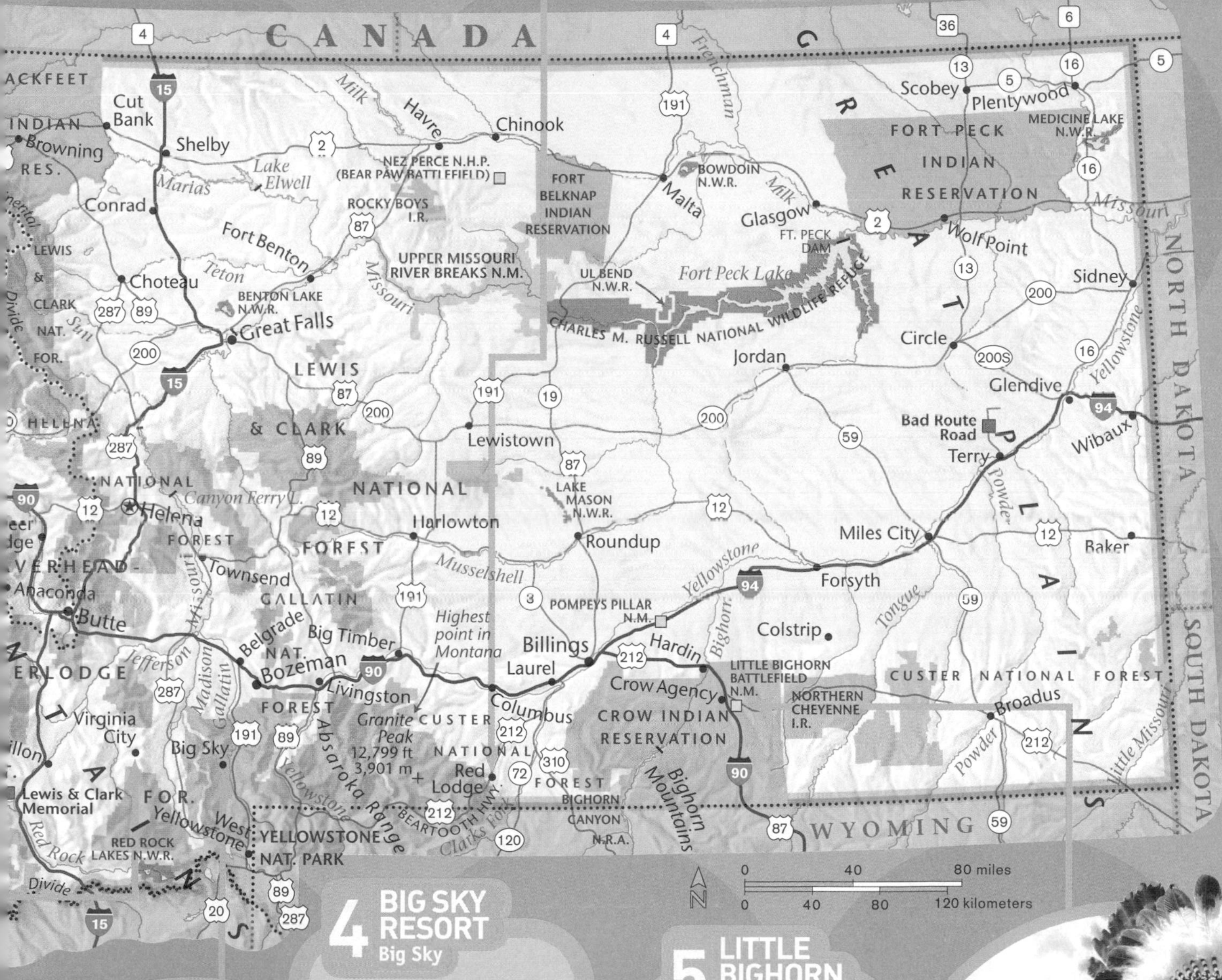

4 BIG SKY RESORT
Big Sky

Conquer a nearly endless supply of ski runs in the winter, or zoom along daredevil bike trails in the summer, at this all-season resort.

5 LITTLE BIGHORN
Crow Agency

Tour the battlefield where Lt. Col. George Armstrong Custer made his famous last stand against Plains Indians warriors.

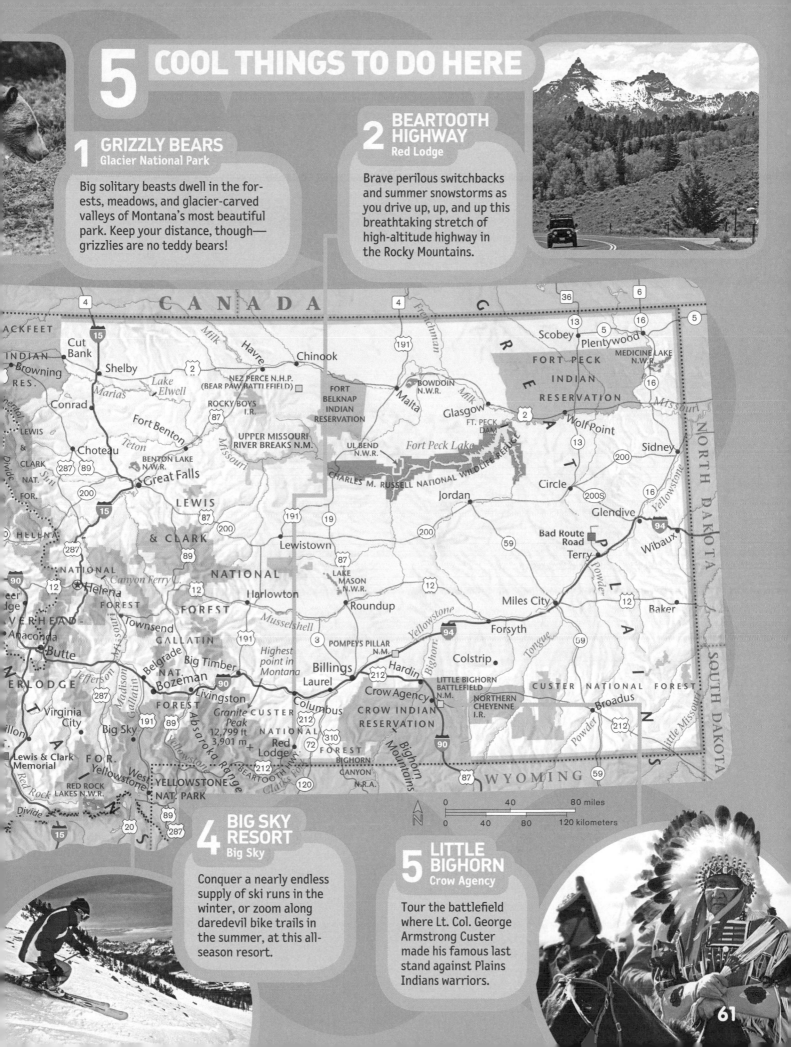

NEBRASKA

The Cornhusker STATE

Roadside Attractions

With its cornfields and cattle ranches sprawling in every direction, this Great Plains state is easy to dismiss as being, well, too plain. Survive the boring drives, however, and you'll find natural wonders and fun attractions all across Nebraska.

CARHENGE

England's prehistoric Stonehenge monument is re-created near the town of Alliance—except with 38 gray-painted vintage automobiles instead of rock slabs.

NATIONAL MUSEUM OF ROLLER SKATING

This small brick building in Lincoln is home to the world's biggest collection of roller skates, including jet-powered skates!

STRATEGIC AIR & SPACE MUSEUM

Visit this aircraft hangar in Ashland to make an up-close inspection of more than 30 fighter jets and cargo planes.

FANTASTIC NEBRASKA FACTS

MAIN ST 300

Chimney Rock, a 300-foot sandstone spire near Bayard, was the most famous landmark along the Oregon Trail. Pioneers bound west often drew pictures of it in their journals.

Nebraska is the only state with a unicameral legislature (meaning just one branch). Every other state has a two-branch legislative system.

Thousands of letters pass through the small wilderness town of Valentine each February 14 to get postmarked with its lovey-dovey name.

BOREDOM BUSTER!

Take a picture of every upturned boot you pass on a fence post—a common cowboy-approved ranch decoration—and see who can get the most!

5 COOL THINGS TO DO HERE

1 SCOTTS BLUFF
Gering

Hike to the 800-foot summit of this sandstone bluff that marked the trail for Pony Express riders and pioneers riding west. You can still see their wagon-wheel ruts 150 years later!

2 SANDHILLS
North-Central Nebraska

Take a stroll through one of the world's geological oddities: a sea of grass-carpeted sand dunes covering a quarter of Nebraska.

3 HENRY DOORLY ZOO
Omaha

Stand within the habitats of gorillas, lemurs, and creatures of the night in this amazing zoo that immerses visitors in its animal kingdoms.

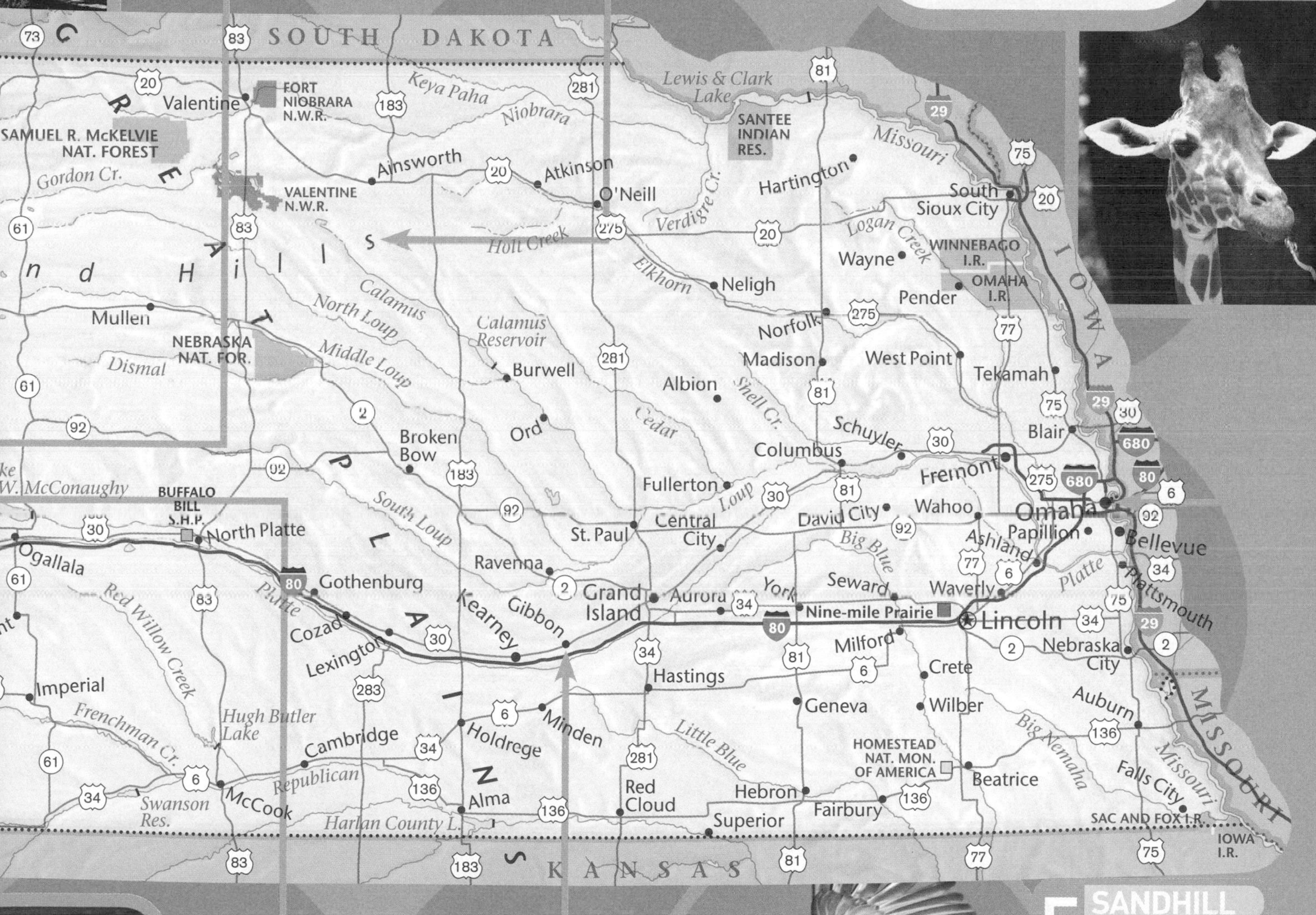

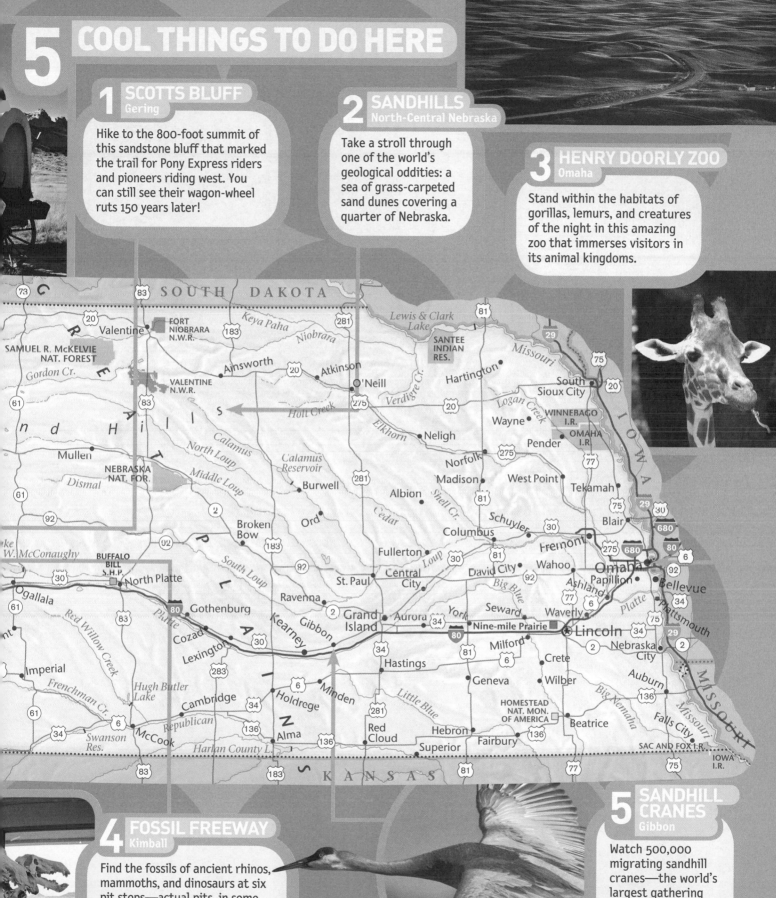

4 FOSSIL FREEWAY
Kimball

Find the fossils of ancient rhinos, mammoths, and dinosaurs at six pit stops—actual pits, in some cases—along this stretch of highway running north from Kimball.

5 SANDHILL CRANES
Gibbon

Watch 500,000 migrating sandhill cranes—the world's largest gathering of these birds—descend in a swirling storm on the Platte River every spring.

STATE BIRD: mountain bluebird

STATE FLOWER: sagebrush

STATE ANIMAL: desert bighorn

NEVADA

The Silver STATE

From the 19th-century miners who struck silver near Reno to the lucky gamblers who win big in Las Vegas's rowdy casinos today, visitors to Nevada have a habit of hitting the jackpot. But with so much of the state's attractions geared toward grown-ups, will kids find any fun stuff here? It's a safe bet.

5 COOL THINGS TO DO HERE

1 LAKE TAHOE
Lake Tahoe State Park

One of America's largest, deepest, and bluest bodies of water, mountain-ringed Lake Tahoe is a paradise for boaters in the summer and ski bums in the winter.

WHAT A SILLY SIGN!

EXTRATERRESTRIAL HIGHWAY 375

Watch the skies as well as Route 375 when you pass this spaced-out sign near Rachel. Nevada officially designated this 98-mile byway as the "Extraterrestrial Highway" after so many motorists reported UFO sightings. The military's supersecret "Area 51" airbase is also nearby. Coincidence?

Roadside Attractions

LAS VEGAS NATURAL HISTORY MUSEUM
One of the few family-friendly attractions in "Sin City," this popular museum features an animatronic T. rex and a shark-infested coral reef.

VIRGINIA CITY
This Wild West boomtown looks just like it did 150 years ago, when prospectors struck silver.

ATOMIC TESTING MUSEUM
The U.S. government, which owns most of Nevada, tested its atomic weapons by nuking the desert north of Las Vegas. See artifacts from the testing program—including a real (but disabled) bomb—at this Vegas museum.

2 MILKY WAY GALAXY
Great Basin National Park

See our planetary neighbors and the luminescent splash of the Milky Way during ranger-led astronomy programs in the nation's darkest stargazing destination.

3 PETROGLYPHS
Valley of Fire State Park

Ancestral Pueblo people chiseled prehistoric graffiti into this park's fascinating red-rock formations.

4 THE STRIP
Las Vegas

An Egyptian pyramid, the Eiffel Tower, lava-spewing volcanoes, the Statue of Liberty, and battling pirate ships are next-door neighbors on the world's most surreal stretch of road.

5 HOOVER DAM
Near Boulder City

Ride an elevator deep into the electricity-generating heart of this engineering marvel.

GPS BOREDOM BUSTER!
Use your car's navigation system to visit each town between Fallon and Ely along Highway 50, the so-called loneliest road in America.

STATE BIRD: purple finch

STATE FLOWER: purple lilac

STATE ANIMAL: white-tailed deer

NEW HAMPSHIRE

The Granite STATE

Spend a week exploring this picturesque state and you'll wind up jealous of the moose that get to live here year-round. Dazzling fall foliage, crystal lakes, granite peaks, country hamlets—everything people love about New England is here in New Hampshire.

Roadside Attractions

AMERICAN CLASSIC ARCADE MUSEUM

The bleeps and blips of vintage video games are preserved forever at this museum that lets you play with the exhibits. Find it in Laconia's Funspot Family Fun Center, the world's largest arcade!

RUGGLES MINE

This mine near Grafton lets you roam its honeycomb of stone passageways. Any precious stones you can chip off the old blocks are yours to keep!

WILDCAT MOUNTAIN ZIPRIDER

Visit this ski resort near Pinkham Notch in the summer for a zooming zip-line ride over spectacular mountain scenery at 45 miles an hour!

5 COOL THINGS TO DO HERE

1 MOOSE
Pittsburg

More than 6,000 of these six-foot-tall beasts roam New Hampshire's forests. The best moose-spotting is along a stretch of Route 3 north of Pittsburg called "Moose Alley."

WHAT A SILLY SIGN!

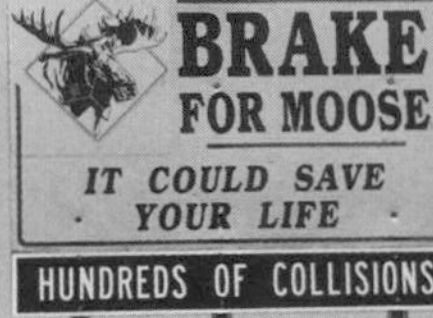

The "Brake for Moose" signs seen in northern New Hampshire may seem a little silly, but their message is no joke! Colliding with one of these half-ton animals is like ramming into a six-foot brick wall—with antlers! Look for their long faces poking from the sides of the roads, and use high beams at night to see the gleam of moose eyeballs.

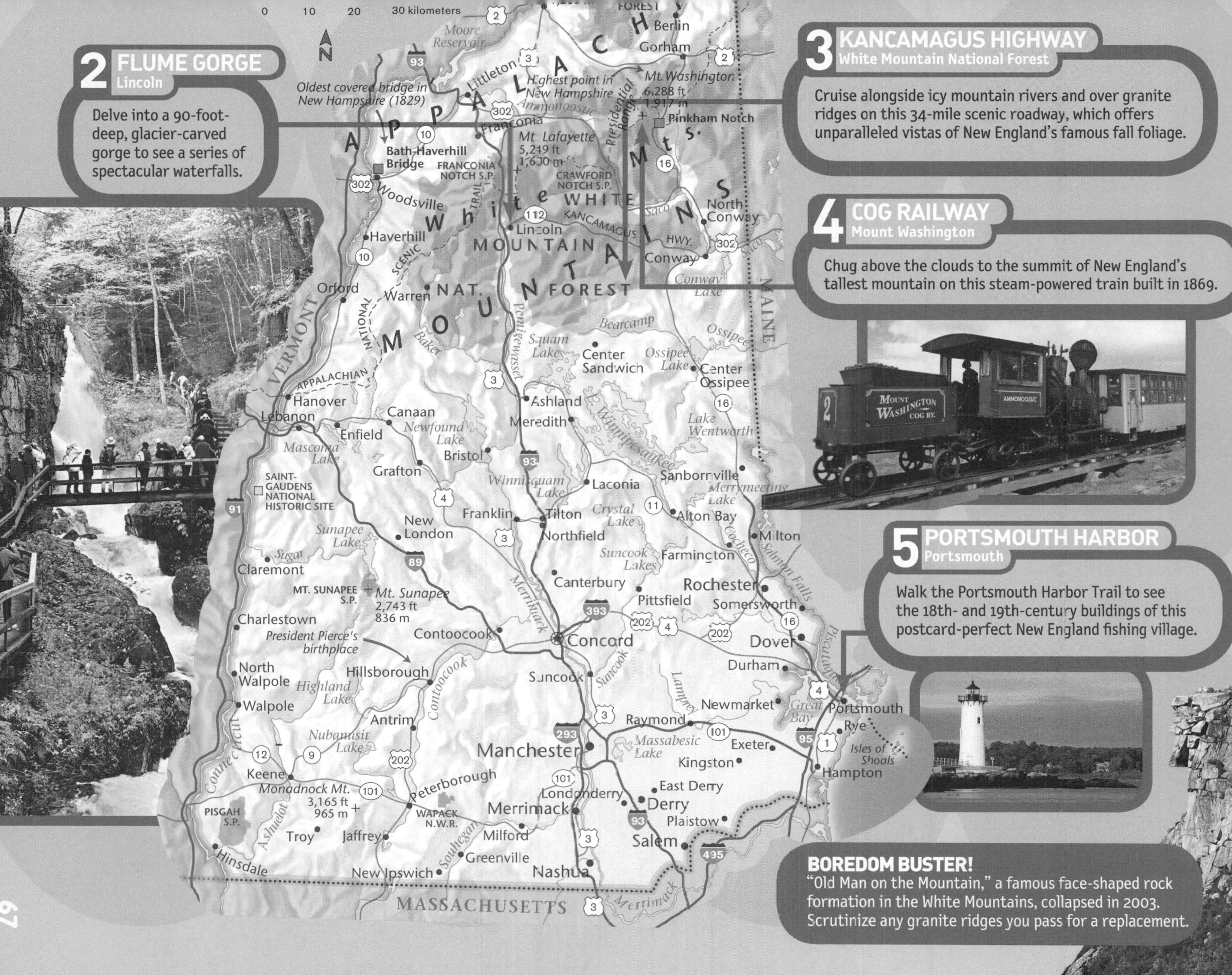

2 FLUME GORGE
Lincoln

Delve into a 90-foot-deep, glacier-carved gorge to see a series of spectacular waterfalls.

3 KANCAMAGUS HIGHWAY
White Mountain National Forest

Cruise alongside icy mountain rivers and over granite ridges on this 34-mile scenic roadway, which offers unparalleled vistas of New England's famous fall foliage.

4 COG RAILWAY
Mount Washington

Chug above the clouds to the summit of New England's tallest mountain on this steam-powered train built in 1869.

5 PORTSMOUTH HARBOR
Portsmouth

Walk the Portsmouth Harbor Trail to see the 18th- and 19th-century buildings of this postcard-perfect New England fishing village.

BOREDOM BUSTER!
"Old Man on the Mountain," a famous face-shaped rock formation in the White Mountains, collapsed in 2003. Scrutinize any granite ridges you pass for a replacement.

STATE BIRD: eastern goldfinch

STATE FLOWER: purple violet

STATE ANIMAL: horse

NEW JERSEY

The Garden STATE

The "Garden State" of New Jersey doesn't live up to its nickname if you see it solely from the traffic-jammed New Jersey Turnpike. Find greener pastures—literally—away from the interstate, along with lots of fun in the sun.

TRAFFIC LAWS YOU WON'T BELIEVE

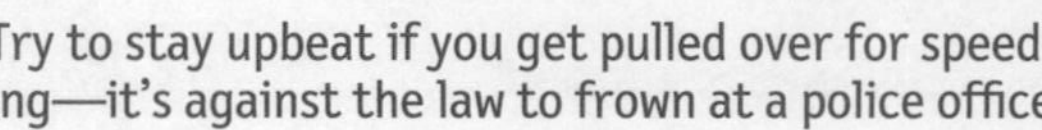

You can't drive past a skateboarder without honking first.

Try to stay upbeat if you get pulled over for speeding—it's against the law to frown at a police officer!

You're not allowed to pump your own gas.

Roadside Attractions

LUCY THE ELEPHANT
Built in 1881, this elephant-shaped house in Margate City has become a Jersey Shore icon.

DISCOVERY SEASHELL MUSEUM
Prepare to be shell-shocked when you visit this Ocean City museum crammed with thousands of seashells from around the world.

LARGEST SPOON COLLECTION
If being a medieval fortress in the New Jersey countryside isn't strange enough, Paterson's Lambert Castle is also home to the world's largest spoon collection!

5 COOL THINGS TO DO HERE

1 DUKE FARMS
Hillsborough

See how the Garden State got its nickname when you tour the greenhouses and lush grounds of this sprawling estate.

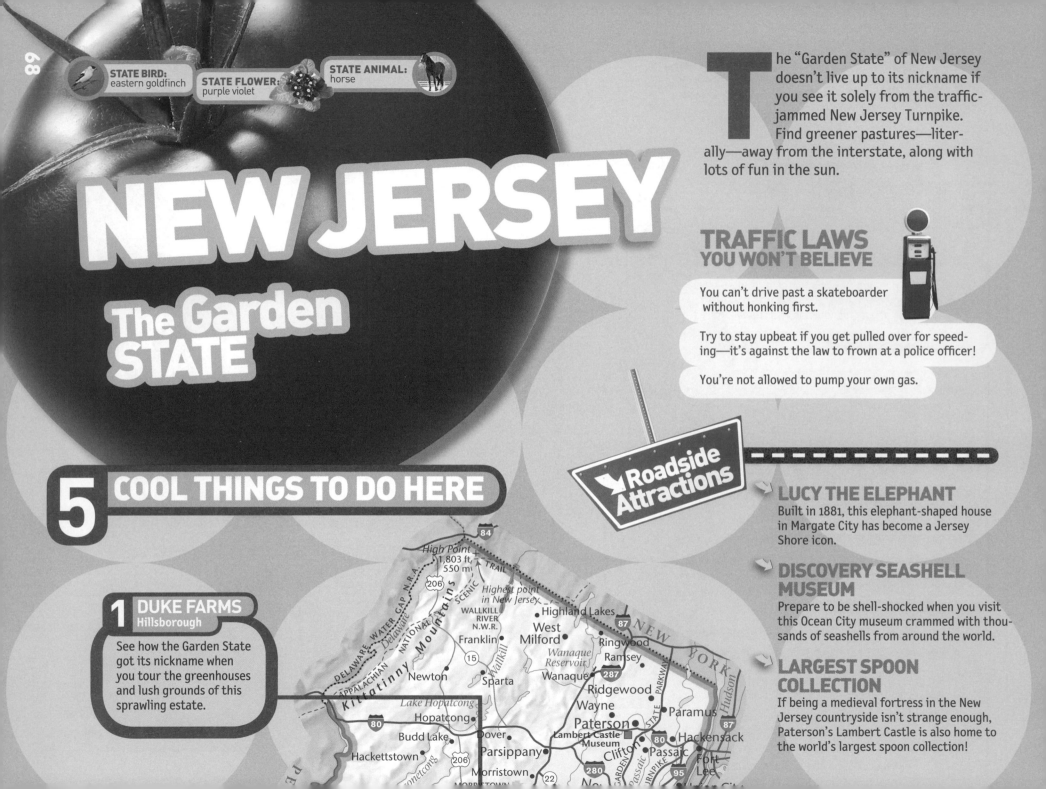

2 ADVENTURE AQUARIUM
Camden

Scratch sharks behind the gills and feed stingrays by hand. Don't forget to say hello to the hippos!

3 CAPE MAY
Cape May

Walk along a serene stretch of the Jersey Shore in this old-fashioned beach town full of quaint cottages and historic inns.

4 INSECTROPOLIS
Toms River

Meet every kind of creepy crawler at this big bug zoo.

5 THE BOARDWALK
Atlantic City

Find all the thrill rides and deep-fried funnel cakes you can stomach at this rowdy stretch of Jersey Shore—the inspiration for the Monopoly game board.

GPS BOREDOM BUSTER!
Use your car's navigation system to count all the boardwalk amusement parks along the Jersey Shore.

STATE BIRD: roadrunner
STATE FLOWER: yucca
STATE ANIMAL: black bear

NEW MEXICO

Land of Enchantment

From the pastel mesas that dominate the desert to the mud-colored adobe homes of the suburbs, New Mexico's landscape is inescapable. Even the original Native American residents became one with the rugged terrain, creating palaces in the sandstone cliffs deep in the heart of the stark Southwest.

FANTASTIC NEW MEXICO FACTS

The northwest corner of New Mexico is the only border spot where you can stand in four states simultaneously.

Native Americans have lived in an adobe house in Taos for 800 years, making it the country's oldest continuously inhabited building.

Infamous outlaw Billy the Kid has two graves at Fort Sumner, where he was gunned down at age 22. Neither grave is real, although one sports his true tombstone.

5 COOL THINGS TO DO HERE

1 SKY CITY
Acoma Pueblo

Explore this Native American town set atop a 370-foot sheer-walled mesa, established 450 years before the first English colonies.

2 PUYE CLIFF DWELLINGS
Española

Every room has a view in this mile-long village cut into a cliff face over a thousand years ago by the Native American Pueblo people.

Roadside Attractions

UFO MUSEUM
The U.S. government denies that an alien spaceship crashed in Roswell in 1947. Investigate the incident for yourself at the International UFO Museum and Research Center.

ICE CAVE
Need a break from the New Mexico heat? Take a refreshing hike into a perpetually icy cave at the Bandera Volcano near Grants.

BRADBURY SCIENCE MUSEUM
Try fun science experiments and learn about the race to build the atomic bomb in this museum at the Los Alamos National Laboratory.

Only spot in the U.S. where the borders of four states come together

3 SANDIA PEAK TRAMWAY
Albuquerque

Ascend 4,000 feet in 15 minutes for a panoramic view of New Mexico's rugged and varied landscape.

4 BATS
Carlsbad Caverns

Watch thousands of Mexican free-tailed bats swarm out of Carlsbad Caverns each summer night in search of yummy bugs.

5 WHITE SANDS
Near Alamogordo

It may look like a winter wonderland, but the White Sands National Monument is actually the world's largest white-gypsum desert. Come in the summer for a midnight hike under a full moon!

BOREDOM BUSTER!
As you ride through the state's beige terrain, keep your eyes peeled for a flash of blue—it's a mountain bluebird! Try to snap a photo of one.

STATE BIRD: bluebird

STATE FLOWER: rose

STATE ANIMAL: beaver

NEW YORK

The Empire STATE

A state with a split personality, New York is best known for its vibrant city of skyscrapers and bustling sidewalks, but outside New York City lies a serene landscape of lakes, mountains, and waterfalls. From wild urban adventures to quiet beach walks at sunrise, the Empire State has an activity for everybody.

TRAFFIC LAWS YOU WON'T BELIEVE

If you need to change clothes in your car, don't do it in Sag Harbor—it's a crime!

Eating in the street is against the law.

Flirting on the street could cost you a $25 fine.

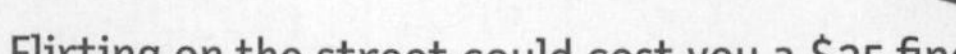

BOREDOM BUSTER!
New York City is home to movie stars and famous musicians. Look for celebrities out and about—and keep your camera handy!

Roadside Attractions

NATIONAL BASEBALL HALL OF FAME

See how America's pastime has evolved over the past 150 years in this Cooperstown shrine to the sport.

CONEY ISLAND

Pig out on hot dogs, then try not to lose your lunch on the thrill rides at this famous boardwalk amusement park in Brooklyn.

SECRET CAVERNS

You'll know you're getting close to this 100-foot subterranean waterfall east of Cobbleskill when you spy its famously funky hand-painted billboards.

5 COOL THINGS TO DO HERE

1 MAID OF THE MIST
Niagara Falls State Park

Don a raincoat and embark on a wet and wild boat ride along the base of the mightiest waterfalls in America.

2 ADIRONDACK PARK
Northern New York

Hike, raft, or ride through the largest state park in the U.S., a lush wilderness of mountains, rivers, and secret lakes.

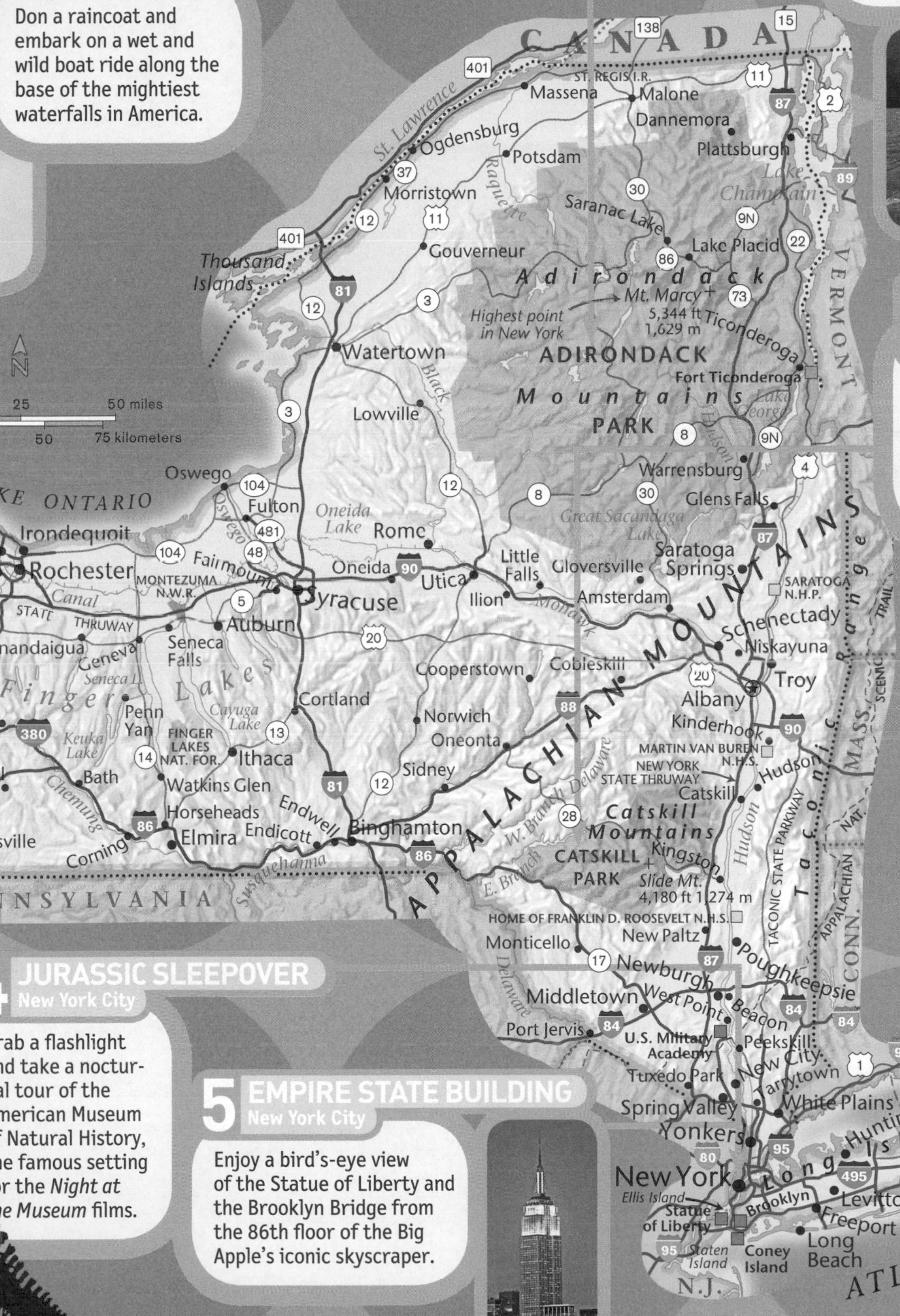

3 CATSKILL MOUNTAINS
Catskill Park

Hunt for hidden waterfalls and explore quaint resort towns in this mountainous forest, a retreat for city slickers seeking a breath of fresh air.

4 JURASSIC SLEEPOVER
New York City

Grab a flashlight and take a nocturnal tour of the American Museum of Natural History, the famous setting for the *Night at the Museum* films.

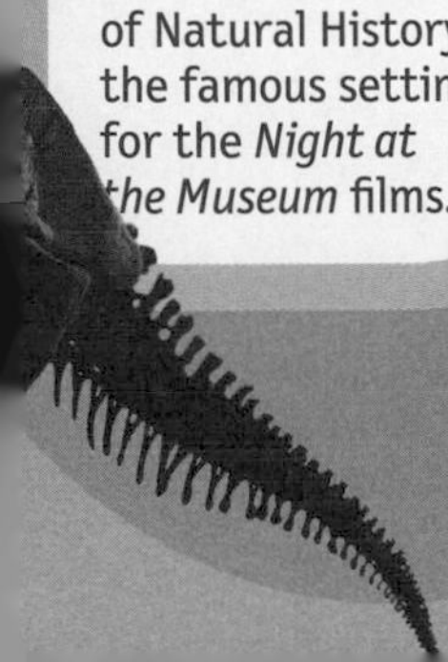

5 EMPIRE STATE BUILDING
New York City

Enjoy a bird's-eye view of the Statue of Liberty and the Brooklyn Bridge from the 86th floor of the Big Apple's iconic skyscraper.

STATE BIRD: cardinal

STATE FLOWER: dogwood

STATE ANIMAL: gray squirrel

NORTH CAROLINA

The Tar Heel STATE

Bordered by the misty Blue Ridge Mountains to the west and miles of Atlantic Ocean beaches to the east, North Carolina is a state of towering turf and pristine surf. In between lie old tobacco plantations, furniture factories, high-tech cities, and detours to America's past.

TRAFFIC LAWS YOU WON'T BELIEVE

Better hope you don't have an allergy attack in Asheville. Sneezing on the street is a crime!

It is forbidden to hurl rocks at the roads in Dunn.

Rollerblading on state highways isn't just a bad idea—it's illegal in Southern Shores.

Roadside Attractions

TEACH'S HOLE

Learn all about the bloodthirsty pirate Blackbeard, aka Edward Teach, whose buccaneering career came to a gruesome end off Ocracoke Island.

WORLD'S LARGEST DRESSER

This four-story chest of drawers in High Point even has a pair of gigantic dangling socks. Better hope they're not stinky!

THE BLOWING ROCK

Snow has been known to blow upside down at this 4,000-foot cliff near the town of the same name.

GPS BOREDOM BUSTER!

Plot a course along the Blue Ridge Parkway using your car's navigation system. Stop at the scenic overlooks to snap postcard-worthy pics!

5 COOL THINGS TO DO HERE

1 BLUE RIDGE PARKWAY
Cherokee

Buckle up for a hilly, curvy, topsy-turvy drive through the spectacular Appalachian Mountains.

2 SEA TURTLES
Cape Hatteras National Seashore

Watch endangered sea turtles bury their eggs on the sandy beaches of the Outer Banks, a chain of barrier islands rich in wildlife and pirate lore.

3 BILTMORE ESTATE
Asheville

Explore this amazing mansion and imagine living in a house with 65 fireplaces and a basement swimming pool.

4 MOUNT MITCHELL
Near Burnsville

Peer down upon the clouds from atop the tallest peak east of the Mississippi—more than a mile high!

5 OLD SALEM
Winston-Salem

Travel back in time to a 19th-century town, where you will find costumed actors reenacting daily life in America's early years.

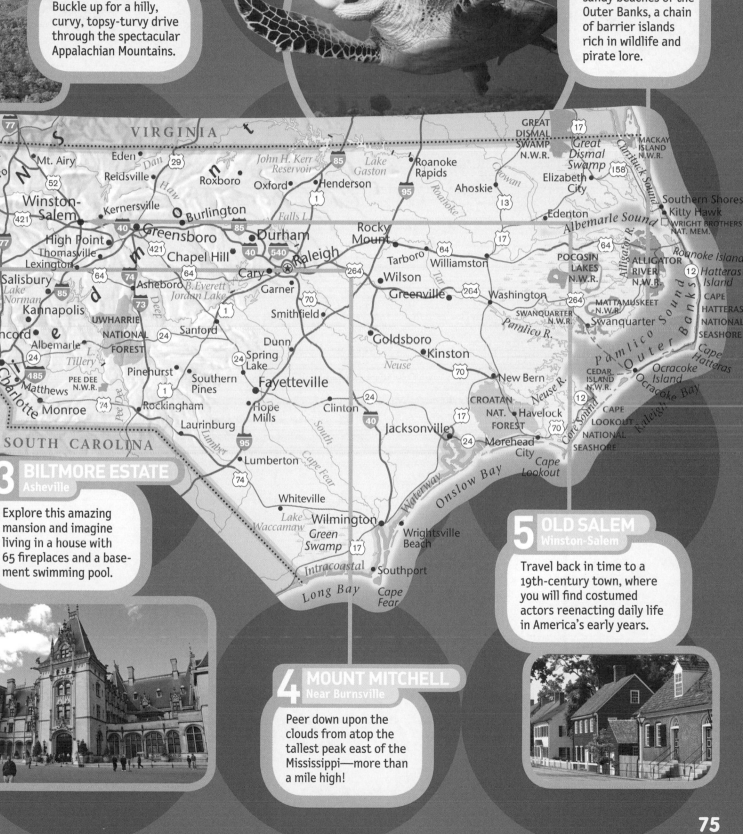

5 COOL THINGS TO DO HERE

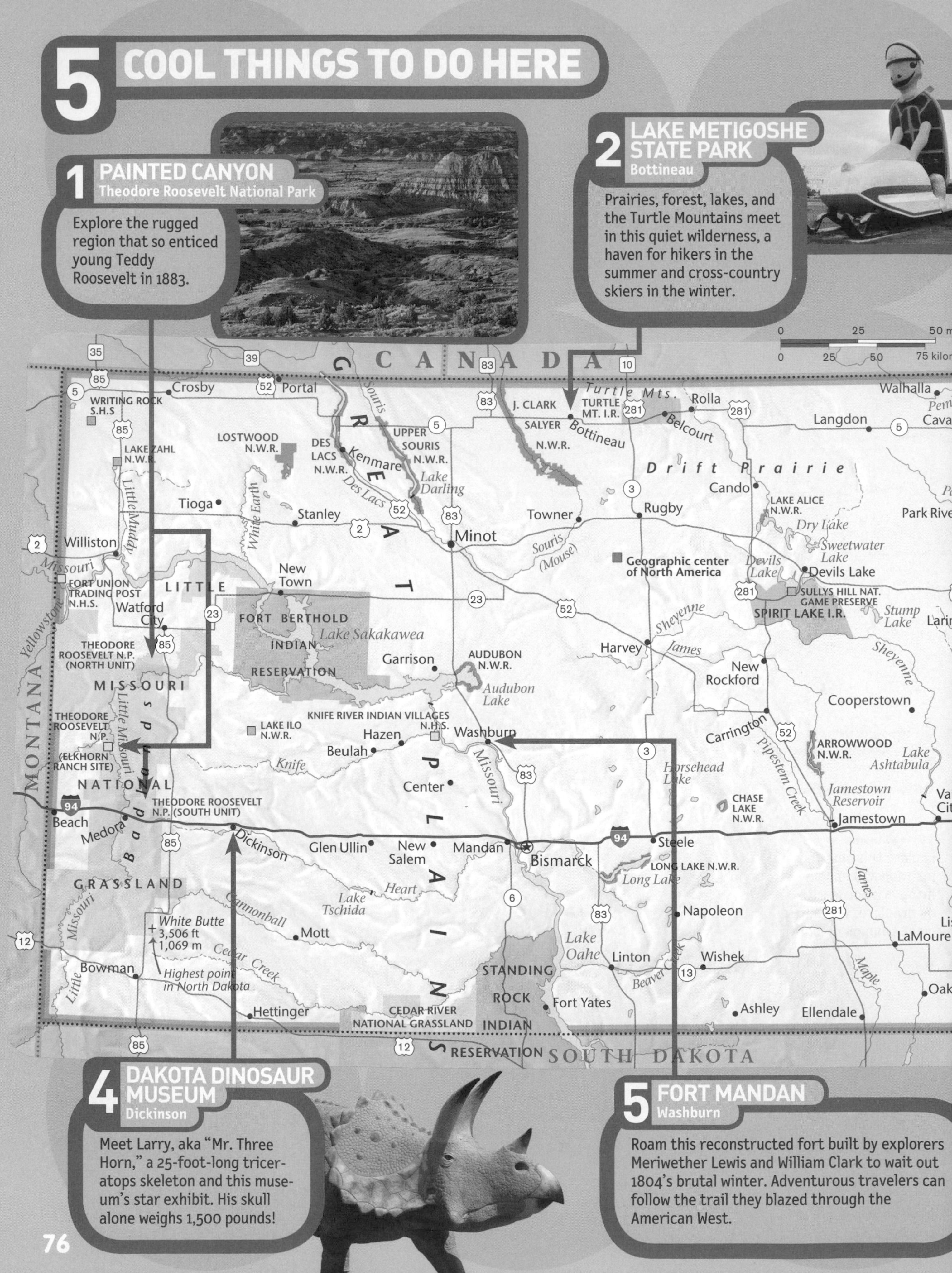

1 PAINTED CANYON
Theodore Roosevelt National Park

Explore the rugged region that so enticed young Teddy Roosevelt in 1883.

2 LAKE METIGOSHE STATE PARK
Bottineau

Prairies, forest, lakes, and the Turtle Mountains meet in this quiet wilderness, a haven for hikers in the summer and cross-country skiers in the winter.

Map of North Dakota showing:

CANADA

Walhalla · Peml · Caval · Langdon · Crosby · Portal · WRITING ROCK S.H.S. · Rolla · Belcourt · Park Rive · Kenmare · UPPER SOURIS N.W.R. · Turtle Mts. · J. CLARK · TURTLE MT. I.R. · SALYER N.W.R. · Bottineau · LOSTWOOD N.W.R. · LAKE ZAHL N.W.R. · DES LACS N.W.R. · Lake Darling · Drift Prairie · Cando · LAKE ALICE N.W.R. · Dry Lake · Tioga · Stanley · White Earth · Des Lacs · Rugby · Sweetwater Lake · Williston · Minot · Towner · Devils Lake · Souris (Mouse) · Geographic center of North America · Devils Lake · Park Rive · FORT UNION TRADING POST N.H.S. · LITTLE · New Town · SULLYS HILL NAT. GAME PRESERVE · Stump Lake · Larin · Watford City · FORT BERTHOLD INDIAN RESERVATION · Lake Sakakawea · SPIRIT LAKE I.R. · THEODORE ROOSEVELT N.P. (NORTH UNIT) · MISSOURI · Harvey · James · Sheyenne · New Rockford · Cooperstown · THEODORE ROOSEVELT N.P. · Garrison · AUDUBON N.W.R. · Audubon Lake · KNIFE RIVER INDIAN VILLAGES N.H.S. · Washburn · Carrington · ARROWWOOD N.W.R. · Lake Ashtabula · (ELKHORN RANCH SITE) · LAKE ILO N.W.R. · Hazen · Beulah · Knife · Center · Missouri · Horsehead Lake · Jamestown Reservoir · Val Cit · NATIONAL · Beach · Medora · THEODORE ROOSEVELT N.P. (SOUTH UNIT) · Dickinson · Glen Ullin · New Salem · Mandan · Bismarck · Steele · CHASE LAKE N.W.R. · Jamestown · GRASSLAND · Heart · LONG LAKE N.W.R. · James · Lake Tschida · Long Lake · Napoleon · LaMoure · Lis · White Butte 3,506 ft 1,069 m · Mott · Cannonball · Cedar Creek · Lake Oahe · Linton · Wishek · Highest point in North Dakota · Bowman · STANDING ROCK INDIAN RESERVATION · Fort Yates · Ashley · Ellendale · Oak · Hettinger · CEDAR RIVER NATIONAL GRASSLAND · RESERVATION · Beaver Creek · Maple · Pipestem Creek · Sheyenne · MONTANA · Yellowstone · Little Muddy · Little Missouri · Missouri

SOUTH DAKOTA

Scale: 0 25 50 mi / 0 25 50 75 kilom

4 DAKOTA DINOSAUR MUSEUM
Dickinson

Meet Larry, aka "Mr. Three Horn," a 25-foot-long triceratops skeleton and this museum's star exhibit. His skull alone weighs 1,500 pounds!

5 FORT MANDAN
Washburn

Roam this reconstructed fort built by explorers Meriwether Lewis and William Clark to wait out 1804's brutal winter. Adventurous travelers can follow the trail they blazed through the American West.

STATE BIRD: western meadowlark

STATE FLOWER: wild prairie rose

STATE TREE: American elm

NORTH DAKOTA

The Roughrider STATE

Tour the schoolhouses, workshops—even the jail—of an authentic pioneer village.

If the grain silos, ghost towns, and endless wheat fields of eastern North Dakota don't sound like sights you need to see, then go west, young road-tripper! You'll find the bison-filled badlands that made a man out of Theodore Roosevelt, America's most rough-and-tumble President.

FANTASTIC NORTH DAKOTA FACTS

The exact middle of North America is in the small North Dakota town of Rugby.

Farms and ranches cover 90 percent of North Dakota.

When three outlaws stole Teddy Roosevelt's boat on the Missouri River in 1886, he built a new one and chased down the thieves!

BOREDOM BUSTER! Take a photo of every ghost town you pass and see who can get the most!

Roadside Attractions

ENCHANTED HIGHWAY
Artist Gary Greff decorated this 32-mile stretch of roadway east of Dickinson with scrap-metal sculptures of bugs, birds, and fanciful beasts.

WORLD'S LARGEST BUFFALO
Herds of buffalo roam the state's badlands, but the biggest stands 26 feet tall near Jamestown, North Dakota's "Buffalo City."

MEDORA DOLL HOUSE
This old house, a historic landmark in Medora, is filled wall-to-wall with antique dolls and toys from the days before AA batteries.

STATE BIRD: cardinal

STATE FLOWER: red carnation

STATE ANIMAL: white-tailed deer

OHIO
The Buckeye STATE

Travel from one end of Ohio to the other and you'll have a tough time believing you're still in the same state. Smoke-belching factories along the Ohio River give way to forests in the south, while horse-drawn buggies outnumber automobiles in the quaint Amish communities of the state's heart.

TRAFFIC LAWS YOU WON'T BELIEVE

It might sound like common sense, but you're not allowed to ride on the roof of a taxi in Youngstown.

If you want to roller-skate in New Canton, you better ask the police first.

You could get a ticket for riding your horse over five miles an hour in Lowell.

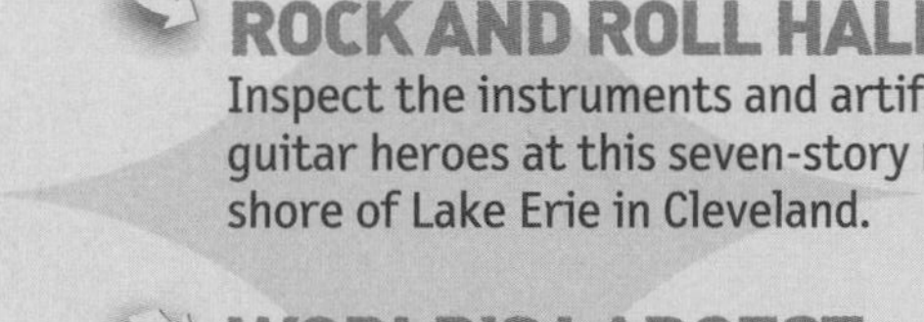

ROCK AND ROLL HALL OF FAME
Inspect the instruments and artifacts of legendary guitar heroes at this seven-story museum on the shore of Lake Erie in Cleveland.

WORLD'S LARGEST APPLE BASKET
New York City may be the Big Apple, but the biggest apple basket is actually here in Frazeysburg. Standing 20 feet tall, it's nearly overflowing with phony oversize fruit.

PRO FOOTBALL HALL OF FAME
Gridiron greats score the ultimate honor at this Canton museum of the National Football League.

5 COOL THINGS TO DO HERE

1 STEEL BEASTS
Sandusky

Give your stomach the topsy-turvy treatment at Cedar Point, an amusement park famous for its roller coasters.

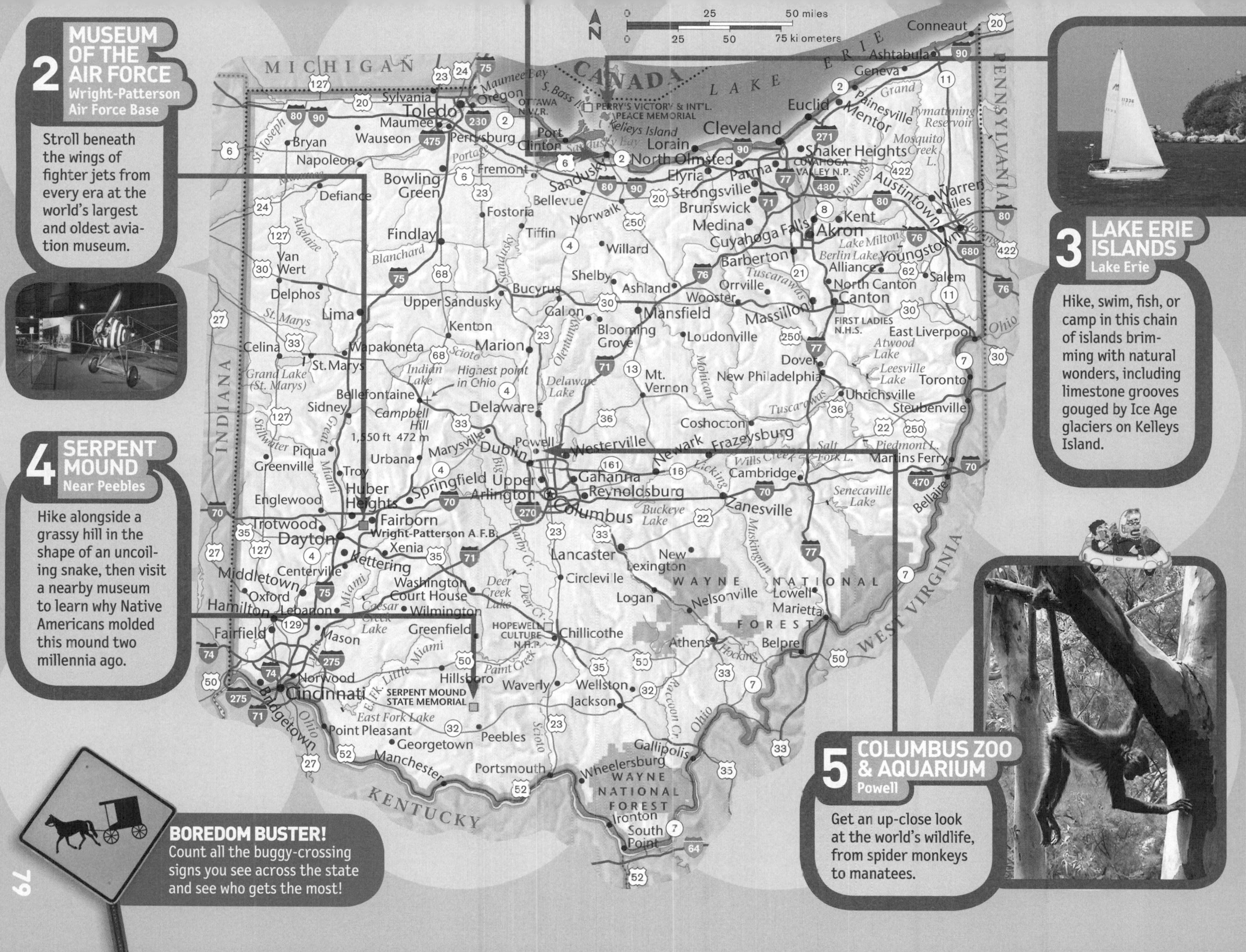

2 MUSEUM OF THE AIR FORCE
Wright-Patterson Air Force Base

Stroll beneath the wings of fighter jets from every era at the world's largest and oldest aviation museum.

4 SERPENT MOUND
Near Peebles

Hike alongside a grassy hill in the shape of an uncoiling snake, then visit a nearby museum to learn why Native Americans molded this mound two millennia ago.

3 LAKE ERIE ISLANDS
Lake Erie

Hike, swim, fish, or camp in this chain of islands brimming with natural wonders, including limestone grooves gouged by Ice Age glaciers on Kelleys Island.

5 COLUMBUS ZOO & AQUARIUM
Powell

Get an up-close look at the world's wildlife, from spider monkeys to manatees.

BOREDOM BUSTER!
Count all the buggy-crossing signs you see across the state and see who gets the most!

OKLAHOMA

The Sooner STATE

COLORADO
Cimarron
Black Mesa 4,973 ft 1,516 m
Highest point in Oklahoma
Kenton
Boise City
Guymon
HIGH PLAINS
N.M.
KIOWA AND RITA BLANCA NATIONAL GRASSLANDS
OPTIMA N.W.R.
Optima Lake

Great Depression dust storms, terrible twisters, forced Native American migrations—unhappy history haunts Oklahoma, an oddly shaped state that few think to visit. Don't let its ugly-duckling early days drive you away. Neither dull nor dusty, Oklahoma is worth another look!

TRAFFIC LAWS YOU WON'T BELIEVE

If you have a house in Bartlesville, you better not let rain drip from your roof onto the sidewalk!

It's against the law to trip a horse.

You can't hit a home run on the streets of Bartlesville.

GPS BOREDOM BUSTER!

Nearly 400 miles of historic Route 66 still stretch across Oklahoma—from Texola to Quapaw. Use your car's navigation system and some detective work to trace the famous highway's path.

Roadside Attractions

THE BLUE WHALE

This smiling concrete sperm whale guards a swimming hole off old Route 66 near Catoosa.

WINDMILL MUSEUM & PARK

More than 50 vintage windmills—some from the 1800s—sprout from this sprawling shrine to wind power in Shattuck.

GOLDEN DRILLER

Like some fossil-fuel-powered superhero, this gold-painted oil worker looms over Tulsa as a monument to the city's days as the "oil capital of the world."

4 BLACK MESA
Kenton

Hike to the flat top of this mesa covered in black volcanic rock. Nearly 5,000 feet above sea level, it's Oklahoma's highest point.

5 WICHITA MOUNTAINS WILDLIFE REFUGE
Lawton

See herds of bison, longhorn cattle, elk, and other Great Plains regulars roam this rocky region popular with climbers.

5 COOL THINGS TO DO HERE

1 OKLAHOMA ROUTE 66 MUSEUM
Clinton

Route 66, the two-lane "Main Street of America" that once linked Chicago and Los Angeles, is an icon of American road-tripping. Stop by this museum to learn about the route's vibrant days before it was replaced by superhighways.

2 FRONTIER CITY
Oklahoma City

Only a bronco bucks harder than the roller coasters at this Wild West–themed amusement park.

3 CHEROKEE HERITAGE MUSEUM
Tahlequah

The Cherokee were one of many Native American tribes forced to resettle in Oklahoma in the early 1800s. See demonstrations of Native American games and weapons at this re-creation of a 17th-century village.

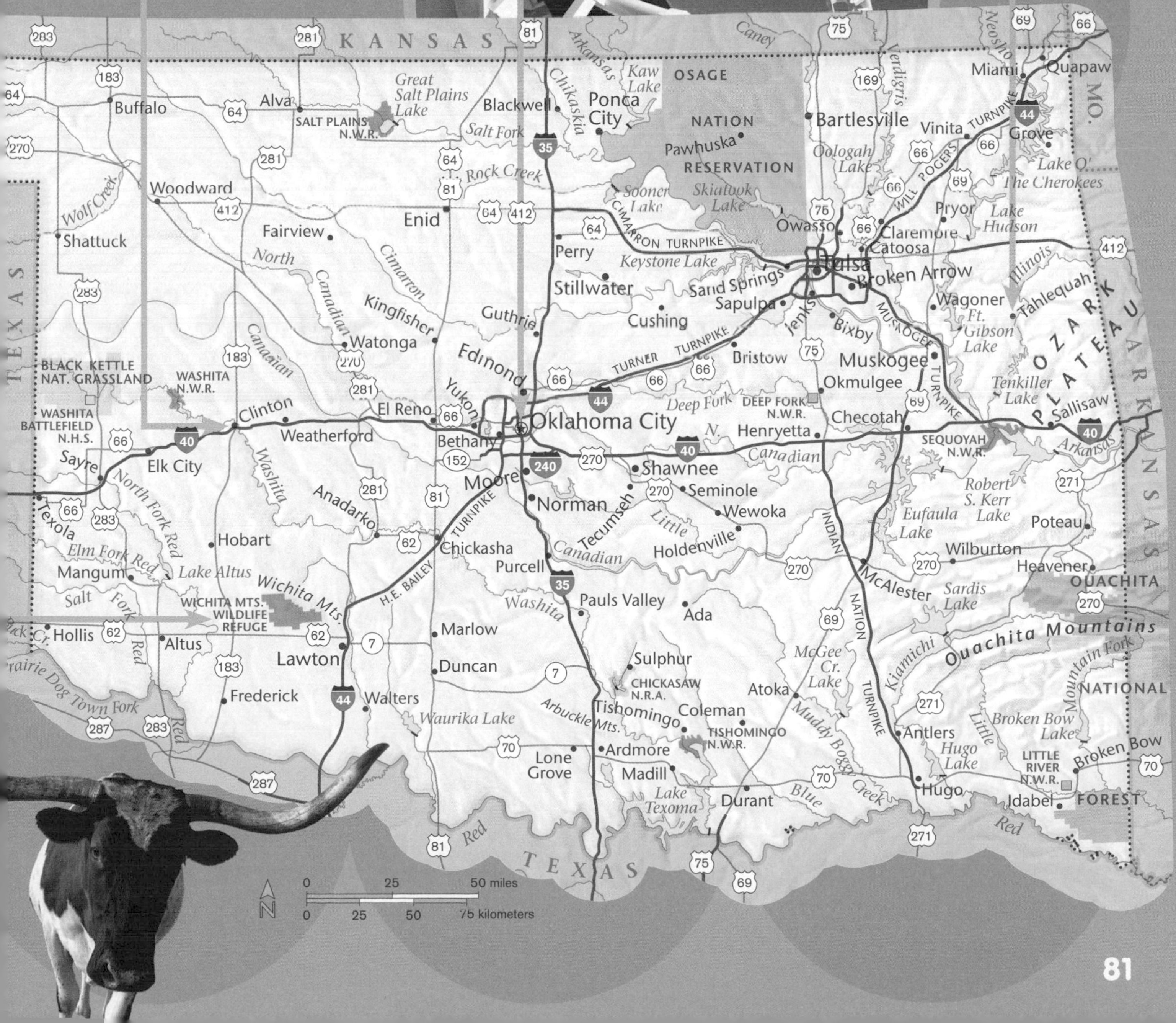

STATE BIRD: western meadowlark

STATE FLOWER: Oregon grape

STATE ANIMAL: American beaver

OREGON

The Beaver STATE

Promises of wide-open land and the good life lured enterprising pioneers west along the 2,000-mile Oregon Trail in the 1840s. Not much has changed! Today's visitors to Oregon find an incredible variety of landscapes and sophisticated cities offering every type of attraction.

TRAFFIC LAWS YOU WON'T BELIEVE

Don't leave your car door open longer than you have to—it's a crime!

You can't let a truck tow you on roller skates in Portland.

You're not allowed to compete in a push-up contest while driving on the highway.

BOREDOM BUSTER!
Deserts, forests, mountains, jagged coastline—Oregon's range of terrain is vast! Try to capture each environment on your camera as you travel through the state.

Roadside Attractions

A.C. GILBERT'S DISCOVERY VILLAGE
The real attraction of this interactive museum in Salem is its sprawling backyard playground, featuring a gigantic Erector set, a miniature village, a woolly mammoth dig site, and lots of other stuff to climb on.

EVERGREEN AVIATION & SPACE MUSEUM
This hangar in McMinnville is home to more than 200 aircraft—including the Spruce Goose, one of the largest planes ever built!

VACUUM MUSEUM
The shelves of Stark's Vacuums store in Portland are lined with hundreds of dirt-devouring contraptions from throughout housecleaning history. One model requires two people to operate!

1 MOUNT HOOD
Mount Hood National Forest

The snowcapped peak of Oregon's tallest mountain makes a stunning backdrop for hiking, camping, and mountain biking.

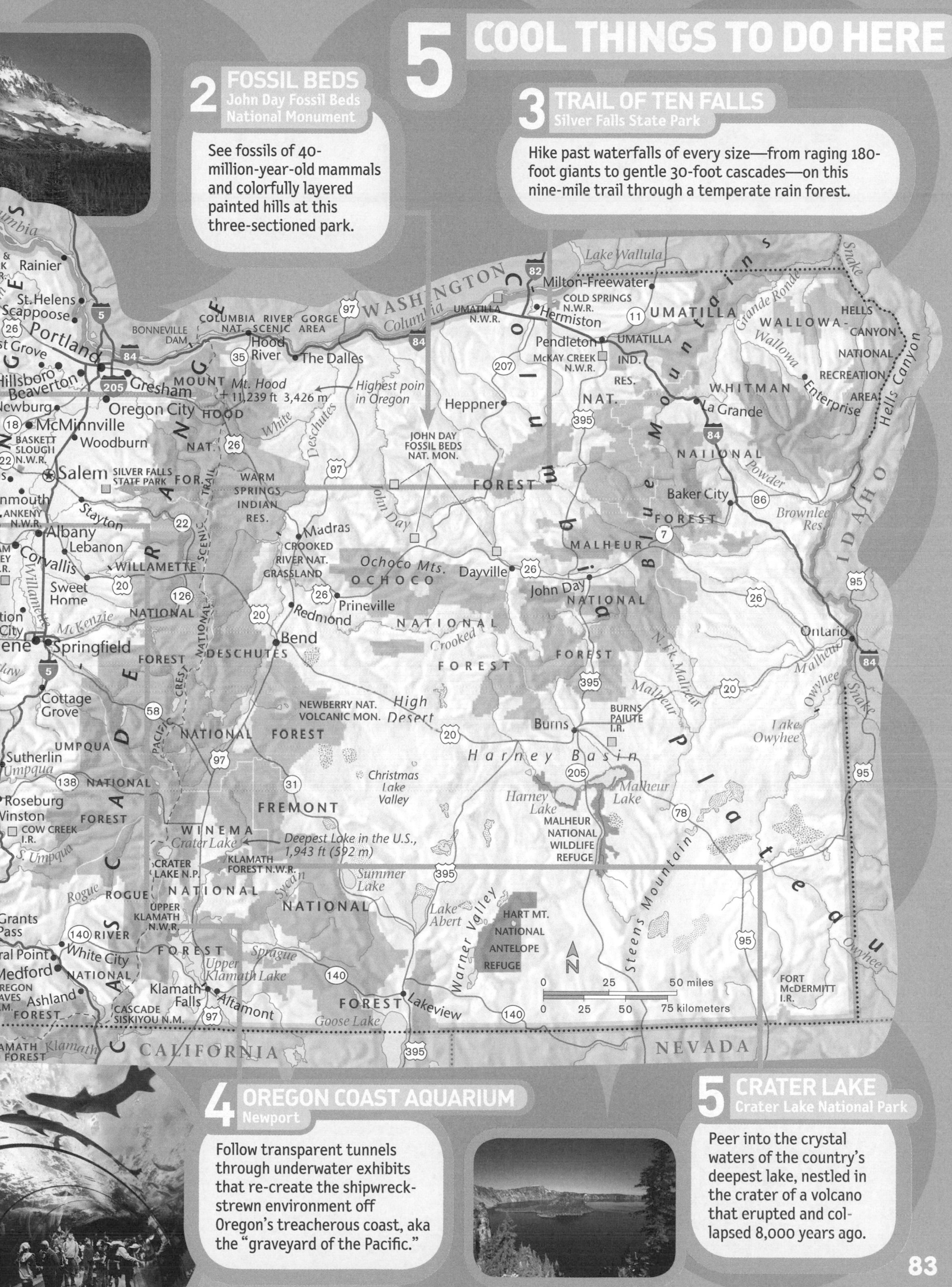

5 COOL THINGS TO DO HERE

2 FOSSIL BEDS
John Day Fossil Beds National Monument

See fossils of 40-million-year-old mammals and colorfully layered painted hills at this three-sectioned park.

3 TRAIL OF TEN FALLS
Silver Falls State Park

Hike past waterfalls of every size—from raging 180-foot giants to gentle 30-foot cascades—on this nine-mile trail through a temperate rain forest.

4 OREGON COAST AQUARIUM
Newport

Follow transparent tunnels through underwater exhibits that re-create the shipwreck-strewn environment off Oregon's treacherous coast, aka the "graveyard of the Pacific."

5 CRATER LAKE
Crater Lake National Park

Peer into the crystal waters of the country's deepest lake, nestled in the crater of a volcano that erupted and collapsed 8,000 years ago.

PENNSYLVANIA

The Keystone STATE

Talk about a state with a history! America's founding principles were drafted in Philadelphia, but Pennsylvania's story goes back another 16,000 years to the oldest known human shelter in North America. What's made the "Keystone State" such a hot spot since the Ice Age? Hit the turnpike and find out!

TRAFFIC LAWS YOU WON'T BELIEVE

You can tie your dog—but not your horse—to a streetlight pole in Tarentum.

All fire hydrants have to be inspected an hour before a fire in Danville Borough.

Better call your donkey a cab in Pittsburgh. They're not allowed on trolleys!

Roadside Attractions

MÜTTER MUSEUM

You don't have to be a medical student to visit this collection of anatomical oddities—from human skulls to barbaric surgical instruments—in Philadelphia.

THE CRAYOLA FACTORY

See how Crayola crayons and markers are made and then color and create to your heart's desire at this cool and colorful visitor center in Easton.

KAVERNPUTT

This 18-hole mini-golf course in Farmington is set inside a creepy artificial cave right next to Laurel Caverns, Pennsylvania's largest cave.

GPS BOREDOM BUSTER!

The Pennsylvania Turnpike was America's first super-highway. Use your car's navigation system to track all the major cities linked by this famous route.

3 ROBOWORLD
Pittsburgh

Get inside the mechanical minds of the world's smartest robots—and even challenge one to a basketball game—at the Carnegie Science Center.

5 COOL THINGS TO DO HERE

1 MEADOWCROFT ROCKSHELTER
Avella

Try wielding the primitive tools and weapons of pre-historic people who used this mountain cave as a campsite 16,000 years ago.

2 INDEPENDENCE HALL
Philadelphia

Visit the chamber where America's founding fathers signed the Declaration of Independence and the U.S. Constitution, just across the street from the famous Liberty Bell.

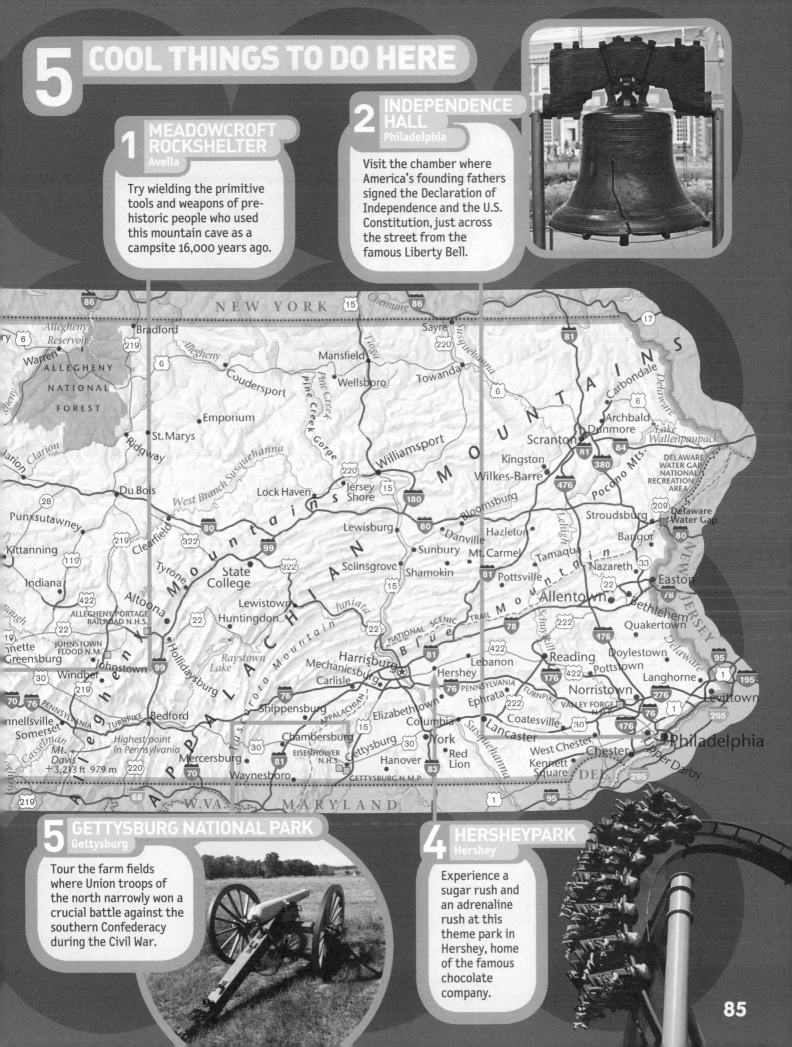

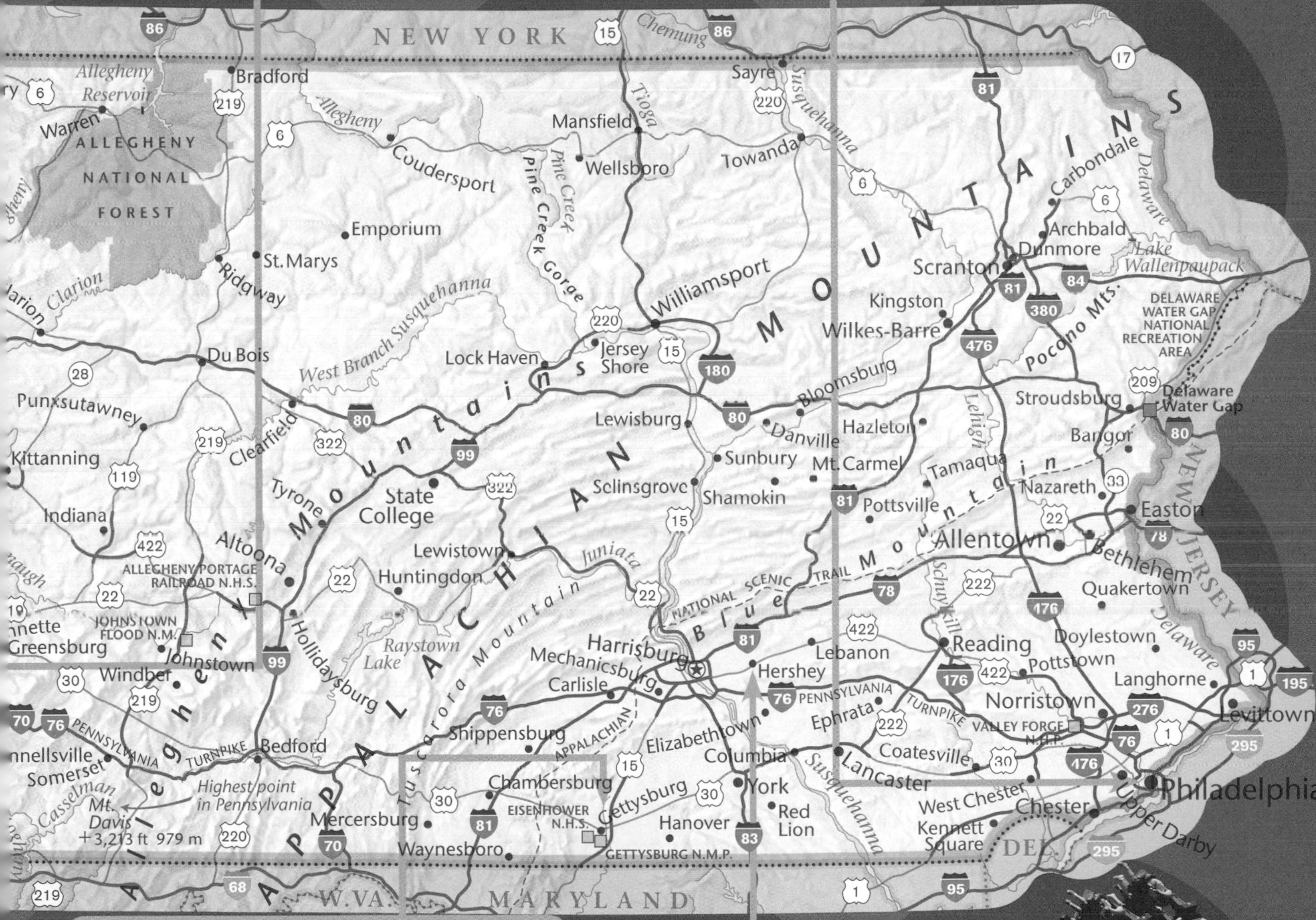

5 GETTYSBURG NATIONAL PARK
Gettysburg

Tour the farm fields where Union troops of the north narrowly won a crucial battle against the southern Confederacy during the Civil War.

4 HERSHEYPARK
Hershey

Experience a sugar rush and an adrenaline rush at this theme park in Hershey, home of the famous chocolate company.

STATE BIRD: Rhode Island red chicken

STATE FLOWER: violet

STATE TREE: red maple

RHODE ISLAND

The Ocean STATE

It may be the nation's tiniest state—just over half the size of the second smallest, Delaware—but Rhode Island delivers big on sights worth seeing. White-sand beaches, lush woodlands, and countless historic landmarks fill an area smaller than some American cities.

TRAFFIC LAWS YOU WON'T BELIEVE

Throwing pickle juice on a trolley is a crime.

Never pass a car on the left without honking your horn first.

It's against the law to race horses on the highway.

Roadside Attractions

FLYING HORSE CAROUSEL

In Watch Hill, take a spin on the hand-carved wooden horses of the oldest carousel of its kind in the country.

BIG BLUE BUG

Watch out for the titanic termite looming over Interstate 95 in Providence! (It's actually the famous fiberglass mascot of a pest-control company.)

THE BREAKERS MANSION

Admire the crystal chandeliers, marble walls, and stunning Atlantic views of this 70-room Newport summer home modeled after a 16th-century palace.

GPS BOREDOM BUSTER!

Use your car's navigation system to see how long it would take to drive through Rhode Island. Compare it to a trip across the largest state, Alaska.

5 COOL THINGS TO DO HERE

1 ROGER WILLIAMS PARK ZOO
Providence

Watch snow leopards prowl and penguins waddle at one of the nation's oldest zoos.

2 SCHOONER SAIL
Newport

Sail Narragansett Bay in 19th-century style aboard the passenger yachts that depart from Newport.

3 FORT ADAMS
Newport

Patrol the bastions and explore the tunnels of the largest coastal fortification in America, built to protect Narragansett Bay in the 1800s.

4 LIGHTHOUSE KEEPER
Rose Island

Don't visit this lighthouse inn expecting a good night's sleep. It's your job to operate the beacon just like it was done back in 1912!

5 BLOCK ISLAND
Block Island

Hop a ferry to this quaint island and spend the day hiking, bird-watching, or just sunbathing on a quiet beach.

MASSACHUSETTS
CONNECTICUT
N.Y.

Woonsocket
Slatersville
Glendale
Harrisville
Pascoag Lake
Pascoag
Chepachet
Highest point in Rhode Island
Jerimoth Hill 812 ft 247 m
Harmony
Greenville
North Scituate
Foster Center
Rice City
Johnston
Coventry Center
Hope
Harris
Anthony
West Warwick
Providence
Cranston
Warwick
East Greenwich
Austin
Exeter
Wyoming
Hope Valley
Ashaway
Bradford
Westerly
Watch Hill
Napatree Point
West Kingston
Carolina
Shannock
Charlestown
Jerusalem
Galilee
Point Judith
Quonochontaug
Watch Hill

Union Village
Manville
Cumberland Hill
Ashton
Valley Falls
Lonsdale
Saylesville
Esmond
Central Falls
Pawtucket
North Providence
East Providence
Barrington
Warren
Bristol
Hamilton
Allenton
Saunderstown
Wickford
Conanicut Island
Jamestown
Kingston
Wakefield
Narragansett Pier
Point Judith Pond
Point Judith

Tiverton
Island Park
Portsmouth
Nonquit Pond
Adamsville
Little Compton
Middletown
Newport
Rose Island
SACHUEST POINT N.W.R.
Sakonnet Point

Rhode Island
Prudence Island
Narragansett Bay
Mount Hope Bay
Stafford Pond
Sakonnet River

RHODE ISLAND SOUND
ATLANTIC OCEAN

Block Island Sound
BLOCK ISLAND N.W.R.
Sandy Point
Block Island

NARRAGANSETT INDIAN RES.
Watchaug Pond
Ninigret Pond
NINIGRET N.W.R.
TRUSTOM POND N.W.R.
PETTAQUAMSCUTT COVE N.W.R.
Great Swamp
Worden Pond
Quonochontaug Pond

Scituate Reservoir
Flat River Reservoir
Tiogue L.
Woonasquatucket Reservoir
Ponaganset Res.
Wallum Lake
Pawtucket Reservoir
Blackstone
Woonasquatucket
Pawtuxet
Providence
Palmer
Moosup
Wood
Queen
Pawcatuck

0 5 10 miles
0 5 10 15 kilometers

87

STATE BIRD: Carolina wren
STATE FLOWER: yellow jessamine
STATE ANIMAL: white-tailed deer

SOUTH CAROLINA

The Palmetto STATE

South Carolina is a state for every sort of buff. Blackbeard buffs come to learn about the pirate king's 1718 blockade of Charleston. Civil War buffs climb the walls of Fort Sumter, unchanged since the war's first battle. Fitness buffs tan their buff bodies on Myrtle Beach's stand of golden sand. What sort of buff are you? Find out in the Palmetto State!

FANTASTIC SOUTH CAROLINA FACTS

South Carolina was the first state to secede from the Union in the Civil War.

Built in 1735, Charleston's Dock Street Theatre is said to be one of America's most haunted buildings.

South Carolina grows more peaches than any state east of the Mississippi.

BOREDOM BUSTER!
More and more films are being shot in the Carolinas. Follow Hollywood's lead and use your camera to make a movie of your South Carolina vacation!

Roadside Attractions

MIDDLETON PLACE
Footpaths meander around a butterfly-shaped lake and beneath dangling Spanish moss at this old Charleston plantation once described as the "premier garden of the thirteen colonies."

MINI-GOLF CAPITAL OF THE WORLD
Putt-putt pros could spend a lifetime in Myrtle Beach, home to 50 miniature golf courses fitting every theme, from Jurassic lizards to scurvy pirates.

WORLD'S LARGEST PEACH
Standing four stories tall alongside Interstate 85 in Gaffney, this tasty-looking peach—actually a water tower—is a monument to the state's juiciest crop.

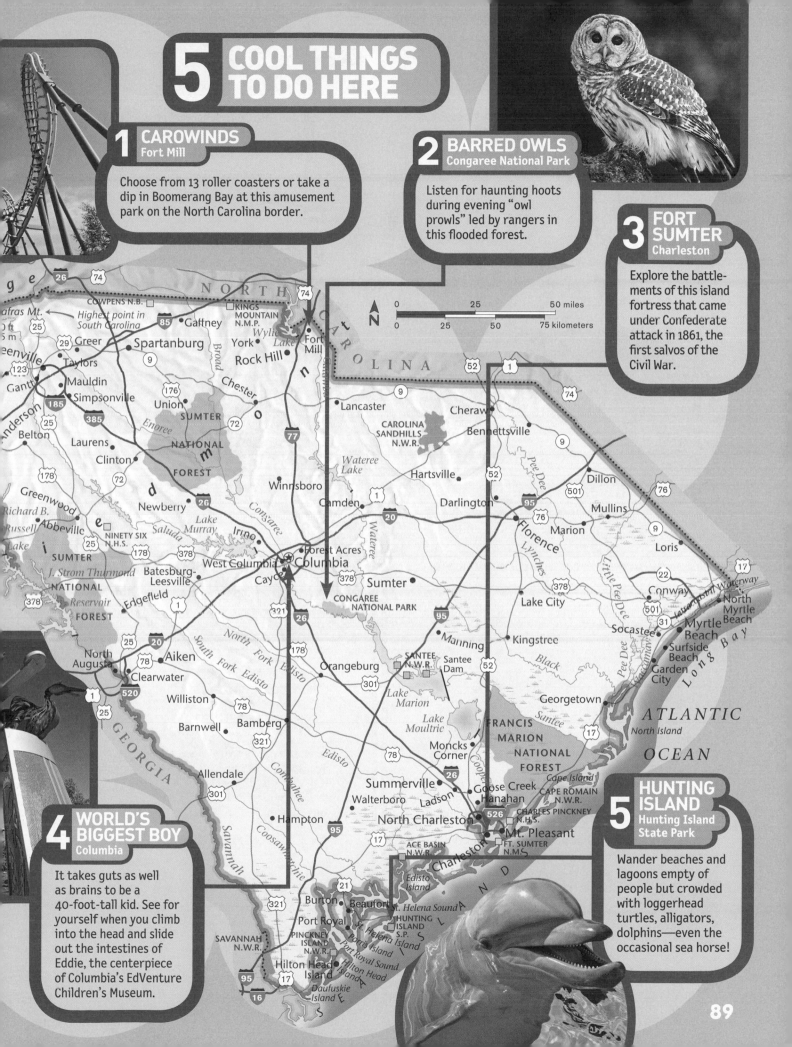

5 COOL THINGS TO DO HERE

1 CAROWINDS
Fort Mill

Choose from 13 roller coasters or take a dip in Boomerang Bay at this amusement park on the North Carolina border.

2 BARRED OWLS
Congaree National Park

Listen for haunting hoots during evening "owl prowls" led by rangers in this flooded forest.

3 FORT SUMTER
Charleston

Explore the battlements of this island fortress that came under Confederate attack in 1861, the first salvos of the Civil War.

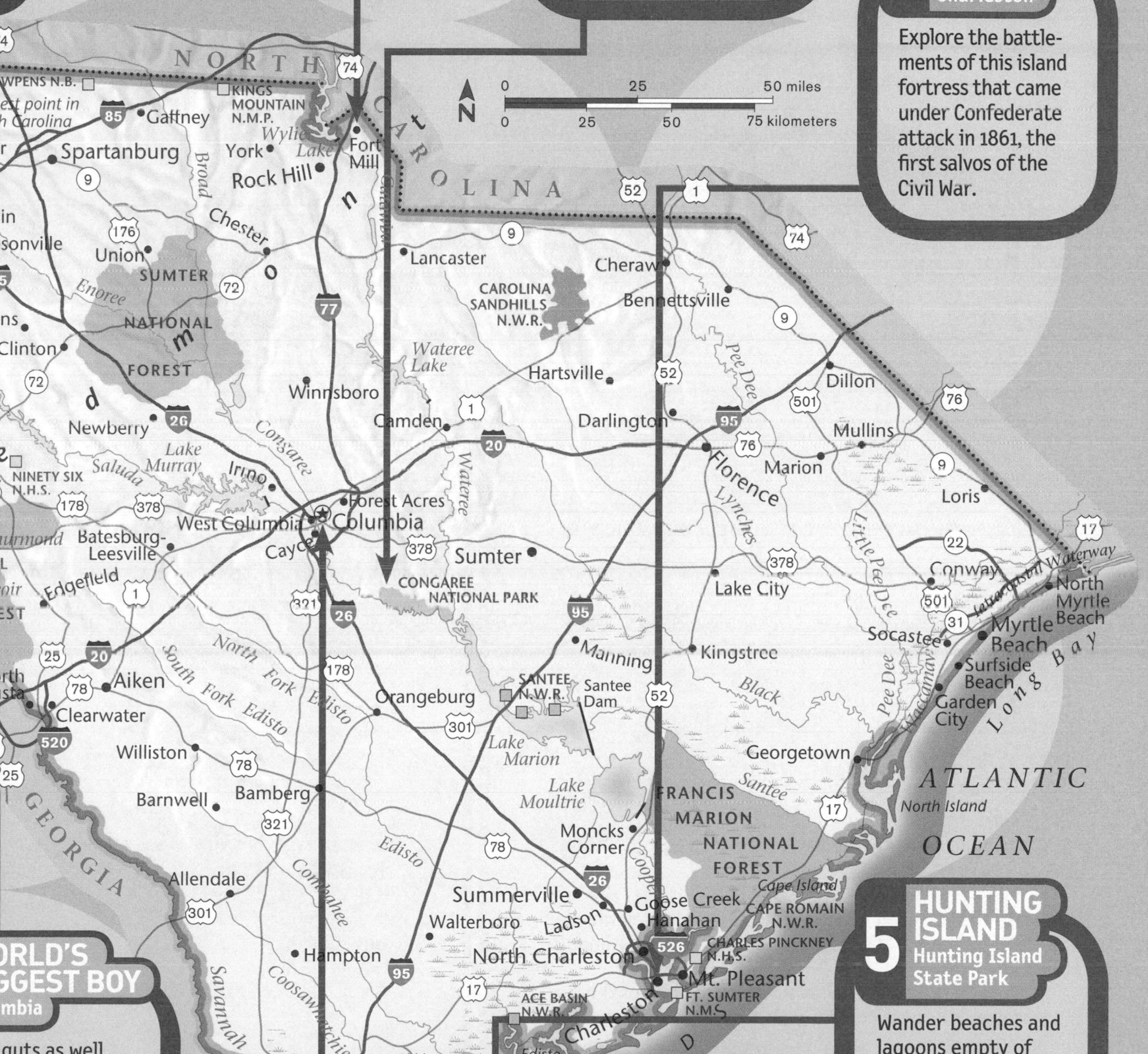

4 WORLD'S BIGGEST BOY
Columbia

It takes guts as well as brains to be a 40-foot-tall kid. See for yourself when you climb into the head and slide out the intestines of Eddie, the centerpiece of Columbia's EdVenture Children's Museum.

5 HUNTING ISLAND
Hunting Island State Park

Wander beaches and lagoons empty of people but crowded with loggerhead turtles, alligators, dolphins—even the occasional sea horse!

STATE BIRD: ring-necked pheasant
STATE FLOWER: pasqueflower
STATE ANIMAL: coyote

SOUTH DAKOTA

The Mount Rushmore STATE

South Dakota may be home to America's biggest rock stars—the dynamite-sculpted presidential noggins of Mount Rushmore—but don't limit your visit to just this Black Hills attraction. Otherworldly landscapes and an enduring Native American heritage make this Great Plains state a fascinating place to explore.

FANTASTIC SOUTH DAKOTA FACTS

More than 90 percent of Mount Rushmore was carved using TNT.

Sculptors are in the process of carving Crazy Horse atop his steed at his mountainside memorial, which will be the world's largest sculpture when finished.

More than 60,000 Native Americans—one of the nation's largest populations—live in South Dakota.

GPS BOREDOM BUSTER!
Use your car's navigation system to see how many buffalo ranches you can find, then take photos of the big furry beasts!

Roadside Attractions

THE MAMMOTH SITE

Built over a dried-up pond in Hot Springs, this enclosed research facility has unearthed the bones of 55 Ice Age woolly mammoths. Visitors can watch paleontologists make new discoveries daily!

WALL DRUG

What started as a tiny drugstore in the town of Wall is now a full-fledged mall famous for its Wild West souvenirs and mini–Mount Rushmore.

MINUTEMAN MISSILE SITE

A holdover from America's Cold War with the Soviet Union, this remote launch facility near Wall has turned its intercontinental ballistic missile site into a tourist attraction.

1 MOUNT RUSHMORE
Black Hills

Stand face to 60-foot face before exalted Presidents George Washington, Thomas Jefferson, Theodore Roosevelt, and Abraham Lincoln at this "shrine of democracy."

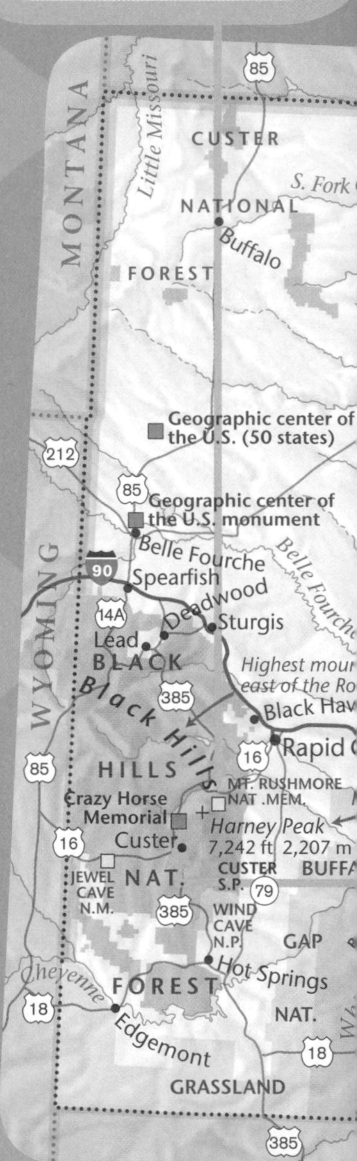

3 THE BADLANDS
Badlands National Park

You'll think you landed on the surface of the moon when you visit this desolate, wind-worn landscape.

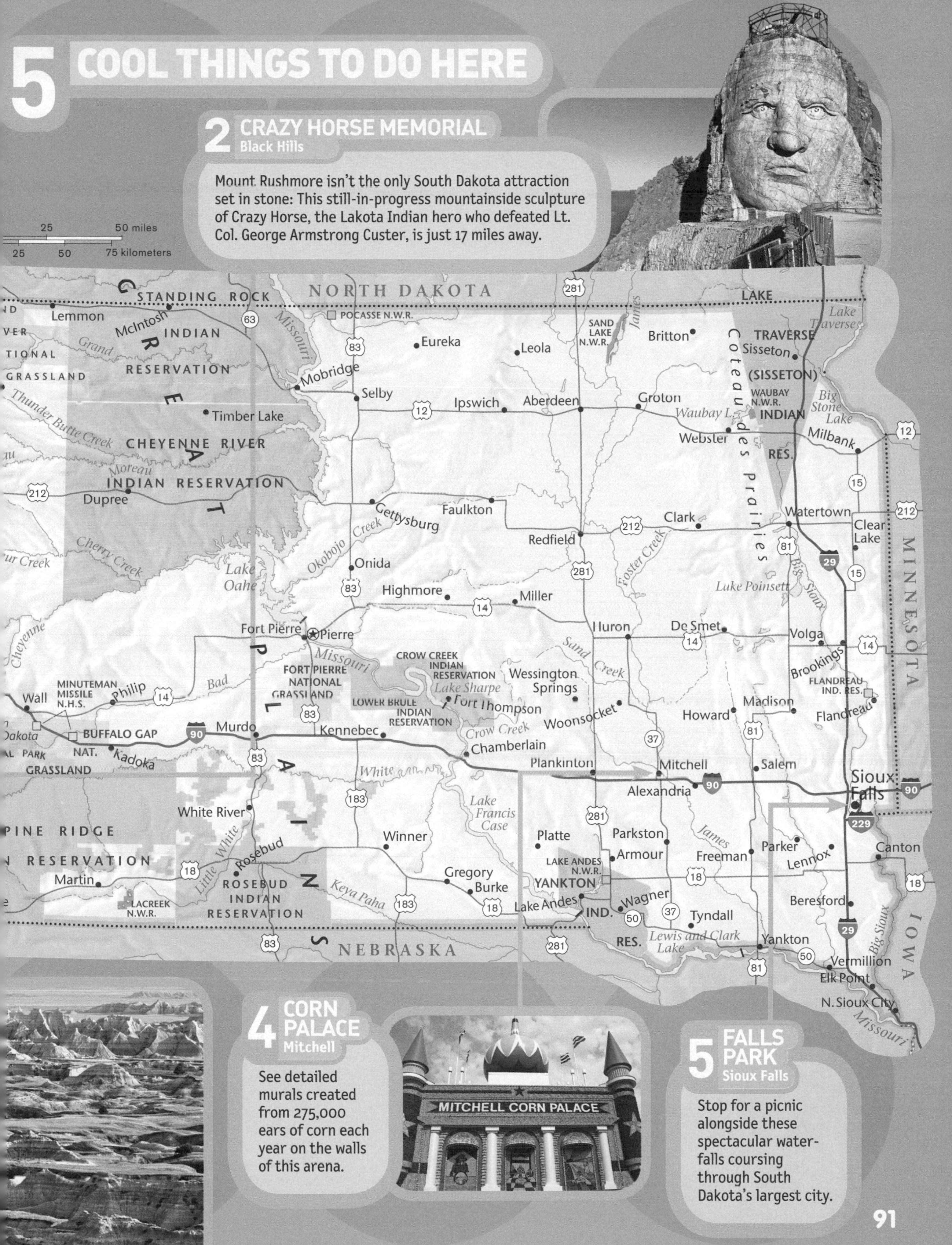
5 COOL THINGS TO DO HERE
2 CRAZY HORSE MEMORIAL
Black Hills
Mount Rushmore isn't the only South Dakota attraction set in stone: This still-in-progress mountainside sculpture of Crazy Horse, the Lakota Indian hero who defeated Lt. Col. George Armstrong Custer, is just 17 miles away.
25 50 miles
25 50 75 kilometers
NORTH DAKOTA
STANDING ROCK INDIAN RESERVATION
GREAT PLAINS
Lemmon
McIntosh
Grand
Missouri
POCASSE N.W.R.
SAND LAKE N.W.R.
James
LAKE TRAVERSE (SISSETON) INDIAN RES.
Lake Traverse
Britton
Sisseton
Coteau des Prairies
Eureka
Leola
Mobridge
Selby
Ipswich
Aberdeen
Groton
WAUBAY N.W.R.
Waubay L.
Webster
Big Stone Lake
Milbank
Timber Lake
Thunder Butte Creek
CHEYENNE RIVER INDIAN RESERVATION
Moreau
Dupree
Gettysburg
Faulkton
Clark
Watertown
Clear Lake
Redfield
Foster Creek
Lake Poinsett
Big Sioux
Cherry Creek
Okobojo Creek
Onida
Lake Oahe
Highmore
Miller
MINNESOTA
Cheyenne
Fort Pierre
Pierre
Huron
De Smet
Volga
Brookings
Sand Creek
CROW CREEK INDIAN RESERVATION
FORT PIERRE NATIONAL GRASSLAND
Missouri
Lake Sharpe
Wessington Springs
FLANDREAU IND. RES.
Flandreau
MINUTEMAN MISSILE N.H.S.
Wall
Philip
Bad
LOWER BRULE INDIAN RESERVATION
Fort Thompson
Woonsocket
Howard
Madison
BUFFALO GAP NAT. GRASSLAND
Murdo
Kennebec
Crow Creek
Chamberlain
Kadoka
Plankinton
Mitchell
Salem
Alexandria
Sioux Falls
White
Lake Francis Case
White River
PINE RIDGE RESERVATION
Platte
Parkston
James
Winner
Armour
Freeman
Parker
Lennox
Canton
Rosebud
Little White
LAKE ANDES N.W.R.
Gregory
Burke
YANKTON IND. RES.
Martin
ROSEBUD INDIAN RESERVATION
Keya Paha
Lake Andes
Wagner
Tyndall
Beresford
LACREEK N.W.R.
NEBRASKA
Lewis and Clark Lake
Yankton
Big Sioux
IOWA
Vermillion
Elk Point
N. Sioux City
Missouri
4 CORN PALACE
Mitchell
See detailed murals created from 275,000 ears of corn each year on the walls of this arena.
MITCHELL CORN PALACE
5 FALLS PARK
Sioux Falls
Stop for a picnic alongside these spectacular water-falls coursing through South Dakota's largest city.

STATE BIRD: mockingbird

STATE FLOWER: iris

STATE ANIMAL: raccoon

TENNESSEE

The Volunteer STATE

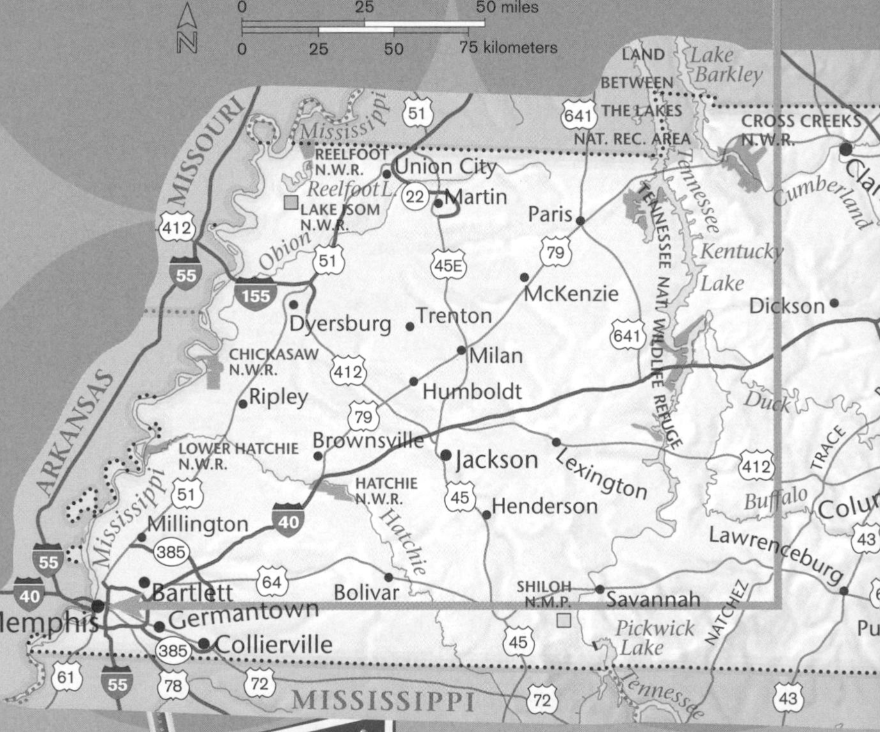

There's a lot to see in Tennessee—a state of misty mountains, sprawling farmland, and rolling hills—but there's even more to hear. The home of rock-and-roll and country music, Tennessee adds rhythm to any cross-country road trip.

TRAFFIC LAWS YOU WON'T BELIEVE

You're not allowed to shoot any animals from a moving car—except for whales.

Chowing down on roadkill is illegal.

You can't drive any skunks into the state.

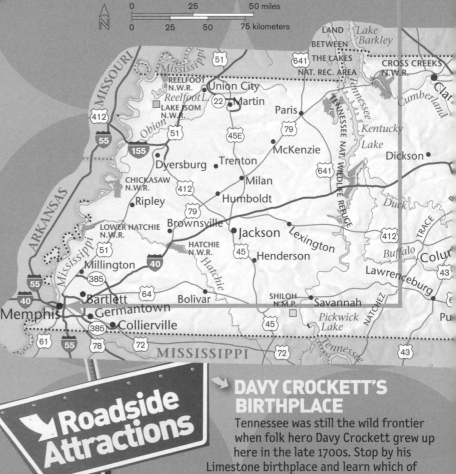

Roadside Attractions

DAVY CROCKETT'S BIRTHPLACE

Tennessee was still the wild frontier when folk hero Davy Crockett grew up here in the late 1700s. Stop by his Limestone birthplace and learn which of Crockett's tall tales are actually true.

DOLLYWOOD

Songstress Dolly Parton opened this country-music-themed amusement park in Pigeon Forge, complete with a roller coaster that plunges through an actual mountain.

GPS BOREDOM BUSTER!

Use your car's navigation system to track down Elvis-themed sights as you cruise across the late superstar's home state.

5 COOL THINGS TO DO HERE

1 GRACELAND
Memphis

Tour the ludicrously lavish mansion of Elvis Presley, the hip-swaying king of rock-and-roll. One jungle-themed room even has its own waterfall!

2 COUNTRY MUSIC HALL OF FAME
Nashville

Tap your cowboy boots to catchy tunes and learn the rich history of honky-tonk.

3 CLINGMANS DOME
Great Smoky Mountains National Park

The grueling half-mile hike to this remote observation post is worth it for the spectacular 360-degree views of the Great Smoky Mountains.

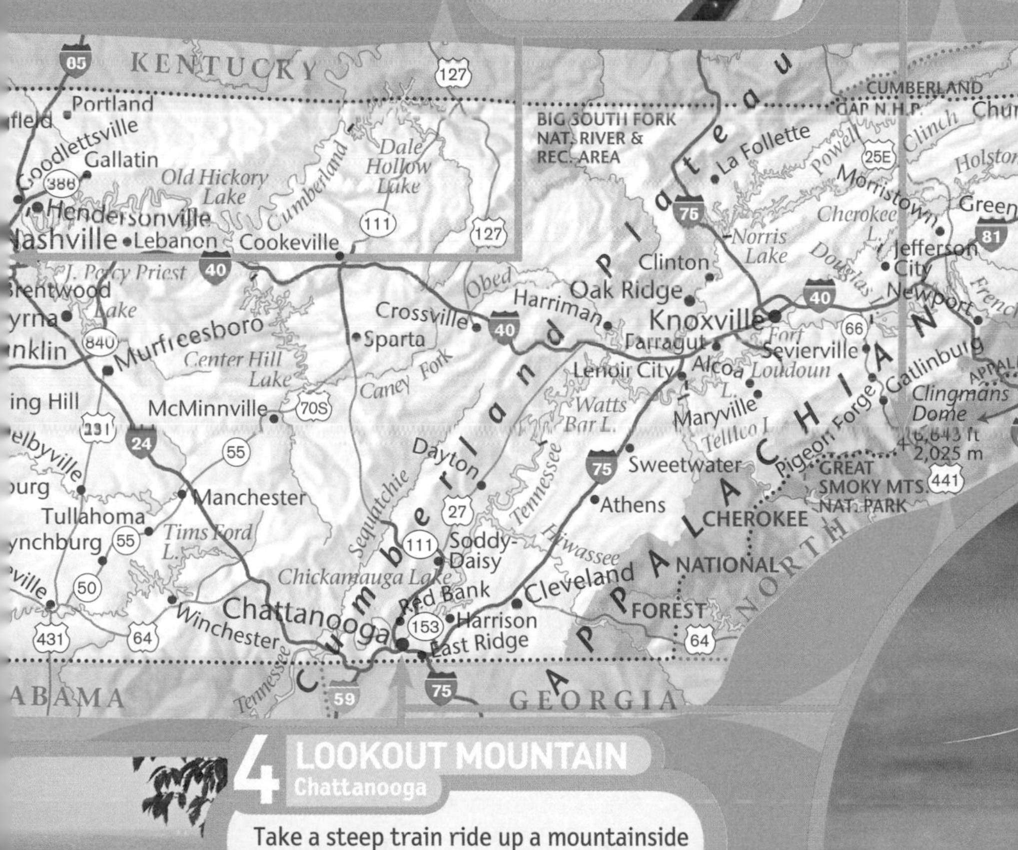

4 LOOKOUT MOUNTAIN
Chattanooga

Take a steep train ride up a mountainside for panoramic views of seven states.

5 RIVER OTTERS
Chattanooga

Watch these rambunctious mammals play silly games at the Tennessee Aquarium, the world's largest freshwater aquarium.

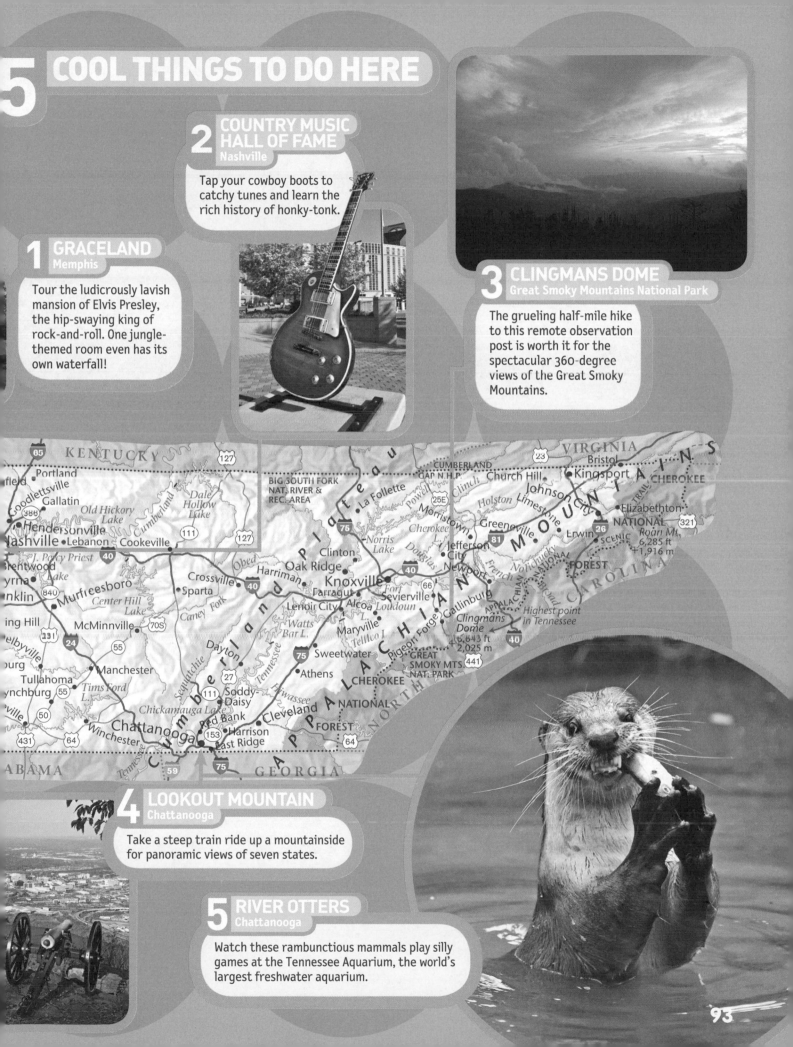

STATE BIRD: mockingbird

STATE FLOWER: bluebonnet

STATE ANIMAL: Texas longhorn

TEXAS

The Lone Star STATE

1 GRAND CANYON OF TEXAS
Palo Duro Canyon State Park

Take a horseback ride through this 800-foot-deep painted canyon in the Texas Panhandle.

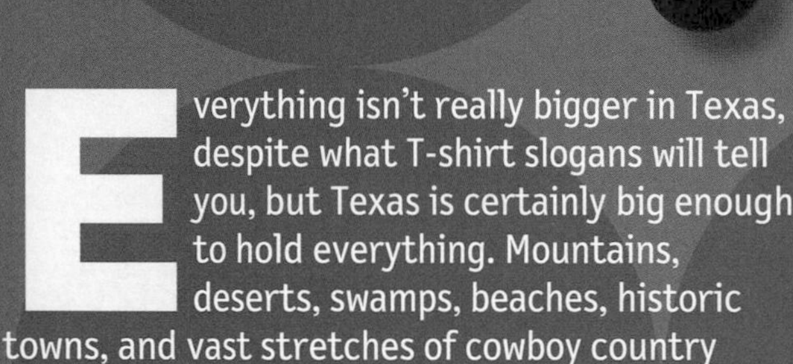

Everything isn't really bigger in Texas, despite what T-shirt slogans will tell you, but Texas is certainly big enough to hold everything. Mountains, deserts, swamps, beaches, historic towns, and vast stretches of cowboy country make up this land of unlimited adventure.

FANTASTIC TEXAS FACTS

Mission controllers in Houston were the first people on Earth to speak with men on the moon.

Texas' official state sport is rodeo.

Famous frontier adventurers Davy Crockett and James Bowie both died at the Battle of the Alamo.

CADILLAC RANCH
Ten graffiti-splattered Cadillacs stick trunk-first from the sunbaked ground just west of Amarillo on Interstate 40. Planted by an eccentric millionaire in the 1970s, they've become America's most famous example of road art.

NATIONAL COWGIRL MUSEUM
This Fort Worth hall of fame features galleries and hands-on exhibits celebrating legendary women of the American West.

SCHLITTERBAHN WATERPARKS
It doesn't take long to work up a sweat in steamy Texas. Cool your heels at one of the wild Schlitterbahn Waterparks, located in Galveston, New Braunfels, and South Padre Island.

BOREDOM BUSTER!
Take camera phone pictures of any oil pumps you pass and see who can get the most!

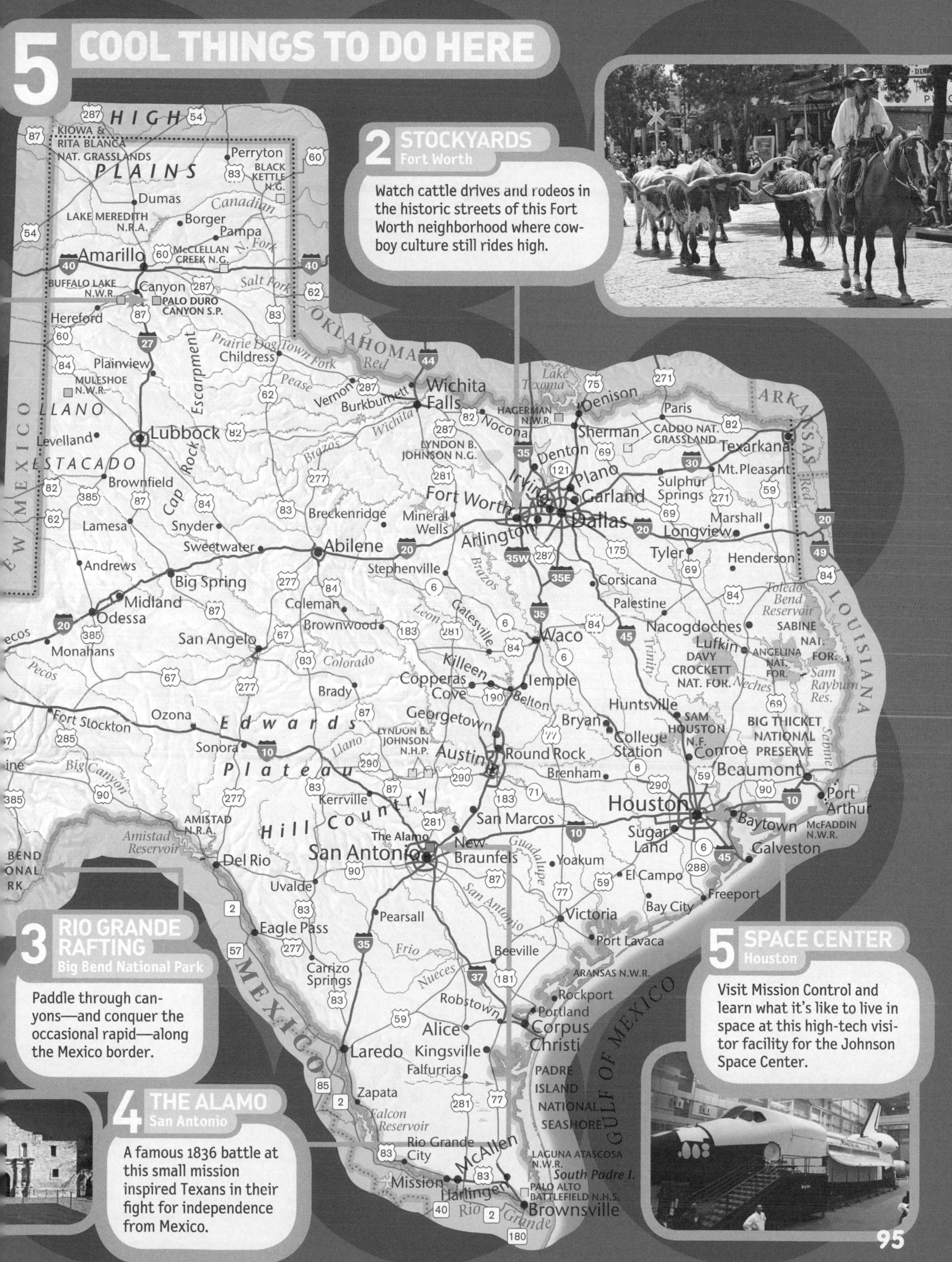
5 COOL THINGS TO DO HERE
2 STOCKYARDS
Fort Worth
Watch cattle drives and rodeos in the historic streets of this Fort Worth neighborhood where cowboy culture still rides high.
3 RIO GRANDE RAFTING
Big Bend National Park
Paddle through canyons—and conquer the occasional rapid—along the Mexico border.
4 THE ALAMO
San Antonio
A famous 1836 battle at this small mission inspired Texans in their fight for independence from Mexico.
5 SPACE CENTER
Houston
Visit Mission Control and learn what it's like to live in space at this high-tech visitor facility for the Johnson Space Center.
HIGH PLAINS
KIOWA & RITA BLANCA NAT. GRASSLANDS
Perryton
BLACK KETTLE N.G.
Dumas
Canadian
LAKE MEREDITH N.R.A.
Borger
Pampa
McCLELLAN CREEK N.G.
Amarillo
BUFFALO LAKE N.W.R.
Canyon
PALO DURO CANYON S.P.
Salt Fork
Hereford
Prairie Dog Town Fork
Childress
OKLAHOMA
Red
Plainview
MULESHOE N.W.R.
Pease
LLANO ESTACADO
Escarpment
Cap Rock
Lubbock
Levelland
Brownfield
Lamesa
Snyder
Sweetwater
Andrews
Big Spring
Midland
Odessa
Monahans
Pecos
San Angelo
Vernon
Burkburnett
Wichita Falls
Wichita
Brazos
Nocona
HAGERMAN N.W.R.
Lake Texoma
Denison
Sherman
Paris
CADDO NAT. GRASSLAND
ARKANSAS
Texarkana
LYNDON B. JOHNSON N.G.
Denton
Plano
Irving
Garland
Fort Worth
Dallas
Arlington
Mt. Pleasant
Sulphur Springs
Marshall
Longview
Tyler
Henderson
Breckenridge
Mineral Wells
Abilene
Stephenville
Corsicana
Palestine
Coleman
Brownwood
Leon
Gatesville
Waco
Nacogdoches
Lufkin
DAVY CROCKETT NAT. FOR.
ANGELINA NAT. FOR.
SABINE NAT. FOR.
Toledo Bend Reservoir
Sam Rayburn Res.
LOUISIANA
Trinity
Neches
Colorado
Brady
Killeen
Copperas Cove
Temple
Belton
Huntsville
SAM HOUSTON N.F.
BIG THICKET NATIONAL PRESERVE
Sabine
Fort Stockton
Ozona
Edwards Plateau
Sonora
Llano
LYNDON B. JOHNSON N.H.P.
Georgetown
Austin
Round Rock
Bryan
College Station
Conroe
Beaumont
Port Arthur
Brenham
Houston
Baytown
McFADDIN N.W.R.
Big Canyon
Kerrville
Hill Country
San Marcos
Sugar Land
Galveston
AMISTAD N.R.A.
Amistad Reservoir
Del Rio
The Alamo
San Antonio
New Braunfels
Guadalupe
Yoakum
El Campo
Bay City
Freeport
Uvalde
San Antonio
Victoria
Port Lavaca
Eagle Pass
Pearsall
Frio
Carrizo Springs
Nueces
Beeville
ARANSAS N.W.R.
Rockport
Robstown
Portland
Corpus Christi
Alice
Kingsville
Laredo
MEXICO
GULF OF MEXICO
Falfurrias
Zapata
PADRE ISLAND NATIONAL SEASHORE
Falcon Reservoir
Rio Grande City
McAllen
Mission
Harlingen
LAGUNA ATASCOSA N.W.R.
South Padre I.
PALO ALTO BATTLEFIELD N.H.S.
Brownsville
Rio Grande
NEW MEXICO
BEND NATIONAL PARK

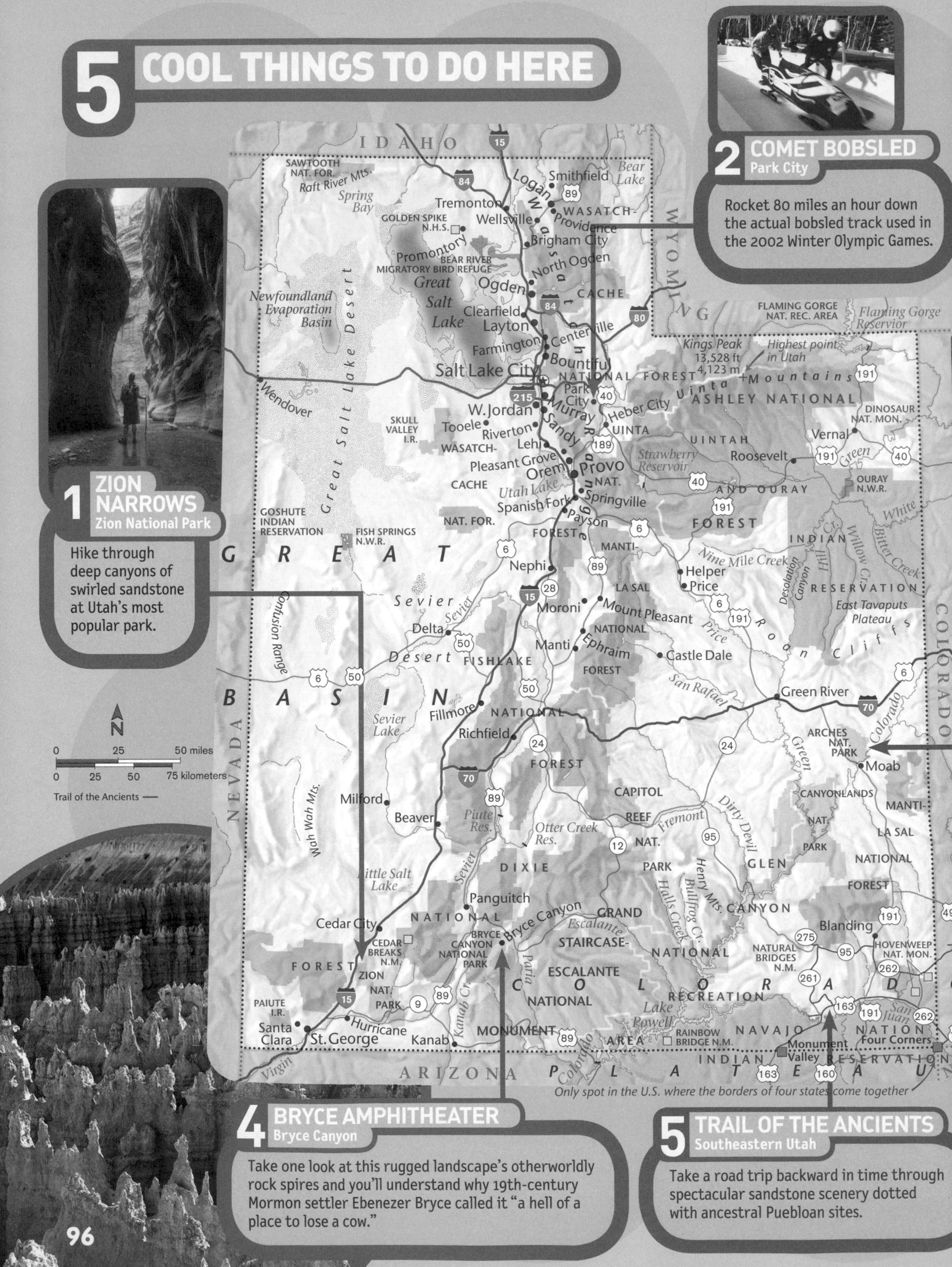
5 COOL THINGS TO DO HERE
1 ZION NARROWS
Zion National Park
Hike through deep canyons of swirled sandstone at Utah's most popular park.
2 COMET BOBSLED
Park City
Rocket 80 miles an hour down the actual bobsled track used in the 2002 Winter Olympic Games.
4 BRYCE AMPHITHEATER
Bryce Canyon
Take one look at this rugged landscape's otherworldly rock spires and you'll understand why 19th-century Mormon settler Ebenezer Bryce called it "a hell of a place to lose a cow."
5 TRAIL OF THE ANCIENTS
Southeastern Utah
Take a road trip backward in time through spectacular sandstone scenery dotted with ancestral Puebloan sites.
IDAHO
WYOMING
COLORADO
ARIZONA
NEVADA
GREAT BASIN
COLORADO PLATEAU
Great Salt Lake
Great Salt Lake Desert
Salt Lake City
Logan
Ogden
Provo
Park City
St. George
Cedar City
Moab
Green River
Bryce Canyon
Kings Peak 13,528 ft 4,123 m
Highest point in Utah
Only spot in the U.S. where the borders of four states come together
Four Corners
Monument Valley
0 25 50 miles
0 25 50 75 kilometers
Trail of the Ancients

UTAH

The Beehive STATE

STATE BIRD: California gull

STATE FLOWER: sego lily

STATE ANIMAL: Rocky Mountain elk

3 AMAZING ARCHES
Arches National Park

Eons of erosion carved this wonderland of gravity-defying sandstone bridges and precariously balanced boulders.

Utah has a long history as a sacred land, first to the Native Americans who built dwellings in its sandstone cliffs, and then to the Mormon pioneers who sought religious refuge near its Great Salt Lake. Today, Utah's wild range of terrain is pure heaven for outdoor enthusiasts.

TRAFFIC LAWS YOU WON'T BELIEVE

Salt Lake County auctioneers can't blow whistles on the street to advertise their services.

You're not allowed to fish from the saddle of your horse.

Watch out for any low-flying birds on the highway—they have the right-of-way!

BOREDOM BUSTER!
Keep your eyes peeled for the rare Utah prairie dog—a threatened species—and try to capture one of these cute critters with your camera.

Roadside Attractions

HOLE N' THE ROCK
Probably the homiest cave you'll ever visit, this 14-room house—complete with a deep stone bathtub—was carved out of a massive sandstone rock near Moab.

BONNEVILLE SALT FLATS
Like the nearby Great Salt Lake, this lifeless 30,000-acre desert of salt is a remnant of an ancient inland sea. It's now a hot spot for lead-footed drivers drawn by the flats' lack of speed limits.

FANTASY CANYON
They may look like manmade sculptures, but Mother Nature gets the credit for carving these fanciful stone formations south of Vernal.

VERMONT

The Green Mountain STATE

STATE BIRD: hermit thrush
STATE FLOWER: red clover
STATE ANIMAL: Morgan Horse

The syrup that flows from Vermont's sugar maple trees isn't the state's sweetest attraction. Forests, mountains, and quaint villages here have remained unspoiled thanks to conservation programs and a ban on billboards. Come autumn, the countryside erupts in fall colors rivaling a fireworks finale.

FANTASTIC VERMONT FACTS

Vermont produces more than 500,000 gallons of maple syrup a year, more than any other state.

The state has the highest ratio of dairy cows to people.

Farmers let their hogs pig out on Vermont's famous Ben & Jerry's ice cream. Mint Oreo is the only flavor they won't eat.

Roadside Attractions

NEW ENGLAND MAPLE MUSEUM

Centuries ago, Native Americans discovered they could cook the sap of a maple tree to make tasty syrup. Learn the full history of Vermont's sweetest export at this Rutland museum.

SANTA'S LAND

Santa's home away from the North Pole, this whimsical village in Putney features a petting zoo with llamas, potbellied pigs, and miniature ponies.

5 COOL THINGS TO DO HERE

1 JAY PEAK
Jay

Located a few miles from the border with Canada, this resort is a powdery heaven for extreme skiers and snowboarders.

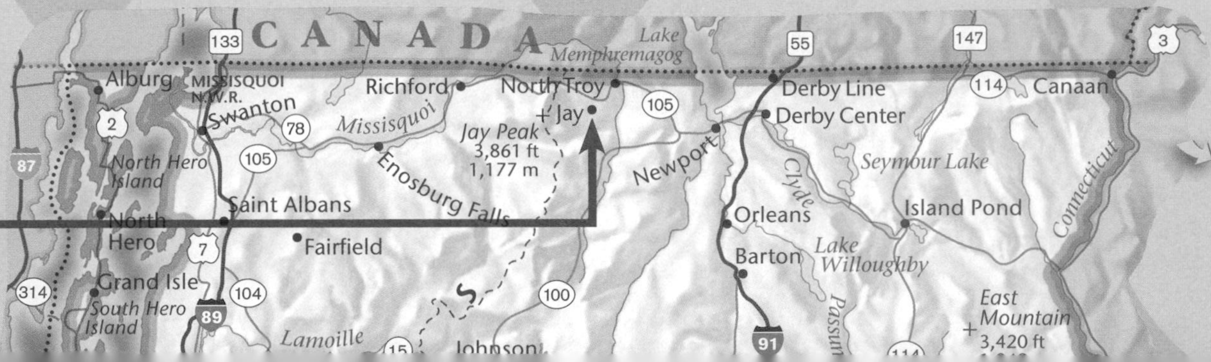

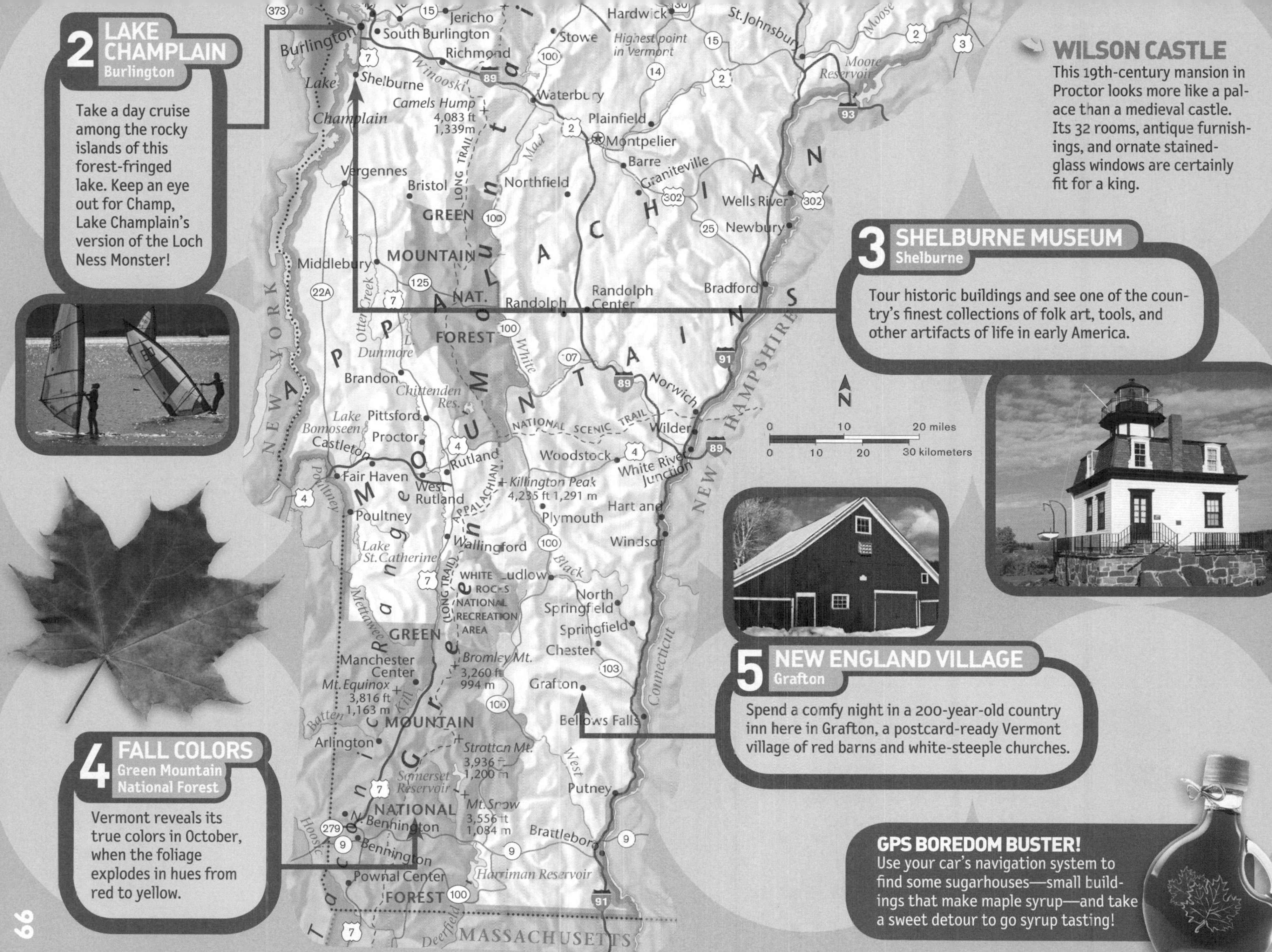

2 LAKE CHAMPLAIN
Burlington

Take a day cruise among the rocky islands of this forest-fringed lake. Keep an eye out for Champ, Lake Champlain's version of the Loch Ness Monster!

WILSON CASTLE

This 19th-century mansion in Proctor looks more like a palace than a medieval castle. Its 32 rooms, antique furnishings, and ornate stained-glass windows are certainly fit for a king.

3 SHELBURNE MUSEUM
Shelburne

Tour historic buildings and see one of the country's finest collections of folk art, tools, and other artifacts of life in early America.

5 NEW ENGLAND VILLAGE
Grafton

Spend a comfy night in a 200-year-old country inn here in Grafton, a postcard-ready Vermont village of red barns and white-steeple churches.

4 FALL COLORS
Green Mountain National Forest

Vermont reveals its true colors in October, when the foliage explodes in hues from red to yellow.

GPS BOREDOM BUSTER!
Use your car's navigation system to find some sugarhouses—small buildings that make maple syrup—and take a sweet detour to go syrup tasting!

STATE BIRD: cardinal

STATE FLOWER: American dogwood

STATE ANIMAL: foxhound

VIRGINIA

The Old Dominion STATE

1 SKYLINE DRIVE
Shenandoah National Park

Take a dazzling road trip through the Blue Ridge Mountains, a lush sea of green in summer and a riot of reds in fall.

America's roots run deepest in Virginia, home of the first English colony and the birthplace of several Founding Fathers. But you don't have to be a history buff to appreciate the state's mountains, valleys, bays, and rivers.

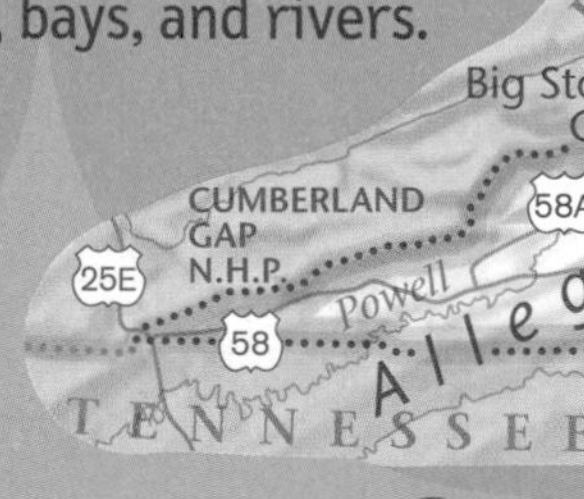

TRAFFIC LAWS YOU WON'T BELIEVE

You can't pass another car without first honking your horn.

Washing mules on the sidewalk is forbidden in Culpeper.

It's against the law to ride on a bicycle's handlebars in Virginia Beach.

BOREDOM BUSTER!
Use a smart phone to research the Founding Fathers so you'll be an expert when you tour their historic haunts.

Roadside Attractions

NATURAL BRIDGE
Marvel at the natural forces that created this 20-story stone arch outside Lexington.

LURAY CAVERNS
Millions of years in the making, this subterranean wonderland in Luray is a maze of stalactites and stalagmites.

5 COOL THINGS TO DO HERE

2 MONTICELLO
Charlottesville

Thomas Jefferson wrote the Declaration of Independence, but was he any good at designing a home? See for yourself as you tour his grand residence and gardens.

3 MOUNT VERNON
Mount Vernon

Explore the mansion and 500-acre farm of George Washington, which has been restored to its condition during his presidency in 1789.

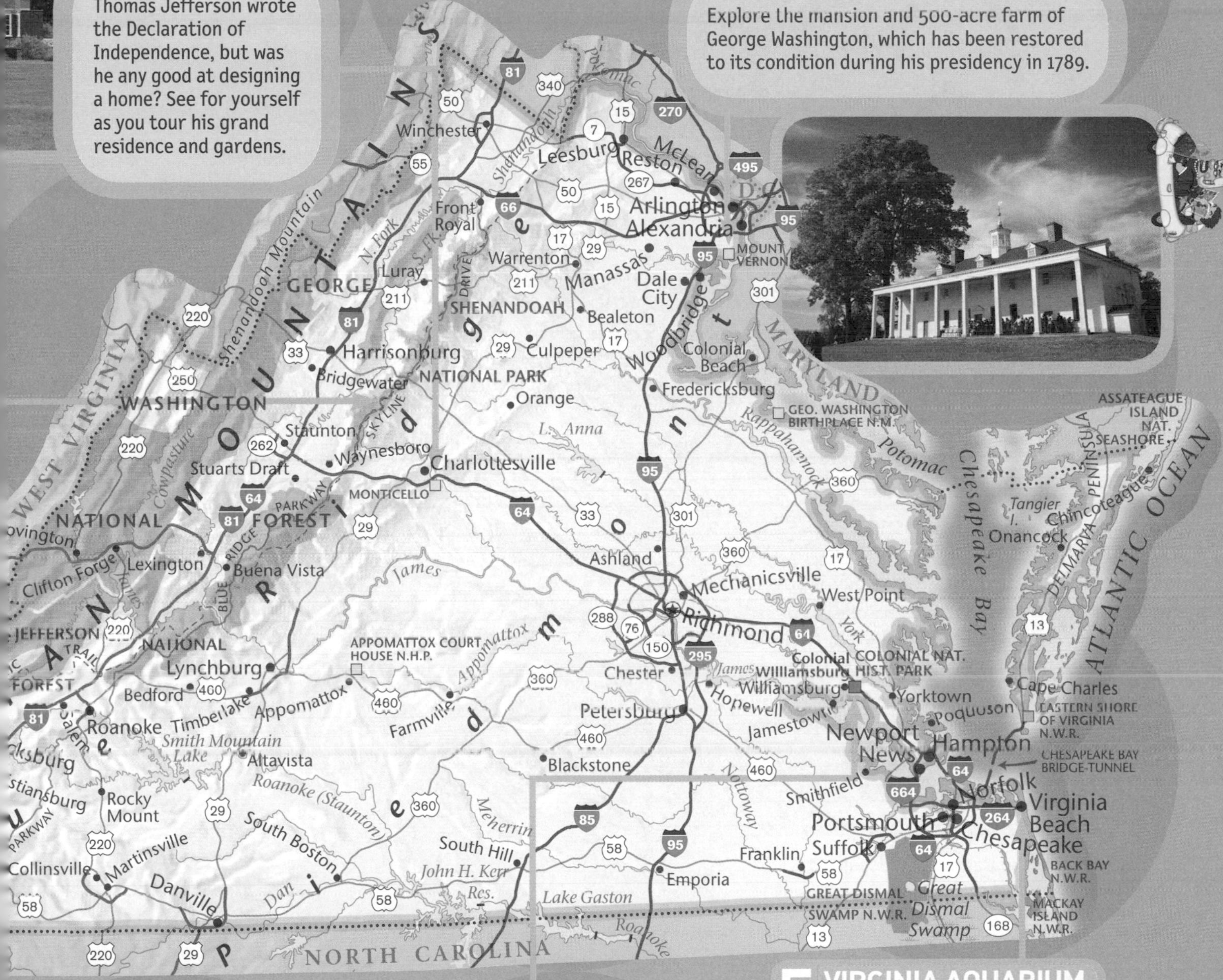

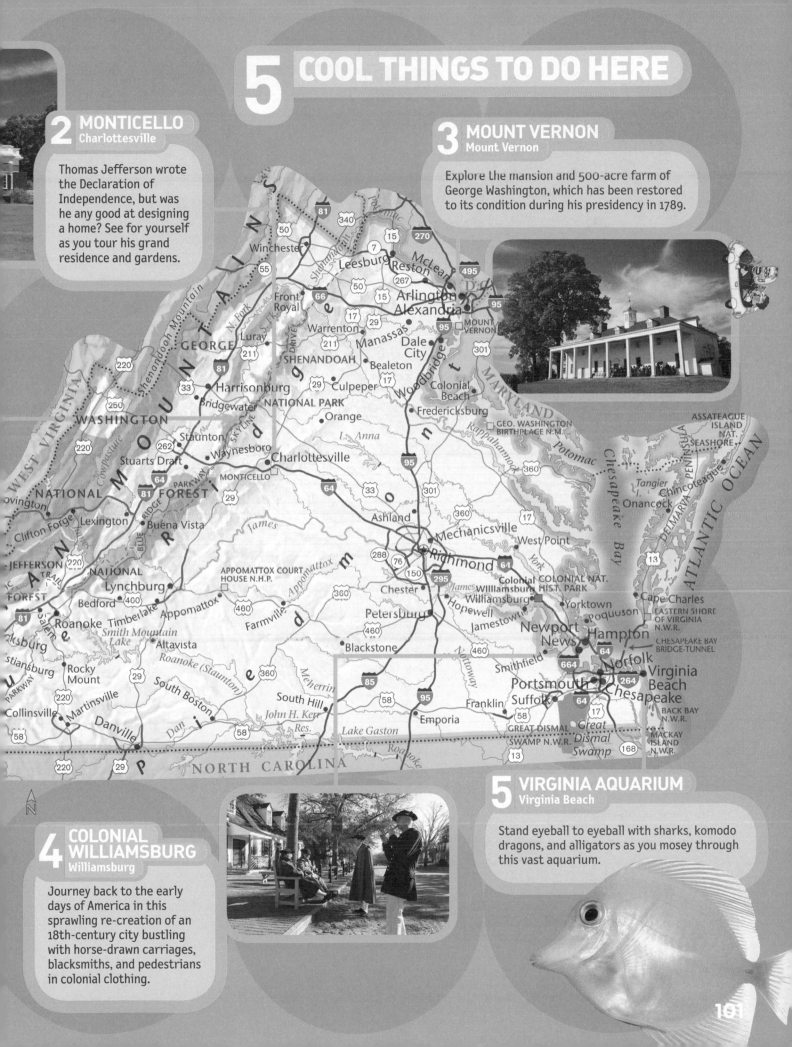

4 COLONIAL WILLIAMSBURG
Williamsburg

Journey back to the early days of America in this sprawling re-creation of an 18th-century city bustling with horse-drawn carriages, blacksmiths, and pedestrians in colonial clothing.

5 VIRGINIA AQUARIUM
Virginia Beach

Stand eyeball to eyeball with sharks, komodo dragons, and alligators as you mosey through this vast aquarium.

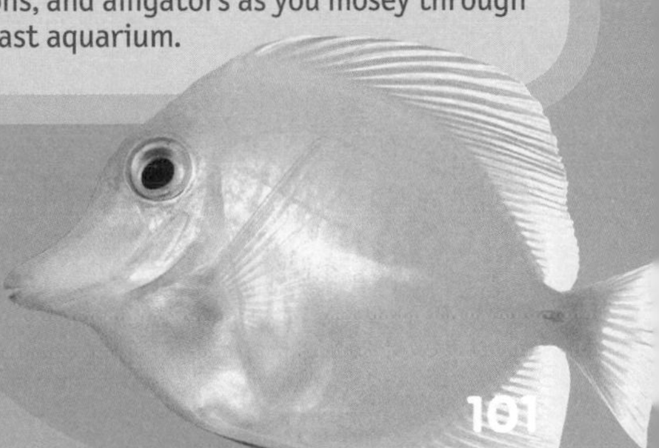

5 COO

WASHINGTON

The Evergreen STATE

You don't always see what you get in Washington. The famously fickle rain and fog of the Pacific Northwest can obscure attractions that lie just outside your window. Don't let a little wet weather keep you from exploring the state's spectacular mountains, rain forests, and seascapes.

FANTASTIC WASHINGTON FACTS

More than a thousand feet of Mount St. Helens vaporized in the blink of an eye when an earthquake triggered its eruption in 1980.

Washington is the only state named after a U.S. President.

This sleepless state has the most coffee-bean roasters per person.

PIKE PLACE MARKET
Not so much a roadside attraction as a Seattle institution, this lively farmers market is home to fishmongers famous for playing catch with today's catch.

MUSEUM OF GLASS
This Tacoma gallery displays delicate glass artwork from many cultures. Come see artists blow glass into fantastical shapes!

YE OLDE CURIOSITY SHOP
In business since 1899, this Seattle souvenir shop entices tourists with its gallery of oddball artifacts, including several mummies and a vampire-killer kit.

0 25 50 miles
0 25 50 75 kilometers
N
Strait of Juan de Fuca
Cape Flattery
MAKAH I.R.
OZETTE I.R.
OLYMPIC COAST NATIONAL MARINE SANCTUARY
LOWER ELWHA I.R.
OLYMPIC NAT. FOR.
Port Angel
Sol Duc
Olympic
QUILEUTE I.R.
101
7,965 ft 2,428 m Mt. Olym
HOH I.R.
Mountains
OLYMPIC NAT. PA
PACIFIC OCEAN
Queets
QUINAULT INDIAN RES.
FOR
COAST
Hoquiam
Ocean Shores
Aberdeen
12
Grays Harbor
SHOALWATER I.R.
Raymo
Willapa Bay
WILLAPA N.W.R.
4
Cape Disappointment
101
JULIA BUTLER HANSEN REF.

BOREDOM BUSTER!
The Pacific Northwest is the alleged stomping ground of Bigfoot, the mythical apelike beast. Unlike all Bigfoot photographers before you, try to capture a steady shot with your camera!

THINGS TO DO HERE

1 SPACE NEEDLE
Seattle

Take in a panoramic view of Puget Sound and the Seattle skyline from the observation deck of this famous three-legged landmark built for the 1962 World's Fair.

2 ORCAS
San Juan Islands

Watch for six-foot dorsal fins slicing through the water on an orca safari around this spectacular island chain.

3 MOUNT ST. HELENS
Mount St. Helens National Volcanic Monument

See this still active volcano that blew its top—literally—in 1980, flattening more than 200 square miles of surrounding forest.

4 OLYMPIC NATIONAL PARK
Olympic Peninsula

It would take a lifetime to see all of this spectacular park's snow-capped peaks, wildflower-covered meadows, waterfalls, lakes, rain forests, and rugged coastline.

5 MOUNT RAINIER
Mount Rainier National Park

Drive or hike past waterfalls and glaciers in the shadow of this snowcapped slumbering volcano.

WEST VIRGINIA

The Mountain STATE

Coal mining and timber cutting have done little to tarnish the natural beauty of this mountainous state. West Virginia attracts outdoor enthusiasts looking for an adrenaline rush—and maybe some good ol' Appalachian music from the days when moonshine flowed from stills hidden in the hills.

TRAFFIC LAWS YOU WON'T BELIEVE

Sleeping on a train is not allowed.

If you spot some tasty roadkill, you're allowed to take it home for dinner!

It's against the law to take a leopard, lion, or tiger for a walk—even on a leash!

BOREDOM BUSTER!
West Virginia is full of quaint towns. Snap a photo of every one you visit and make a map of your West Virginia road trip!

Roadside Attractions

THE KRUGER STREET TOY & TRAIN MUSEUM

You won't find books or teachers in this old Wheeling schoolhouse, now a repository for every type of toy, from model trains to Legos.

GREENBRIER BUNKER

Once a classified underground refuge for members of Congress in the event of World War III, this decommissioned bunker in White Sulphur Springs is a fascinating monument to the Cold War.

NATIONAL RADIO ASTRONOMY OBSERVATORY

A 485-foot-tall radio telescope—the largest of its kind—looms above the countryside in Green Bank. Stop by to see how this observatory helps astronomers explore the universe and search for alien life.

1 COAL MINE
Beckley

Ride a mine car 1,500 feet under a mountain to see the dirty work of old-fashioned coal mining. Not for the claustrophobic!

Ravenswood
Point Pleasant
Kanawha
Sissonville
Ohio
Hurricane
Kenova
Huntington
Nitro
St. Albans
South Charleston
Big Sandy
Madison
KENTUCKY
Tug Fork
Logan
Williamson
VIRGINIA

5 COOL THINGS TO DO HERE

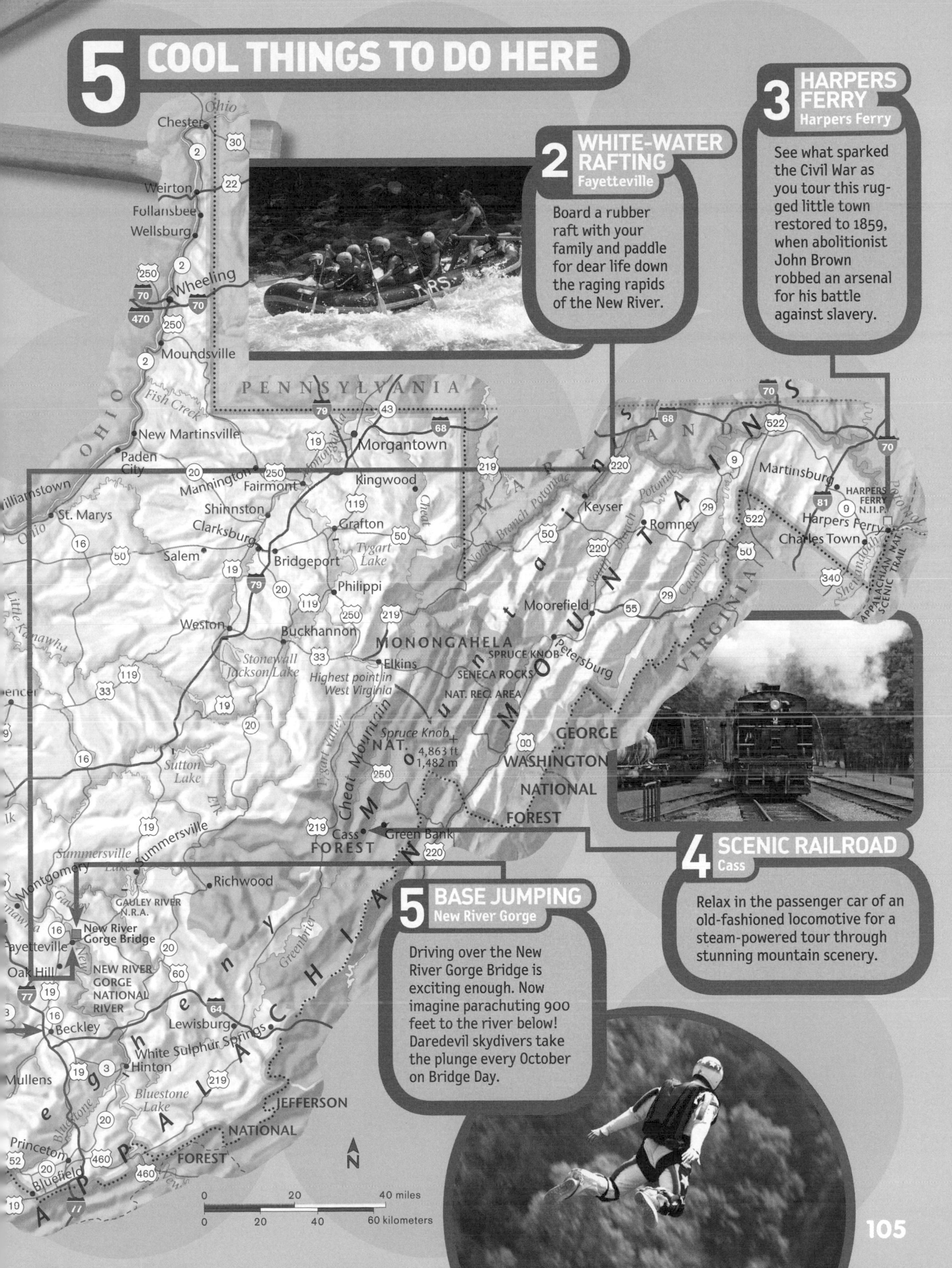

2 WHITE-WATER RAFTING
Fayetteville

Board a rubber raft with your family and paddle for dear life down the raging rapids of the New River.

3 HARPERS FERRY
Harpers Ferry

See what sparked the Civil War as you tour this rugged little town restored to 1859, when abolitionist John Brown robbed an arsenal for his battle against slavery.

4 SCENIC RAILROAD
Cass

Relax in the passenger car of an old-fashioned locomotive for a steam-powered tour through stunning mountain scenery.

5 BASE JUMPING
New River Gorge

Driving over the New River Gorge Bridge is exciting enough. Now imagine parachuting 900 feet to the river below! Daredevil skydivers take the plunge every October on Bridge Day.

STATE BIRD: robin

STATE FLOWER: wood violet

STATE ANIMAL: badger

WISCONSIN

The Badger STATE

It's hardly an insult to call someone a "cheesehead" in Wisconsin, a state with so many dairy farms that one-fifth of the population speaks in moos. But with its thousands of lovely lakes and unspoiled state parks, Wisconsin is much more than America's cheesiest state.

TRAFFIC LAWS YOU WON'T BELIEVE

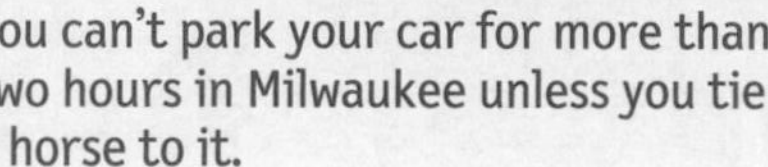

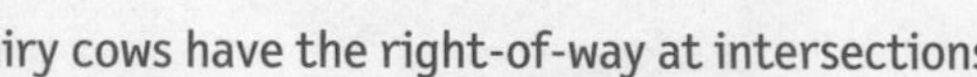

You can't park your car for more than two hours in Milwaukee unless you tie a horse to it.

Dairy cows have the right-of-way at intersections.

If you want to sit on someone's parked car in Hudson, you have to ask for permission first.

Roadside Attractions

MARS' CHEESE CASTLE

Sample Wisconsin's signature goodies at this roadside fortress in Kenosha.

HOUSE ON THE ROCK

The result of an eccentric architect's imagination run amok, this sprawling compound in Spring Green is full of fanciful creatures and even has its own carousel.

WORLD'S LARGEST BICYCLE

Over 30 feet tall, this old-time, fiberglass high wheeler greets visitors to Sparta, dubbed the "bicycling capital" of the world for its many riding trails.

5 COOL THINGS TO DO HERE

1 APOSTLE ISLANDS
Bayfield

Canoe, kayak, or sail beneath the dramatic cliffs of these island jewels in Lake Superior, the world's largest freshwater body.

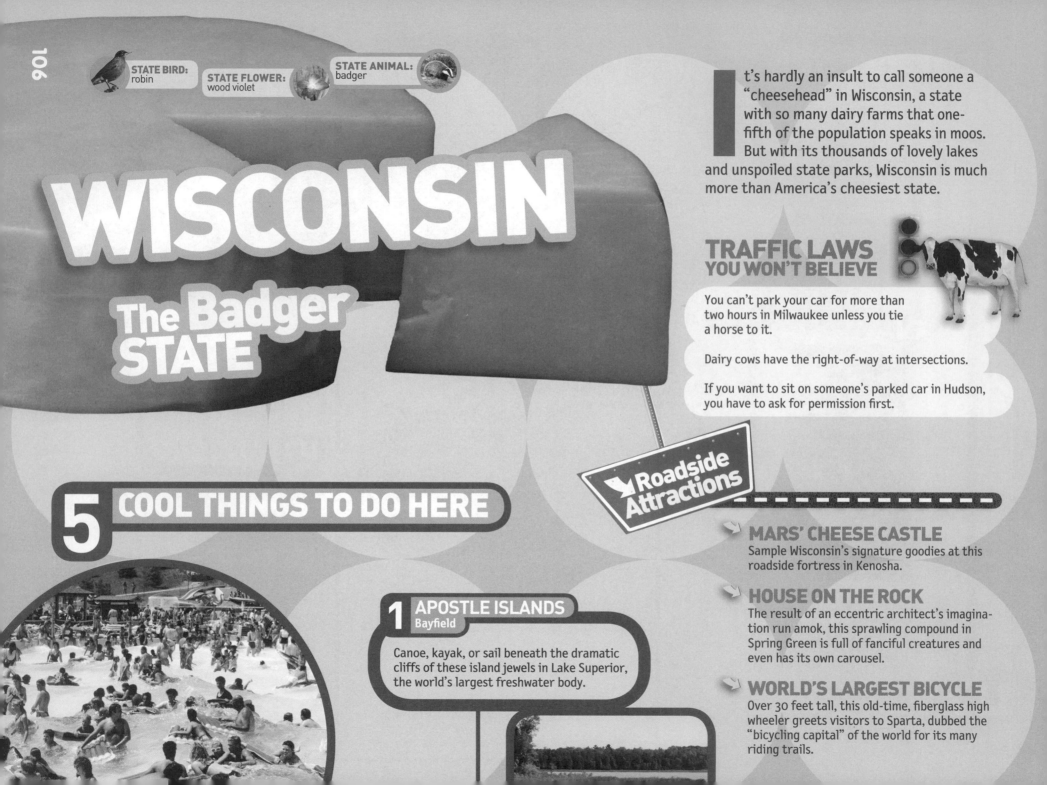

2 NOAH'S ARK
Wisconsin Dells

There's never a dry moment at the largest waterpark in the world, overflowing with snaking slides, lazy rivers, and churning wave pools.

BOREDOM BUSTER!
Take a picture of every cow-crossing sign you pass and see who can get the most!

3 EAA AIRVENTURE
Oshkosh

Climb into the cockpits of stomach-flipping flight simulators and build your own airplane at this museum for experimental aircraft, home to the world's wildest annual airshow.

4 CIRCUS WORLD
Baraboo

A three-ring spectacle runs all summer long at this former big-top base of the Ringling Brothers Circus. Tour its colorful museum of circus artifacts in the off-season.

5 DOOR COUNTY
Near Green Bay

More than two million people flock to this peninsula on Lake Michigan each year for its five state parks, 11 lighthouses, and 300 miles of scenic shoreline.

STATE BIRD: meadowlark

STATE FLOWER: Indian paintbrush

STATE ANIMAL: buffalo

WYOMING

The Equality STATE

1 OLD FAITHFUL
Yellowstone National Park

You can practically set your watch to the iconic geyser at the country's oldest national park. Old Faithful blasts a steamy shower 150 feet into the air about every 90 minutes.

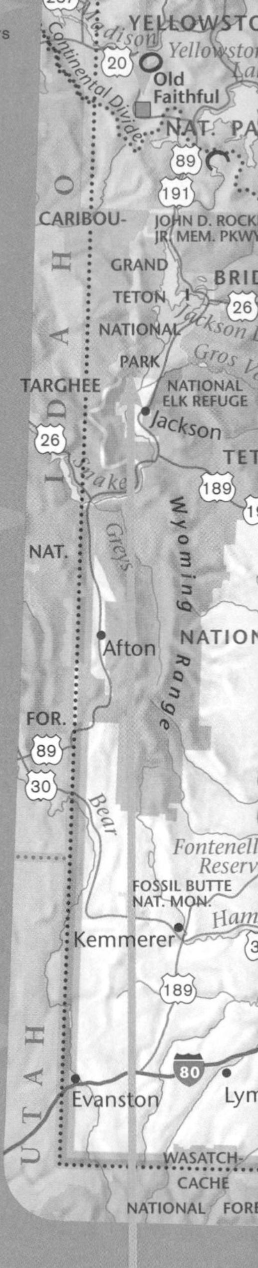

It almost seems a crime to ride anything that isn't fueled by oats through Wyoming's wide-open prairies and rugged badlands. Throw on a Stetson hat and hop into the saddle—this state's made for cowboys and cowgirls!

Roadside Attractions

FRONTIER DAYS OLD WEST MUSEUM
Stagecoaches, saddles, firearms, and hundreds of other Wild West artifacts await in Cheyenne.

AMES PYRAMID
Off Interstate 80 near the town of Laramie, this cryptic granite monument to two railroad tycoons rises 60 feet above the barren landscape.

JACKALOPE SQUARE
Half-jackrabbit, half-antelope, the elusive jackalope is Wyoming's official mythological creature. Its legend began in Douglas, where jackalope sightings are frequent.

FANTASTIC WYOMING FACTS

Although Wyoming is the ninth largest state, it's home to the fewest people!

Wyoming is nicknamed "The Equality State" because it pioneered the right for women to vote. It was also the first state to elect a female governor.

Two-thirds of the world's geysers are in Yellowstone.

GPS BOREDOM BUSTER!
Use your navigation system to find Buford, the smallest town in Wyoming. It has just one resident—and he has his own zip code!

3 GRAND TETONS
Grand Teton National Park

Hike beneath these dramatically jagged peaks, the youngest of the Rocky Mountains.

5 COOL THINGS TO DO HERE

2 DEVIL'S TOWER
Northeastern Wyoming

Marvel at this unearthly stub of volcanic rock rising 1,267 feet above the Belle Fourche River.

4 CODY NIGHT RODEO
Cody

Watch cowboys cling to bucking bulls at this nightly summer rodeo. Can't make the show? Gallop to the nearby Buffalo Bill Historical Center instead.

5 DINOSAUR DIG
Thermopolis

Spend a day helping paleontologists dig Jurassic giants out of the Bighorn Basin at the Wyoming Dinosaur Center.

TRY THESE BOREDOM-BUSTING **GAMES AND ACTIVITIES** ON YOUR NEXT FAMILY ROAD TRIP (OR EVEN ON A RIDE TO THE STORE).

SCAVENGER HUNT

Race your family! See who is the fastest to spot these items from the car windows.

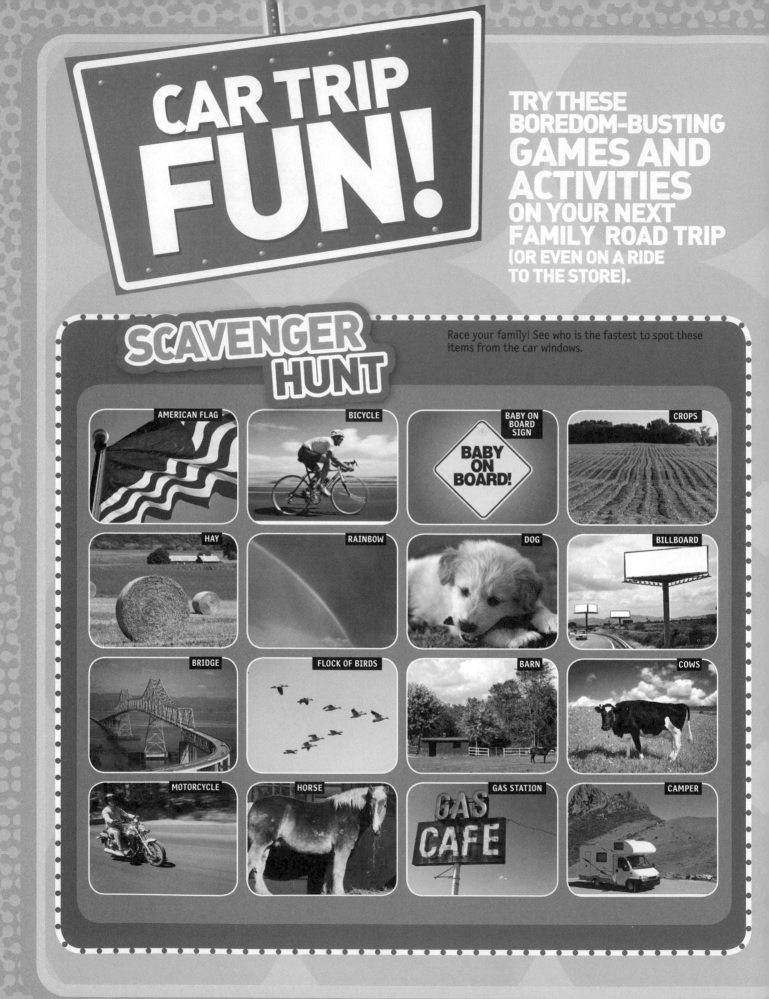

AMERICAN FLAG

BICYCLE

BABY ON BOARD SIGN

CROPS

HAY

RAINBOW

DOG

BILLBOARD

BRIDGE

FLOCK OF BIRDS

BARN

COWS

MOTORCYCLE

HORSE

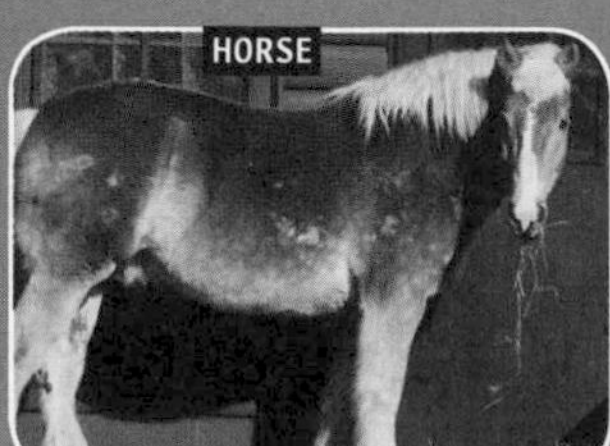

GAS STATION

CAMPER

STUMP YOUR PARENTS

Are your parents really as smart as they think they are? Test their brain power with these trivia questions.

>CITIES

True or False?

1. The Empire State Building in New York City is the tallest building in the United States.
2. The most famous Mardi Gras celebration in the U.S. is in New Orleans, Louisiana.
3. The National Mall is a shopping center in Washington, D.C.
4. The famous Golden Gate Bridge in San Francisco is the longest bridge over open water in the world.
5. Austin is the capital of Texas and is located north of Houston and south of Dallas.

>SUMMER FUN

True or False?

1. You can see a reproduction of the Eiffel Tower at Walt Disney World's Magic Kingdom in Florida.
2. The first known recipe for s'mores—graham crackers, chocolate, and marshmallows—appeared in a book for Girl Scouts.
3. Yellowstone National Park, which spans parts of Wyoming, Montana, and Idaho, has more geysers than anywhere else on Earth.
4. The Sky Rocket roller coaster at the Kennywood amusement park in West Mifflin, Pa takes you form 0 to 50 miles an hour in less than 3 seconds!

>BEACHES

True or False?

1. The popular summer vacation spot Cape Cod is on the coast of Maine.
2. There are more than a hundred beaches on Hawaii's Big Island.
3. The Wright brothers made their first flight in the beach town of Kill Devil Hills in North Carolina's Outer Banks.
4. The beautiful town of Laguna Beach is a located on the Oregon Coast.

Fun Park

Wacky stuff is going on in this amusement park. Find at least ten things that are wrong in this scene.

ANSWERS ON PAGE 122

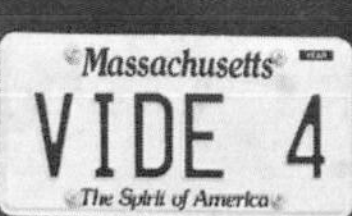

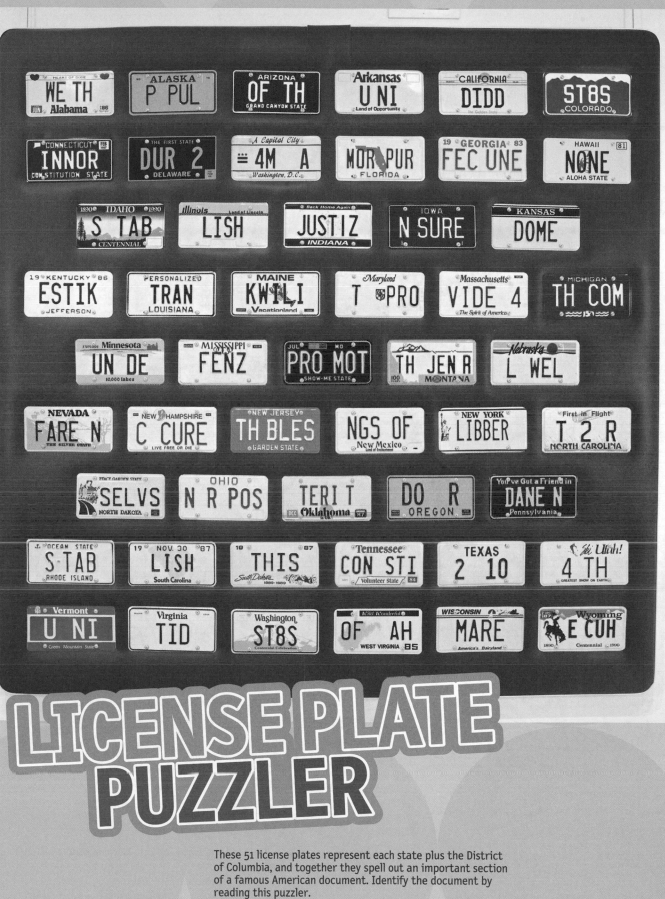

LICENSE PLATE PUZZLER

These 51 license plates represent each state plus the District of Columbia, and together they spell out an important section of a famous American document. Identify the document by reading this puzzler.

ANSWERS ON PAGE 122

Ant Invasion

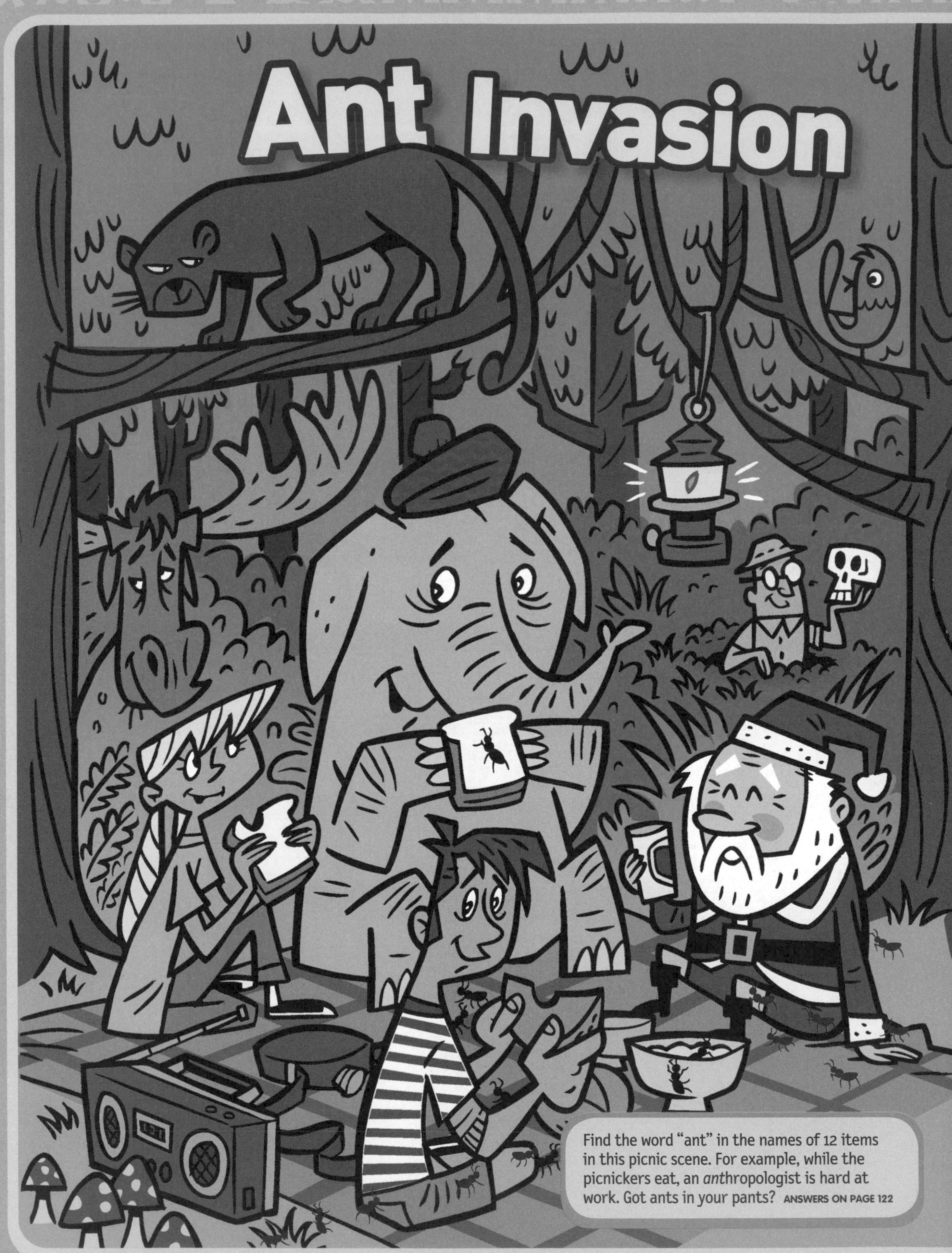

Find the word "ant" in the names of 12 items in this picnic scene. For example, while the picnickers eat, an *ant*hropologist is hard at work. Got ants in your pants? ANSWERS ON PAGE 122

SPLASHDOWN!

Crazy stuff is happening at the water park. Find at least 15 things that are wrong in the scene.

ANSWERS ON PAGE 122

Photo Find Beach Daze

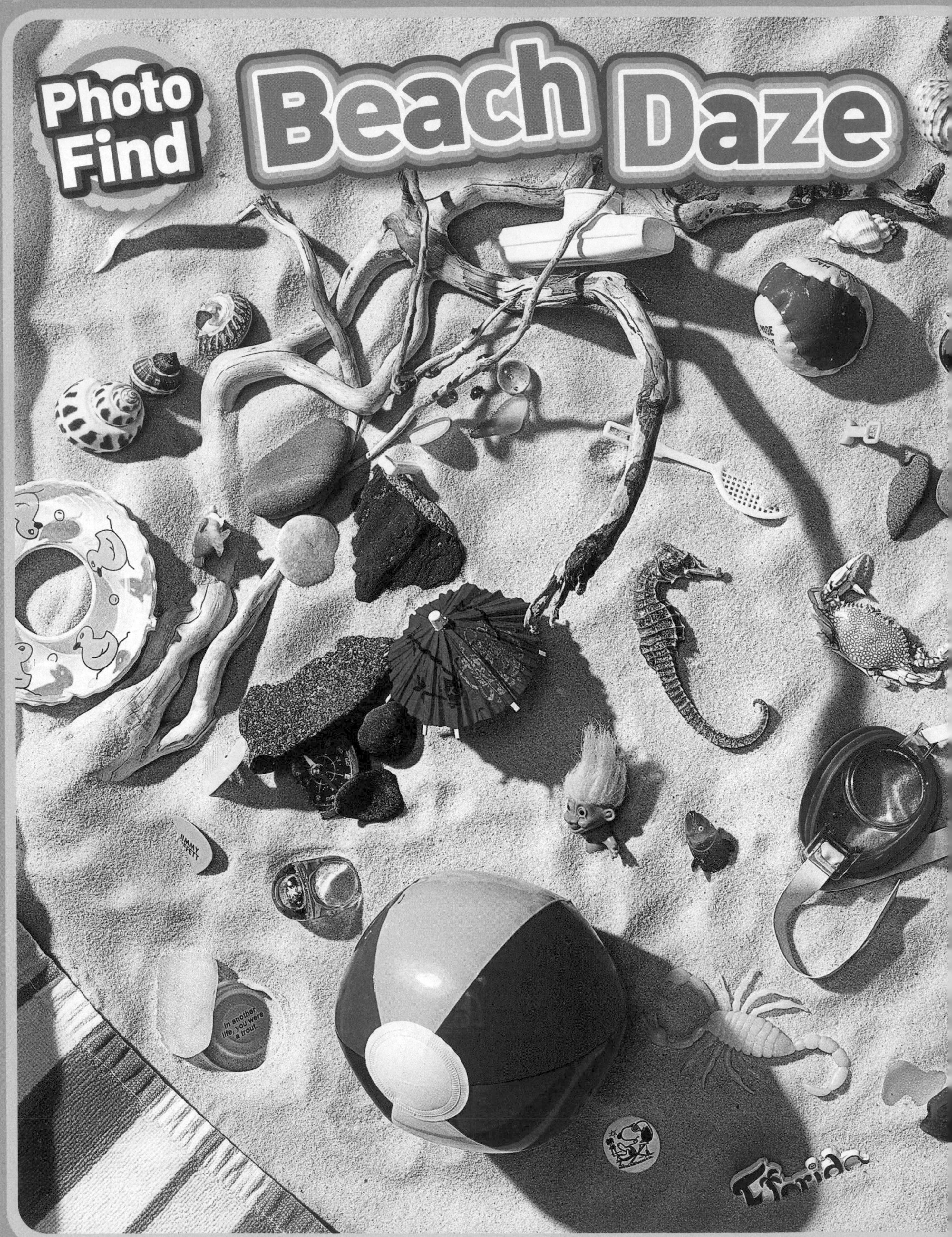

The beach party's over!

ANSWERS ON PAGE 123

There are lots of things that need to go to the Lost and Found. Find these:

key	barrette	guitar pick
Statue of Liberty	bottle cap	ring
crayon	photograph	beagle
tennis racket	car	2 state names
2 goldfish	compass	kazoo
3 marbles	sunglasses	purple monster
4 balls	pearl	shovel

BONUS: Which objects on this beach would a metal detector locate?

Teeing Off

Find at least 30 items on this miniature golf course that start with the letter *T*.

ANSWERS ON PAGE 123

ROAD TRIP

Aunt Bertha has to make five stops without making any right turns or driving on the same path twice. She must stay on the road and cannot cut through the city blocks. Find the route that will get her from home to the places on her list in order, and then home again.

ANSWERS ON PAGE 123

TO DO:
1. TOLL BOOTH
2. FARMERS MARKET
3. BEATRICE'S HOUSE
4. PUMP 'N' GO
5. PARADE

City Sights

There's a lot to see as you stroll through this busy city. Find at least one of each of the following items in this scene.

ANSWERS ON PAGE 123

1. remote-control car
2. police officer
3. yellow flipper
4. person riding a Segway
5. dog on a leash
6. worker down a manhole
7. wheelbarrow
8. men carrying a fish
9. laptop computer
10. golf cart

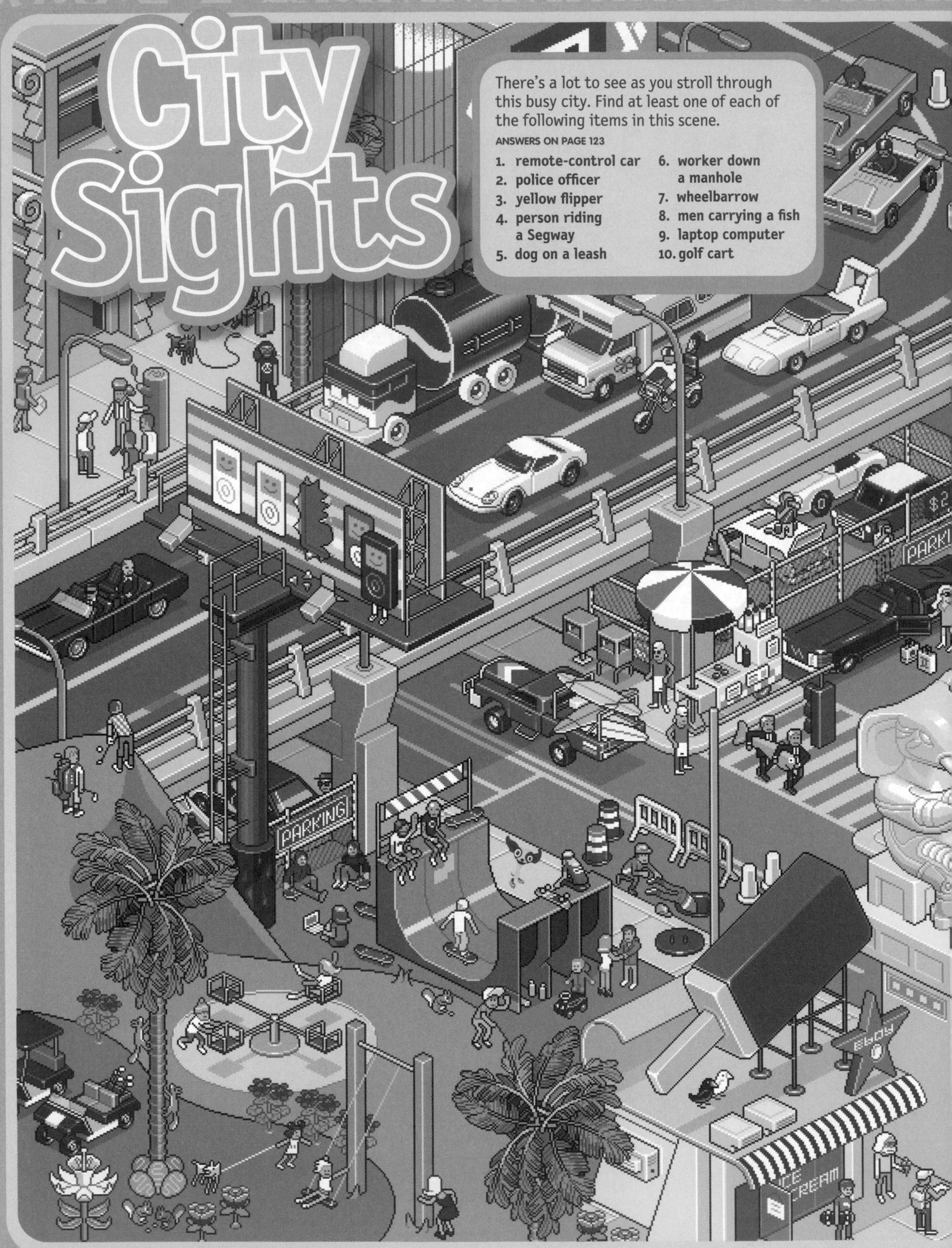

PARK
HELLO
Joe's
moo moo
BIG
BANG

ANSWERS

Stump Your Parents, page 111:

CITIES, 1. False. The Sears Tower in Chicago, Illinois, is the tallest. 2. True. 3. False. The National Mall is the park area that stretches for two miles west from the U.S. Capitol. 4. False. Jiaozhou Bay bridge in China is 26 miles (42 km) long. It connects the port city of Qingdao to the island of Huangdao. The Golden Gate Bridge is 1.7 miles (2.7 kilometers) long. 5. True.

SUMMER FUN, 1. False. The Eiffel Tower reproduction is at Epcot. 2. True. The recipe for s'mores was published in 1927. 3. True. 4. True.

BEACHES, 1. False. Cape Cod is part of Massachusetts. 2. True. 3. True. 4. False. Laguna Beach is located on the Southern California Coast.

Fun Park, page 112:

License Plate Puzzler, page 113:

We the people of the United States, in order to form a more perfect union, establish justice, insure domestic tranquility, provide for the common defense, promote the general welfare, and secure the blessings of liberty to ourselves and our posterity, do ordain and establish this Constitution for the United States of America. (These words are from the Preamble to the U.S. Constitution.)

Ant Invasion, page 114:

anthropologist, plants, pants, radio antenna, ants' antennae, cantaloupe, canteen, elephant, Santa, lantern, antlers, panther.

Splashdown!, page 115:

Beach Daze, pages 116-117:

Teeing Off, page 118:

Road Trip, page 119:

City Sights, pages 120-121:

Aunt Bertha appears 25 times in this book.

INDEX

Illustrations are indicated by **boldface.**

INDEX

Photo Credits

AL = Alamy, IS = iStockphoto.com, NG = NationalGeographicStock.com, NGMS = National Geographic My Shot, SS = Shutterstock

Front matter: 2, Olaf Simon/IS; 2, Dmitry Kosterev/SS; 2, J. Helgason/SS; 3, Ivaschenko Roman/SS; 4, Talvi/SS; 4, vm/SS; 4, Jonathan G/SS; 4, Steve Byland/SS; 4, Good Shots; 4, John A. Anderson/SS; 4, Terrance Emerson/IS; 4, Eric Isselée/SS; 5, urmoments/SS; 5, Steve Noakes/SS; 5, urmoments/SS; 5, Edwin Verin/SS; ALABAMA: 10 (top left), Vishnevskiy Vasily/SS; 10 (top center), Guo Yu/SS; 10 (top right), Ned Therrien/Visuals Unlimited/Getty Images; 10 (left center), violetkaipa/SS; 10 (right center), Elnur/SS; 10 (bottom right), Richard T. Nowitz; 11 (top left), Peter M. Wilson/AL; 11 (top right), Walter G Arce/SS; 11 (bottom left), Shout It Out Design/SS; 11 (bottom center), John Eder/Taxi/Getty Images; 11 (bottom right), Jeffrey M. Frank/SS; ALASKA: 14 (background top left), Alex Staroseltsev/SS; 14 (center), Joy Prescott/SS; 14 (bottom), Randal Sedler/SS; 14 (top right), Scott Kapich/SS; 14 (top left), TTphoto/SS; 14 (top center left), Martin Fowler/SS; 14 (top center right), Arnold John Labrentz/SS; 15 (top), Steven J. Kazlowski/NG; 15 (center), Roman Krochuk/SS; 15 (bottom left), Kirk Geisler/SS; 15 (bottom right), Steve Faber/SS; ARIZONA: 12 (top left), Paul S. Wolf/SS; 12 (left center), Lebrecht Music and Arts Photo Library/AL; 12 (bottom left), tezzstock/SS; 12 (bottom right), Catherine Karnow/Corbis; 12 (bottom center), Richard T. Nowitz; 12, (center) Darla Hallmark/SS; 12, (top) DLILLC/Corbis; 13 (top right), Caitlin Mirra/SS; 13 (top left), topseller/SS; 13 (bottom left), Jill Fromer/IS; 13 (bottom right), Kenneth Sponsler/SS; ARKANSAS: 16 (bottom), Buddy Mays/AL; 16 (top), Terry Smith Images Arkansas Picture Library/AL; 17 (top left), Michelle Connolly Photography; 17 (top center left), Chesapeake Images/SS; 17 (top center right), Stas Volik/SS; 17 (top right), Christina Richards/SS; 17 (center), Eric Isselée/SS; 17 (bottom), Portrait painted by Simmie Knox/Whitehouse.gov; 17 (background top right), AptTone/IS; CALIFORNIA: 18 (background top left), Alex Staroseltsev/SS; 18 (top left), Tom Reichner/SS; 18 (top center left), LianeM/SS; 18 (top center right), Andy Z./SS; 18 (top right), Christopher Elwell/SS; 19 (top), a.v.ley/SS; 19 (left center), Rene Mattes/Hemis/Corbis; 19 (right center), Richard Cummins/Corbis; 19 (bottom right), Sasha Buzko/SS; 19 (bottom left), Tiago Estima/IS; COLORADO: 20 (background top left), Skip ODonnell/IS; 20 (top left), Robert Shantz/AL; 20 (top center left), Casey Chinn Photography/SS; 20 (top center right), Bwilson/SS; 20 (left center), titelio/SS; 20 (top right), iofoto/SS; 20 (right center), Karina Bakalyan/SS; 20 (bottom left), Bruce Works/SS; 20 (bottom right), Duncan Gilbert/SS; 21 (top), John Hoffman/SS; 21 (bottom), David Gaylor/SS; CONNECTICUT: 22 (left), Kate Rose/AL; 22 (center), worldswildlifewonders/SS; 22 (right), Lana Sundman/AL; 23 (left center), Danita Delimont/AL; 23 (background top right), Rich Koele/SS; 23 (top left), Sebastian Knight/SS; 23 (top center), hd connelly/SS; 23 (top right), Peter Allinson/NGMS; 23 (bottom), hd connelly/SS; DELAWARE: 24 (top center left), browndogstudios/IS; 24 (top left), Susan Schmitz/SS; 24 (top center), Chyrko Olena/SS; 24 (top right), Russell Wood Jr./IS; 24 (bottom center), shippee/SS; 24 (bottom), Pincasso/SS; 25 (left), Martin Bluhm/AL; 25 (bottom), Mary Terriberry/SS; 25 (top), Danita Delimont/AL; 25 (right), Robert Clay/AL; FLORIDA: 26 (background top left), Good Shots; 26 (top left), John A. Anderson/SS; 26 (top center), Terrance Emerson/IS; 26 (top right), Eric Isselée/SS; 26 (left center), vm/SS; 26 (right center), Talvi/SS; 26 (bottom right), Steve Byland/SS; 26 (bottom left), Jonathan G/SS; 27, (center) urmoments/SS; 27, (right) Steve Noakes/SS; 27, (top) urmoments/SS; 27, (bottom) Edwin Verin/SS; GEORGIA: 28 (background top left), RedHelga/IS; 28 (top left), Tom Hirtreiter/SS; 28 (top center left), Science Photo Library/AL; 28 (top center right), Darryl Brooks/SS; 28 (top right), Aksenova Natalya/SS; 29 (right center), Edward Chin/SS; 29 (bottom), kurdistan/SS; 29 (top left), SeanPavonePhoto/SS; 29 (top right), Ritu Manoj Jethani/SS; 29 (bottom left), Kristian Sekulic/SS; 29 (bottom right), Stephen Saks Photography/AL; HAWAII: 30 (center), Stephen Coburn/SS; 30 (top left), Wunson/SS; 30 (top center left), JCREATION/SS; 30 (top center right), Zack Woolwine/IS; 30 (bottom), Mana Photo/SS; 30 (top right), Alberto Loyo/SS; 31 (left center), Kato Inowe/SS; 31 (bottom left), Camilla Wisbauer/IS; 31 (top), frantisekhojdysz/SS; 31 (bottom right), Bryan Busovicki/SS; 31 (right center), Katrina Brown/SS; IDAHO: 32 (top left), Steve Byland/SS; 32 (top center), srdjan draskovic/SS; 32 (top right), Bob Gibbons/AL; 32 (left center), Danny E Hooks/SS; 32 (right center), Haigen G. Pearson; 32 (bottom left), Danita Delimont/AL; 32 (bottom right), Christopher Boswell/SS; 33 (left), fotokik_dot_com/SS; 33 (top right), Robert Crow/SS; 33 (bottom right), Weldon Schloneger/SS; ILLINOIS: 34 (background top left), shinyshot/SS; 34 (top left), Steve Byland/SS; 34 (top center), Volosina/SS; 34 (top right), Christina Richards/SS; 34 (left center), Brooke Whatnall/SS; 34 (right center), Mark Thiessen, NGS Staff; 34 (bottom), Craig Lovell/Eagle Visions Photography/AL; 35 (top right), Jason Patrick Ross/SS; 35 (left), Ira Block/NG; 35 (right center), FloridaStock/SS; 35 (bottom right), Library of Congress; INDIANA: 36 (top left), Steve Byland/SS; 36 (top center), Sergey Ryzhov/SS; 36 (top right), blickwinkel/AL; 36 (left center), TOSP Photo/SS; 36 (right center), pirita/SS; 36 (bottom), Steve Geer/IS; 37 (top right), Bryan Busovicki/SS; 37 (top left), Bill Grove/IS; 37 (bottom left), David R. Frazier Photolibrary, Inc./AL; 37 (right center), Don Smetzer/AL; 37 (bottom right), Oleksiy Mark/IS; IOWA: 38 (background top left), Vaclav Volrab/SS; 38 (top left), Stephen Bonk/SS; 38 (top center), oksana2010/SS; 38 (top right), kosam/SS; 38 (center), Christian Delbert/SS; 38 (bottom), hifashion/SS; 39 (top), Andre Jenny/AL; 39 (bottom left), Johan Knelsen/SS; 39 (bottom center), Emily Howard/IS; 39 (right center), Lyroky/AL; 39 (bottom right), Clint Farlinger/AL; KANSAS: 40 (background top left), Olaf Simon/IS; 40 (top left), Martha Marks/SS; 40 (top center left), photolinc/SS; 40 (top center right), Laz4273/IS; 40 (center), prapass/SS; 40 (bottom left), SimplyCreativePhotography/IS; 40 (top right), Michael Vorobiev/SS; 40 (bottom right), Andre Jenny/AL; 40 (bottom center), Steve Adamson/SS; 41 (top), Sharon Day/SS; 41 (bottom left), Alfie Photography/ShutterPoint Photography; 41 (bottom right), Harry Frank/IS; KENTUCKY: 42 (top center left), Materio/IS; 42 (top left), Steven Russell Smith Photos/SS; 42 (top center), Elena Elisseeva/SS; 42 (top right), Darren Hedges/SS; 42 (bottom center), Image Wizard/SS; 42 (top center right), Daniel Dempster Photography/AL; 42 (bottom), Abramova Kseniya/SS; 43 (top left), Jon Meier/AL; 43 (top right), Amy Nichole Harris/SS; 43 (bottom left), Danita Delimont/AL; 43 (bottom right), Danita Delimont/AL; LOUISIANA: 44 (left), Monkey Business Images/SS; 44 (bottom right), Lori Monahan Borden/SS; 44 (top right), Tetra Images/AL; 45 (left center), Michele Molinari/AL; 45 (background top right), Kathryn8/IS; 45 (top left), Steve Byland/SS; 45 (top center), aerogondo2/SS; 45 (top right), Judy Kennamer/SS; 45 (right center), Fer Gregory/SS; 45 (bottom), Mary Evans Picture Library/AL; MAINE: 46 (top left), Steve Byland/SS; 46 (top center), Ross Frid/AL; 46 (top right), Arnold John Labrentz/SS; 46 (left center), yellowj/SS; 46 (right center), verityjohnson/SS; 46 (bottom), Olivier Asselin/AL; 47 (top left), Jeff Schultes/SS; 47 (top right), Stone Nature Photography/AL; 47 (bottom left), Chee Onn Leong/SS; 47 (bottom right), Nicolaus Czarnecki/ZUMA Press; 47 (bottom center), Bill Florence/SS; MARYLAND: 48 (top left), hagit berkovich /SS; 48 (top center), Chris Hill/SS; 48 (top right), kosam/SS; 48 (bottom left), Caitlin Mirra/SS; 48 (bottom right), Gregory Johnston/SS; 48 (right center), Pyma/SS; 48 (left center), 4736202690/IS; 49 (left), Olga Bogatyrenko/SS; 49 (top right), GlowImages/AL; 49 (right center), Edwin Remsberg/AL; 49 (bottom right), John M. Chase/IS; MASSACHUSETTS: 50 (background top left), Victor Maffe/IS; 50 (top left), Steve Byland/SS; 50 (top center), Anyka/SS; 50 (top right), Ross Frid/AL; 50 (bottom left), M. Unal Ozmen/SS; 50 (bottom right), Jeff Schultes/SS; 51 (top left), Art & Vision/AL; 51 (bottom left), jiawangkun/SS; 51 (top right), Jeffrey M. Frank/SS; 51 (bottom right), Eric Carr/AL; MICHIGAN: 52 (background top left), Aleksandar Bunevski/SS; 52 (top left), Sebastian Knight/SS; 52 (top center), CoolR/SS; 52 (top right), Dhoxax/SS; 52 (bottom), Michael Olson/IS; 52 (top right), Michael G Smith/SS; 53 (top left), Alexey Stiop/SS; 53 (right center), Presselect/AL; 53 (bottom left), Peter Mah/IS; 53 (bottom right), Susan Montgomery/SS; MINNESOTA: 54 (top left), Nancy Bauer/SS; 54 (top right), Holly Kuchera/SS; 54 (top right), Pablo Scapinachis Armstrong/AL; 54 (background top left), zhu difeng/SS; 54 (bottom left), Chris Alcock/SS; 54 (right center), Robert J. Beyers II/SS; 54 (bottom right), Greg Ryan/AL; 55 (left), PhotoStock-Israel/AL; 55 (top right), fotokik_dot_com/SS; 55 (bottom right), Rick & Nora Bowers/AL; 55 (bottom center), Andreas Feininger/Time Life/Getty Images; MISSISSIPPI: 56 (top left), Chesapeake Images/SS; 56 (top center), aerogondo2/SS; 56 (top right), Dhoxax/SS; 56 (background top left), Quang Ho/SS; 56 (bottom left), Vespasian/AL; 56 (bottom right), Anton Gvozdikov/SS; 57 (top left), Don Smetzer/AL; 57 (top right), Andre Jenny/AL; 57 (bottom left), Edna Haden/IS; 57 (bottom center), Dan Brandenburg/IS; MISSOURI: 58 (left), Ilene MacDonald/AL; 58 (bottom right), imagebroker/AL; 58 (top right), Danita Delimont/AL; 59 (left center), picsbyst/SS; 59 (top left), Rob McKay/SS; 59 (top center), Rey Kamensky/SS; 59 (top right), Eric Isselée/SS; 59 (background top), Seregam/SS; 59 (right center), Comstock/Getty Images; 59 (bottom left), Rob McKay/SS; 59 (bottom right), Martin Kraft/SS; MONTANA: 60 (top left), Martha Marks/SS; 60 (top center left), 6015714281/SS; 60 (top center right), Jim Laybourn/National Georgraphic My Shot; 60 (background top), Michael Balderas/IS; 60 (bottom left), B.G. Smith/SS; 60 (top right), ND Johnston/SS; 60 (bottom right), Luc Novovitch/AL; 60 (bottom center), ; 61 (top), Allen Russell/AL; 61 (bottom left), Blaine Harrington III/Corbis; 61 (bottom right), Steven G. Smith/Corbis; NEBRASKA: 62 (top left), Chas/SS; 62 (top center left), Elena Elisseeva/SS; 62 (top center right), Tony Campbell/SS; 62 (background top left), Todd Harrison/IS; 62 (bottom left), Jonathan Larsen/Diadem Images/AL; 62 (bottom right), Michael Snell/AL; 62 (top right), Sharon Day/SS; 63 (top), M. Williams Woodbridge/NG; 63 (center), Bull's-Eye Arts/SS; 63 (bottom), pix2go/SS; NEVADA: 64 (top left), Steve Byland/SS; 64 (top center left), Debbie Frantzen/SS; 64 (bottom center right), Bates Littlehales/NG; 64 (background top left), Pertti Sironen/IS; 64 (right), Gerrit de Heus/AL; 64 (bottom), Tim Fitzharris/Minden/NG; 65 (top right), Prisma Bildagentur AG/AL; 65 (top left), Andy Z./SS; 65 (bottom right), Andy Z./SS; 65 (bottom left), John Elk III/AL; NEW HAMPSHIRE: 66 (top left), Judy Kennamer/SS; 66 (top center), kml/SS; 66 (top right), Steve Byland/SS; 66 (background top left), Bomshtein/SS; 66 (bottom left), Paul Tessier/IS; 66 (bottom right), John Elk III/AL; 67 (left), Daniel Dempster Photography/AL; 67 (top right), Greg Ryan/AL; 67 (bottom right), Superstock/AL; 67, (bottom right) Garry Black/AL; NEW JERSEY: 68 (top left), Raymond Barlow/NGMS; 68 (top center), cosma/SS; 68 (top right), Mike Quinn/NGMS; 68 (background top left), Dmitry Kosterev/SS; 68 (bottom right), Rob Wilson/SS; 69 (top left), AP Images/Jacqueline Larma; 69 (top right), www.insectropolis.com; 69 (bottom left), iShootPhotos, LLC/IS; 69 (right center), dbimages/AL; 69 (bottom right), John Van Decker/AL; NEW MEXICO: 70 (background top left), Ivaschenko Roman/SS; 70 (top left), BenjaminTaggart/NGMS; 70 (top center), Douglas Knight/SS; 70 (top right), Holly Kuchera/SS; 70 (bottom right), Weldon Schloneger/SS; 70 (bottom left), Steve Hamblin/AL; 71 (top right), Pat Canova/AL; 71 (bottom right), M. Williams Woodbridge/NGMS; 71 (bottom center), Phil Degginger/AL; 71 (left), Steve Byland/SS; NEW YORK: 72 (top left), Steve Byland/SS; 72 (top center left), Michaela Murray/NGMS; 72 (top center right), Bill Smith/SS; 72 (background top left), Nikada/SS; 72 (bottom center), ecco/SS; 72 (bottom right), VikaSuh/SS; 72 (top right), Kevin Tavares/SS; 72 (bottom right), Eye Ubiquitous/AL; 73 (top), Ron Chapple/Getty Images; 73 (center), Colin D. Young/SS; 73 (bottom), Tetra Images/Getty Images; NORTH CAROLINA: 74 (top left), Walter Nussbaumer/NGMS; 74 (top center left), Paul Atkinson/SS; 74 (top center right), Ron Rowan Photography/SS; 74 (top right), Brad Whitsitt/SS; 74 (bottom right), Mike Theiss/NG; 74 (bottom left), Stacey Putman/AL; 74 (bottom center), sevenke/SS; 75 (top), Rich Carey/SS; 75 (bottom left), EditorialByDarrellYoung/AL; 75 (bottom right), John Elk III/AL; NORTH DAKOTA: 76 (top left), Danita Delimont/AL; 76 (top right), Franck Fotos/AL; 76 (bottom), Andre Jenny/AL; 77 (top center left), Don Smetzer/AL; 77 (bottom center left), Sue Smith/SS; 77 (bottom), Marie-Dominique Verdier/AL; 77 (top left), Steve Byland/SS; 77 (top center), Weldon Schloneger/SS; 77 (top right), M. Dykstra/SS; 77 (background top right), SeDmi/SS; OHIO: 78 (top left), Jim Nelson/SS; 78 (top center), Simone Andress/SS; 78 (top right), Mike Rogal/SS; 78 (background top left), Craig Barhorst/IS; 78 (bottom right), J. Helgason/SS; 78 (bottom left), James M Phelps, Jr/SS; 79 (top left), Daniel Borzynski/AL; 79 (top right), Tom Uhlman/AL; 79 (bottom right), ODM Studio/IS; 79 (bottom left), Judy Kennamer/SS; OKLAHOMA: 80 (top left), Radius Images/Getty Images; 80 (top center), Hitoshi Kawakami/amana images/Getty Images; 80 (top right), Mark Thiessen, NGS Staff; 80 (background top left), Eliza Snow/IS; 80 (bottom left), Joel Zatz/AL; 80 (left center), Lawrence Manning/Corbis; 80 (bottom right), Carol & Mike Werner/Photolibrary/Getty Images; 81 (top left), Brett Mulcahy/SS; 81 (top right), Danny Lehman/Corbis; 81 (bottom), John Elk III/AL; OREGON: 82 (top left), Laurie L. Snidow/SS; 82 (top center), Colette3/SS; 82 (top right), pix2go/SS; 82 (background top left), Tischenko Irina/SS; 82 (bottom right), Scott Sanders/SS; 82 (bottom left), Greg Vaughn/AL; 83 (top left), Larry Geddis/AL; 83 (bottom left), Steve Estvanik/SS; 83 (right), Russell Kord/AL; PENNSYLVANIA: 84 (top left), Tom Reichner/SS; 84 (top center), Phil64/SS; 84 (top right), George F. Mobley/NG; 84 (background top left), Christopher S. Howeth/SS; 84 (center), Martin Valigursky/IS; 84 (bottom), George Sheldon/AL; 85 (top), David W. Leindecker/SS; 85 (bottom left), Caitlin Mirra/SS; 85 (bottom right), Corbis Bridge/AL; RHODE ISLAND: 86 (top left), Chuck Wagner/SS; 86 (top center), Valerie Potapova/SS; 86 (top right), Maxim Tupikov/SS; 86 (background top left), Tobik/SS; 86 (center), Peter Zijlstra/SS; 86 (bottom), Robert J. Beyers II/SS; 87 (top left), Tim Laman/NG; 87 (bottom left), Albert Knapp/AL; 87 (top right), Michael Dwyer/AL; 87 (bottom right), Peter Casolino/AL; SOUTH CAROLINA: 88 (top left), Steve Byland/SS; 88 (top center left), Florapix/AL; 88 (top center right), Sam Abell/NG; 88 (background top left), Andrea Hil/IS; 88 (bottom), Sashkin/SS; 88 (top right), Daboost/SS; 89 (bottom left), SuperStock/AL; 89 (top), mlorenz/SS; 89 (bottom right), Rick Rhay/IS; SOUTH DAKOTA: 90 (top left), Rob Kemp/SS; 90 (top center), Pi-Lens/SS; 90 (top right), Ed Robertson/NGMS; 90 (background top left), Joseph Sohm/ChromoSohm Inc./Corbis; 90 (center), oneo/SS; 90 (bottom), JCElv/SS; 91 (bottom left), Scott Kemper/AL; 91 (top), Hemis/AL; 91 (bottom right), Peder Digre/SS; TENNESSEE: 92 (top left), Steve Byland/SS; 92 (top center), M. Williams Woodbridge/NG; 92 (top right), Dari Hughes/NGMS; 92 (background top), Markus Gann/SS; 92 (bottom left), Prisma Bildagentur AG/AL; 92 (bottom right), Jon Arnold Images Ltd/AL; 93 (top right), Frank Tozier/AL; 93 (top left), Robert Harding Picture Library Ltd/AL; 93 (bottom left), Pat & Chuck Blackley/AL; 93 (bottom right), Kjersti Joergensen/SS; TEXAS: 94 (top left), picsbyst/SS; 94 (top center), Fedor A. Sidorov/SS; 94 (top right), Mike Flippo/SS; 94 (background top left), J. Helgason/SS; 94 (center), NASA; 94 (bottom), Mike Theiss/NG; 94 (bottom right), LOOK Die Bildagentur der Fotografen GmbH/AL; 95 (bottom left), BenC/SS; 95 (top), Lana Sundman/AL; 95 (bottom right), Houston Space Center; UTAH: 96 (top left), evantravels/SS; 96 (top right), Mark Gibson/AL; 96 (bottom left), alysta/SS; 97 (left center), Darren J. Bradley/SS; 97 (bottom left), Eric Isselée/SS; 97 (bottom right), Sashkin/SS; 97 (background top right), LilKar/SS; 97 (top left), Arvind Balaraman/SS; 97 (top center), Maureen Ruddy Burkhart/AL; 97 (top right), Alfie Photography/SS; VERMONT: 98 (top left), Bates Littlehales/NG; 98 (top center), dabjola/SS; 98 (top right), Melissa Dockstader/SS; 98 (background left), Morgan Lane Photography/SS; 98 (bottom right), Ian Dagnall/AL; 99 (top left), George Robinson/AL; 99 (bottom left), Zoom Team/SS; 99 (right center), Patti McConville/AL; 99 (top right), Hemis/AL; 99 (bottom right), Daniel Wiedemann/SS; VIRGINIA: 100 (top left), Robert Greene/NGMS; 100 (top center left), fstockfoto/SS; 100 (top center right), Terekhov Igor/SS; 100 (background top left), Julian Chojnacki/IS; 100 (top right), Cephas Picture Library/AL; 100 (bottom right), Raymond Gehman/NG; 100 (bottom left), Gilbert Stuart; 101 (top), Richard Nowitz/NG; 101 (bottom left), Lori Epstein/NG; 101 (bottom right), marrio31/SS; WASHINGTON: 102 (top left), Gregg Williams/SS; 102 (top center), LouLouPhotos/SS; 102 (top right), Timothy Epp/SS; 102 (bottom left), GMEVIPHOTO/SS; 102 (bottom right), Robert Harding Picture Library Ltd/AL; 102 (background top), Valentina R./SS; 103 (top left), Jeremy Edwards/IS; 103 (top right), Tory Kallman/NGMS; 103 (bottom), neelsky/SS; WEST VIRGINIA: 104 (top left), Steven Smith/NGMS; 104 (top center), W.E. Garrett/NGMS; 104 (top right), James Galletto/NGMS; 104 (background top), DNY59/IS; 104 (bottom left), Joel Sartore/National Geographic Creative/Getty Images; 104 (bottom right), Roger Ressmeye/Photolibrary; 105 (top), Danita Delimont/AL; 105 (center), Christopher Purcell/AL; 105 (bottom), Aurora Photos/AL; WISCONSIN: 106 (top left), Michael J Thompson/SS; 106 (top center), Chas/SS; 106 (top right), Sue Robinson/SS; 106 (background top left), ; 106 (bottom left), Dennis MacDonald/AL; 106 (bottom center), Steven Newton/SS; 106 (bottom right), Eric Isselée/SS; 107 (top left), Jim W. Parkin/IS; 107 (top right), nokhoog_buchachon/SS; 107 (bottom left), WilsonsTravels Stock/AL; 107 (right center), James A. Sugar/NG; 107 (bottom right), Geoffrey Kuchera/IS; WYOMING: 108 (top left), Martha Marks/SS; 108 (top center), Ocean/Corbis; 108 (top right), Brad Miller/NGMS; 108 (background top), Devon Stephens/IS; 108 (center), naturediver/SS; 108 (bottom), Joerg Metzner/Restless Photography/AL; 109 (top), Mike Norton/SS; 109 (bottom left), Nicholas Rous/AL; 109 (bottom right), Mervyn Rees/AL.

GAMES

110 (A), Digital Stock; 110 (B), Polka Dot Images/Jupiterimages; 110 (C), PhotoObjects.net/Jupiterimages; 110 (D), PhotoDisc; 110 (E), Sonya Etchison/SS; 110 (F), Olga A/SS; 110 (G), Lopatinsky Vladislav/SS; 110 (H), SS Guy/SS; 110 (I), Digital Stock; 110 (J), Glenn Young/SS; 110 (K), Andrew F. Kazmierski/SS; 110 (L), YellowJ/SS; 110 (M), Bart Sadowski/IS; 110 (N), PhotoDisc; 110 (O), Harris Shiffman/SS; 110 (P), Elena Aliaga/SS; 111 (bottom left), Digital Stock; 111 (bottom center), Digital Stock; 111 (bottom right), Digital Stock; 112, Smithsonian American Art Museum, Washington, DC/Art Resource, NY

Published by the National Geographic Society
John M. Fahey, Jr., *Chairman of the Board and Chief Executive Officer*
Timothy T. Kelly, *President*
Declan Moore, *Executive Vice President; President, Publishing*
Melina Gerosa Bellows, *Executive Vice President; Chief Creative Officer, Books, Kids, and Family*

Prepared by the Book Division
Hector Sierra, *Senior Vice President and General Manager*
Nancy Laties Feresten, *Senior Vice President, Editor in Chief, Children's Books*
Jonathan Halling, *Design Director, Books and Children's Publishing*
Jay Sumner, *Director of Photography, Children's Publishing*
Jennifer Emmett, *Editorial Director, Children's Books*
Eva Absher-Schantz, *Managing Art Director*
Carl Mehler, *Director of Maps*
R. Gary Colbert, *Production Director*
Jennifer A. Thornton, *Managing Editor*

Staff for This Book
Priyanka Lamichhane, *Project Editor*
Lori Epstein, *Senior Illustrations Editor*
Eva Absher-Schantz, Ruthie Thompson, Kathryn Robbins, *Designers*
Sven M. Dolling, *Map Research and Production Manager*
Michael McNey, *Map Production*
Grace Hill, *Associate Managing Editor*
Joan Gossett, *Production Editor*
Lewis R. Bassford, *Production Manager*
Susan Borke, *Legal and Business Affairs*
Kate Olesin, *Assistant Editor*
Kathryn Robbins, *Design Production Assistant*
Hillary Moloney, *Illustrations Assistant*
Jennifer Essig, *Photography Intern*

Manufacturing and Quality Management
Christopher A. Liedel, *Chief Financial Officer*
Phillip L. Schlosser, *Senior Vice President*
Chris Brown, *Technical Director*
Nicole Elliott, *Manager*
Rachel Faulise, *Manager*
Robert L. Barr, *Manager*

The National Geographic Society is one of the world's largest nonprofit scientific and educational organizations. Founded in 1888 to "increase and diffuse geographic knowledge," the Society works to inspire people to care about the planet. National Geographic reflects the world through its magazines, television programs, films, music and radio, books, DVDs, maps, exhibitions, live events, school publishing programs, interactive media and merchandise. *National Geographic* magazine, the Society's official journal, published in English and 33 local-language editions, is read by more than 38 million people each month. The National Geographic Channel reaches 320 million households in 34 languages in 166 countries. National Geographic Digital Media receives more than 15 million visitors a month. National Geographic has funded more than 9,400 scientific research, conservation and exploration projects and supports an education program promoting geography literacy. For more information, visit nationalgeographic.com.

For more information, please call
1-800-NGS LINE (647-5463) or
write to the following address:
National Geographic Society
1145 17th Street N.W.
Washington, D.C. 20036-4688 U.S.A.

Visit us online at www.nationalgeographic.com/books

For librarians and teachers:
www.ngchildrensbooks.org

More for kids from National Geographic:
kids.nationalgeographic.com

For information about special discounts for bulk purchases, please contact National Geographic Books Special Sales: ngspecsales@ngs.org

For rights or permissions inquiries, please contact National Geographic Books Subsidiary Rights: ngbookrights@ngs.org

Library of Congress Cataloging-in-Publication Data

Boyer, Crispin.
National Geographic kids ultimate U.S. road trip atlas : maps, games, activities, and more for hours of backseat fun/by Crispin Boyer.—1st ed.
p. cm.
Includes bibliographical references and index.
ISBN 978-1-4263-0933-5 (pbk. : alk. paper)—
ISBN 978-1-4263-0934-2 (lib. bdg. : alk. paper)
1. United States—Maps for children. 2. United States—Description and travel. 3. Recreation areas—United States—Maps. 4. Outdoor recreation—United States—Maps. I. Title. II. Title: Kids ultimate U.S. road trip atlas.
G1200.B75 2012
912.73—dc23

2011034647

Printed in China
12/RRDS/2